DISTINGUISHED SHADES:
Americans Whose Lives Live On

DISTINGUISHED SHADES

Americans Whose Lives Live On

By Louis Filler

Still nursing the unconquerable hope,
Still clutching the inviolable shade
                                    Matthew Arnold, *The Scholar Gypsy*

BELFRY PUBLICATIONS, INC.
P.O. Box 1
OVID, MICHIGAN 48866

Library of Congress Cataloging Publication Data

Filler, Louis
Distinguished Shades.
Bibliographical notes. Includes index.

1. Americans of several eras whose influence continues. 2. The arts, politics, science.
3. Public appreciation and neglect. 4. Death and memory. 5. Non-fiction.

I. Title. II. Distinguished Shades.

Library of Congress Catalog Card Number 91-077228
ISBN 0-9631527-0-X (Hardcover edition)

For
ALLAN NEVINS
*Master-historian of
his generation—
Friend and guide to
historical Reconstruction*

Death be not proud

> John Donne
> *Holy Sonnets*

So set before the echoes fade
    The fleet foot on the sill of shade
And hold to the low lintel up
    The still-defended challenge-cup.

> A.E. Houseman
> "To an Athlete Dying Young"
> *A Shropshire Lad*

There is something beyond the grave;. . .
    and the pale ghost escapes from the vanquished pyre.

> Sextus Propertius
> *Elegies*

[S]ouls departed [are] but the shadows of the living.
All things fall under this name.

> Sir Thomas Browne
> *Urn-Burial*

    Jesus
[Buffalo bill] was a handsome man
    and what i want to know is
how do you like your blue-eyed boy
Mister Death

> e.e. cummings
> *Portraits*

Table of Contents

In The Midst Of Life

"I think," wrote young Stephen Spender in his best-known poem, "continuously of those who were truly great." If we did this more often we would be less tolerant of personalities living or dead created by "presentists" in and out of journalism and academe: personalities who are or were mere functions of fads or youthful ambitions. Such people are ready to flout experience and to anticipate support from others like themselves, or from elders who have lost their faith in life.

Andy Warhol, now a shade, uttered a truly memorable line in believing that "in the future everyone will be world-famous for fifteen minutes." He forgot, however, or did not care, that fame like currency depreciates in value the more it multiplies in the market.

Unfortunately, such mobs of celebrities in circulation complicate things for the truly great. The mobs grow and twist in all directions so that we are all but blinded by their numbers and deafened by their cries. Who is truly great? Who, as the late Johann Wolfgang von Goethe said of a contemporary of his, can help us no more? Whole movements have sought, some successfully, to stamp out memory of persons disruptive of their will, and to raise others to heights. Randolph Bourne's (*q.v.*) friends determined to rear a monument to his memory which would out-face that of such foes as Woodrow Wilson (*q.v.*). They half succeeded.

Union men set up busts and plaques to Samuel Gompers following his death in 1924, but academics foisted an image of him among the young which was that of a "labor faker," rather than a labor statesman. In poetry, Robert Frost's verses were moved out of hearing and his image made that of a family tyrant and mean competitor.

Needed is not a guide to distinction or to past figures who seem to lean toward present interests, but rather a guide to methods by which past or present lions can be given place to assert their qualities for good or ill. This must seem all but futile in an era which all but crowned such people as the Beatles and others of similar cast, not as entertainers but as prophets. One of them had it that he and his fellows had more followers than Jesus Christ. He was not jeered from the headlines. Yet it would be wrong to jeer at such views. Without joining them, one can ask what one wants of those men who were or are truly great, or at least useful. Or women: the feminism of our times itself suggests a question for those who seek among the living or dead.

The mystery of those who have become shades has haunted the living from the earliest times, and by no means only among the primitives. Rome was a proud civilization impossible to tear down—though marble was carried from its Coliseum across the Tiber to build the Vatican, and Vandals smashed and burned much of that proud Roman structure. Yet Rome lived a complex life which related not only to the material world, but also to the world of Gods and the dead—many of them dwelling in Hades but others in the Elysian Fields. Nor were the dead entirely cut off from the living. Gods, shades, men, and women, moved in endless relations in and out of the realms of the dead. For that matter, the tangible world of the living was inhabited by ghosts, monsters, giants, benign spirits, and witches who were not in awe of either beauty or greatness, and who created nightmares in sunny and beautiful climes.

So the shades are not, after all, too far removed from ourselves in our own time, who will ponder forever our Stalins and Hitlers, as well as our Lindberghs and Mother Teresas. And that is what our shades tell us: that we do wrong to try to forget them, for when we do, we forget the living as well. Harry Thurston Peck (*q.v.*) was a phenomenon of learning and understanding, as his monumental *Harper's Dictionary of Classical Literature and Antiques* (1896) reminds us. Yet his empire crumbled overnight, his tragedy forgotten even at his own university, as we learn from a glance at our *Columbia Encyclopedia*.

We are often told that information has become so extensive that no human mind can hold it all. We have problems remembering the names of current bestsellers. How can we hope to make recognized paths into a universal range of people and events? Yet if we ponder our shades as enigmatic, contradictory personages, rather than non-persons no longer in the news, out of date, not even alive, we find that they can offer clues to humanity at any time, to the essence of people, and of their potential—whether living or dead. We can find clues to our own selves—for better or worse.

There are pundits today who, having mastered their specialties enough to wave their prestige before the unprestigious, warn us against "cosmic arrogance:" in effect they order us to see ourselves as insignificant, as mites in the universe, and to *stop thinking about it*. Yet it is rather they who are arrogant in attempting to force us to accept their premises which are, after all, as vulnerable as any. They do not know whence comes matter. They can calculate distances, until they run out of them, but not infinity. And they are required to hold on to their cosmic hypotheses even when they are questioned within their own disciplines.

They are, indeed, in no farther an advanced position than was Herbert Spencer who, more than a century ago, wrote off the "Unknowable" as outside his purview, but who did not prove his case. Much that then seemed unknowable has since become known. Much of it is open to conjecture and experiment, and continues to make life the zestful adventure it has always been despite the shocks and the savagery it momentarily encounters.

These distinguished shades have not been casually selected. They represent aspects of our national life and dilemmas. Others can be found—indeed should be—whose lives illuminate our changing yet related conditions.

Our present shades went into death with many of their questions unanswered; and when left there, questions multiply. Who were they? What do they tell us of their times and ours? What remains if their stage is emptied? Happily, it never is. Shakespeare is an enigma at Stratford, if he is there. But not entirely. As I write, the first recovered movement of Beethoven's "lost" Tenth Symphony is being played in Germany. Musicologists say they have recovered enough from Schubert's musical notations to be able to complete his "Unfinished" Symphony. Boswell's enormous manuscript find has amazed us for the past quarter of a century. One can say quite boldly that more and more surprises and revelations lie ahead of us.

Cerberus awaits us at the River Styx, but his time is not yet. There is a place for a review not of an old stage, but of a continuing stage—one on which our own petty titans can be viewed against the shades of other times, and be seen for what they truly are. We say that So-and-So would "turn in his grave" if he knew what someone we do not like had done; but our So-and-So may have done better than that. He may have suffused the scene so that that deed cannot accomplish what was intended. As the late Robert Browning had it: "A chance, another chance, just one chance more." We are not alone, and we are not unarmed.

LOUIS FILLER

Prefatory Note

Our present era exposes so many breath-taking problems to human perspective, that it would be surprising if our language was not affected: memory being at odds with new communication. There is nothing that can be just now done to adjust these matters to larger social purpose. The word "gay," for example, has lost its traditional meaning; what was once a colloquialism for homosexuals has acquired dictionary sanction. Like the word "liberal," considered below, it has become, at least in its original sense, an endangered species.

"Blacks," in its American context at least, and whatever the subject's color, was once used by bigots, especially in the Old South, to connote those of African ancestry, however remote. The race itself sought recognition for "Colored ladies and gentlemen." Frederick Douglass, the distinguished 19th century black author and activist, employed the word "blacks" mainly when answering those who could not or would not see beyond that color. In our own time it became a banner to militants, even, often, when patently white-skinned. Today the subject is again in flux, as a proper word is sought. Influential groups ponder the use of "Afro-Americans."

"Progressivism" derived from *progress*, and was identified with the political philosophy of the era of both Theodore Roosevelt and Woodrow Wilson (*q.v.*). In this book, the phrase "the Progressive era" refers to that period, when new thinking was not only current but also frequently welcomed. Later it continued to be associated with the attitudes of advocates opposed to monopoly, corruption in government, and limited opportunities for people with small means—seen as features of the bad old times which were passing away. Robert M. LaFollette (*q.v.*) is still a reference point in this connection. More on "Progressivism" below.

"Muckraking" needs to be distinguished from Progressivism, since although the muckrakers were all Progressives, they divided between those who ardently admired Theodore Roosevelt, and others who chose to look beyond him to other causes and personalities. "Muckraking" in the other style was much diminished by 1912, but Progressivism continued through the Woodrow Wilson administration; see Filler, "Armageddon," in *The Muckrakers*, pp. 359 (1976 ed,).

"Liberalism" is another word the meaning and connotation of which have been changed with the times. Its loss of prestige, and devaluation to the status of being no more than an epithet, has been a current phenomenon. In 19th Century England, to Liberal Party supporters, "liberalism" suggested an economic philosophy inspired by self-interest rather than generous feeling. It upheld free trade as the way to prosperity among nations, and opposed war, when possible, as wasteful, uneconomical, and retrogressive.

America had no Liberal Party, but its principles, crossing the Atlantic Ocean, challenged conservatives in both major parties. E.L. Godkin (*q.v.*), transplanted from the United Kingdom, in his later years could not adjust his "liberalism" to the new age Theodore Roosevelt came to symbolize. It is unlikely that the 200-year American liberal tradition can be long submerged. Here, "liberal" is used variously, as should be clear from the contexts.

There are doubtless other words which must be freshened for a new time; seen through examples and appropriate eras, they can cause less perplexity. The best answer to apparent puzzles may be found in Allan Nevins (*q.v.*), who urged that above all one must read—read farther, read varied and opposed books—and thus become masters of current arguments.

To return to "Progressivism," definitions are today especially important because of the evident effort to identify it with negative connotations of capitalism, conservatism, and routine bureaucracy.

One such effort identifies Herbert Hoover as a "forgotten" Progressive, a term he and his following would never have accepted. Another finds Progressivism in bureaucrats who no more than happened to be part of Progressive entourages. An oddity in formal history is that it must inevitably involve people of all trends and qualities. Forthright and competent scholars are likely to work along side of calculating propagandists of a point of view, especially in collaborative works to which they contribute but do not edit. Thus a "dictionary" can become a muddle of harmful and also evocative materials: it is difficult to judge how much of either.

The intelligent reader, reading further, will not be harmed.

The Progressive *Era* was a well-defined time; as Lincoln Steffens (*q.v.*) said in his classic *Autobiography*, he and his fellows knew when times had changed for them. But an apparently helpful compilation like John D. Buenker and Edward R. Kantowicz, editors and contributors, *Historical Dictionary of the Progressive Era, 1890-1920* (1988) is rendered difficult by its combination of contributors, limited by their specialties, or lack of them, and in the hands of editors mixing materials as suited their direction.

Thus, there is *no* entry for William J. Ghent, though he was well respected even by non-socialists, and even thought to serve "radicals" because of one of his theses. There are no entries for Hutchins or Norman Hapgood, though one created a field of socio-cultural contemporary portraits and the other, editor of the famous *Collier's* was a public person of national status.

There is an entry for Frances Willard, noted for feminist education and less universally for her temperance crusade, but *none* for her nephew Josiah Flynt Willard, though he instituted then-modern muckraking. There is a William Isaac Thomas entry, but *no* Norman Thomas (*q.v.*) one—what must one do to be a Progressive? Were Generals Leonard Wood and John J. Pershing, both entried, Progressives? On what evidence and by what definition?

There are numerous institutional pieces such as the American Bar Association, the American Medical Association, and so on; no explanation why. "Tammany Hall" shares space with Ida M. Tarbell, and Finley Peter Dunne, the latter possibly because a branch of the "new History" holds city bosses as having been the real friends of the people they mulcted. Lincoln Steffens famously disputed this view.

There are no entries for George K. Turner, A.H. Lewis, Gov. Slaton (misspelled) (*qq.v.*). There are entries for Kenesaw M. Landis, the baseball "czar," and Harold L. Ickes (*q.v.*) but none on the Ickes scandals, though the monographist mentions the White, Maze book without revealing its contents, and the James M. Landis connection—helping to explain the mystery of Ickes's Progressivism—is obviously not in her thinking span.

The Edwin Markham (*q.v.*) entry does not notice his "Lincoln" poem, though it stirred the nation, and there is *no* entry on Vachel Lindsay (*q.v.*), the truer poet of Progressivism. There is *no* entry on Youth, though such leaders as Randolph Bourne (*q.v.*), as they intended, helped undermine Progressivism. There is a J.P. Morgan entry, but not one for Arthur E. Morgan (*q.v.*), one of the founders of Progressivism in education and environmentalism.

Why Richard Harding Davis, except to help put David Graham Phillips (*q.v.*), in a false category of journalism-fiction? Theodore Dreiser (*q.v.*) is evidently thought of as a Progressive, though a glance at his true biography shows an *anti*-Progressive. Upton Sinclair (*q.v.*), a central Progressive figure, shares a tepid page with others, as do numerous persons deep in Progressivism.

But what do John Reed, "Big Bill" Haywood, the Armory Show of 1913, the I.W.W.—the *I.W.W.!*—*The Masses*, Emma Goldman—exclamation marks fail us, and numerous others—to say nothing of Henry James—have to do with Progressivism, in empathy or opposition?

And what do Robert Lansing, Cotton Futures, Thomas Taggart, Charles Y. Yerkes, the transportation mogul and crook, John Hollis Bankhead, Atlanta as "Progressive," James B. Duke, the tobacco lord, and many, many more have to do with anything Progressive?

Josephine Shaw Lowell (*q.v.*) is not in this "dictionary," though she pioneered arbitration—to say no more of a great lady; and George D. Herron is here as a Christian Socialist, though his disillusionment with reform is unknown in this context. Tom Watson has long been used to besmirch Progressivism, thanks to C. Vann Woodward's conscientious history. But there are truly heroic Southerners, like Willis D. Weatherford, who are yet to be recaptured for a new Pantheon.

So the work goes on, and it is for the reader to determine how or whether such turns and twists affect his thinking or not. If he reads carefully, he will notice that there are oddities or unfulfilled questions in many of the following portraits, as in our very own lives. These are no conventional encyclopedia pieces here which pretend that all is known and explained.

Dr. Benjamin Rush
(1745-1813)

*"Bring Out
    Your Dead!"*

Oₙₑ OF PHILADELPHIA'S MOST
noted citizens of all time, pioneer in the treatment of the sick and insane,
reformer and signer of the Declaration of Independence. Dr. Benjamin Rush
was principal in a famous legal suit which permanently casts a shadow on
his fame.

He was born in Byberry, north of Philadelphia and later incor-
porated into it: then a Quaker agricultural colony, later, possibly coincidentally, as will appear, a center for a lunatic asylum. Rush was of the fifth
generation of his family in America, a child of well-to-do parents, descend-
ed from a comrade at arms of Oliver Cromwell. He attended the College
of New Jersey, later Princeton University, graduating at fifteen. There being
no medical school in the colonies he left for Edinburgh, famous for its
medical facilities. He took his medical degree there, but also drew in the
ideas of such radicals as John Wilkes. He returned home in 1769 to become
the first instructor in chemistry in the colonies, at the College of Philadelphia, which became the University of Pennsylvania.

As involved in radical politics as he was in medicine, he encouraged the British expatriate Thomas Paine to publish the powerfully
effective *Common Sense,* and himself signed the Declaration of Independence and served as Surgeon General in Washington's army. Peace

1

having returned, he became the first citizen of Philadelphia, as a writer against slavery and for women's opportunity, as a founder of Dickinson College, and as a member of the Pennsylvania Convention which ratified the Federal Constitution.

Rush was intensely concerned for every aspect of medicine and its treatments. His *Medical Inquiry and Observations* (1794-1798) was issued in five volumes. In 1772 he became Professor of Institutes of Medicine and Clinical Practice, and later given the whole field as his own. His students preserved the lecture notes of their Professor of Theory and Practice, and took them along to the towns and cities where they opened offices. In 1786 he established the first free dispensary in the country.

When in August of 1793 the Yellow Fever first made its appearance, it found a city unprepared for its dangers. Open barrels of rainwater stood everywhere in William Penn's relatively neat and orderly city, but no connection was to be made between the mosquitoes which comforted themselves on the rainwater's surface and the illness which began to appear in several streets among individuals.

No man could match Dr. Rush in his fearless effort to help the afflicted and study the symptoms which accompanied the course of the disease to returned health or descent to death. Dr. Rush was tireless in going from house to house, as the Yellow Fever caught on, as the cry of "Bring out your dead!" increased in the streets for toughened men to cart away, and as frightened citizens made rude efforts to protect themselves by bolting their doors and windows, avoiding contact with outsiders and even with each other, by wearing camphor around their necks, or by fleeing the city increasingly by wagon, carriage, or on foot.

Dr. Rush opened windows, fed patients wine, or shocked them with cold baths, studied their chills and high fevers, their yellowed eyes and vomit, and stayed up nights to pore over books and manuscripts for cures. His fellow physicians were beside themselves with worry and contradictory solutions, and, some his friends, some foes, themselves came down with the Yellow Fever.

How Dr. Rush hit upon purging and bleeding as the authentic cure, certain to help so long as the patient was not in decline or unwilling to obey orders, makes a lengthy tale of long-established medical theory and practice at home and abroad. It was complicated by the question of whether the disease had commenced at home, or been brought in from abroad. Dr. Rush thought it had been brought in by foreign ships docked in Philadelphia Harbor. Common sense could not function in the hysterical condition sufficiently to remark that dirt, decaying matter, offal, and still other matter were constant in a city of horses, dogs, cats, rats, and careless citizens. The opposing theory at least had the relevance of parts of his theory which prescribed the open windows which brought mosquitoes as well as fresh air.

The key question lay in Rush's prescription of drastic purging and the generous drawing of blood, presumably carrying a variant concept of "humors" which had to be drained from the body. Dr. Rush tried his "cure" on some one hundred patients, and exultantly reported that among those not too far gone to profit from his treatment, recovery had been almost entire. He was no creature of his theory. He himself, who had been more exposed than anyone, first suffered a mild case of the Yellow Fever, then a severe case. He himself ordered generous purging, with his specific of calomel (mercury) and jalap, and bleeding. His own recovery, and recoveries, he reported from his increasingly large, changing, and continuing run of patients. They confirmed him in the unique power of his "cure."

Nevertheless, the continuing cries of "Bring out your dead!" went on, coming eventually to some 4,000—some one-tenth of the entire population of the proud city, at that time Capital of the United States. It was summer, and Philadelphia was almost without Congress or city officials. Heroes of that summer included Negroes, who were maligned, and defended by Richard Allen, founder of the African Methodist denomination, and Stephen Girard. That founder of the later Girard College for fatherless boys was a dour businessman with no pretensions to civic virtue, but he tended the dying and dead, wrapped them in funeral shrouds, and saw them to the flourishing cemeteries.

Dr. Rush walked among scenes of horror, a general with the weapons for overcoming them, and though clung to and sought by frantic citizens in Philadelphia and beyond, was not without infuriating skeptics. A former Princeton classmate, Ebenezer Hazard, was taken with the Yellow Fever, and "plentifully" bled by Rush. Hazard then refused any further ministrations, angering Rush who strode out of the house. That Hazard lived told Rush only that his earlier treatment had laid the "foundations" for his return to health.

A detail which only time would reveal was Dr. Rush's estimate that the body held twenty-five pounds or a bit more of blood. Later analysis would show that it normally contained no more than half that figure, and that drastic as had seemed Dr. Rush's bleedings— taking on occasion some four-fifths of the entire body's holdings—it had been vastly more diminishing of human substance than had been imagined.

Nevertheless, the Yellow Fever finally ran its course by October. The national and city administrations began to take up their work, the people to resume their activities. Dr. Rush went on to write up his experiences and views, to draft lectures and respond to correspondence, to care for his family, and to attend sessions of the American Philosophical Society which his friend Benjamin Franklin had founded.

There was a Yellow Fever case here and there, and in 1797 it struck hard again. Dr. Rush could now consider, despite mutterings and hesitancy here and there, that his cure was established, and no longer required him to be a centerpiece of events. A new factor then entered the scene which he could not ignore.

William Cobbett was an obscure Britisher, self-educated and with wife and family. He had been a British army sergeant. Resentful of the graft and corruption he had observed in the service and because he had voiced his anger, he had been forced to flee to America to avoid arrest. He tutored French immigrants in English while also discovering in himself a home-patriotism which resented invidious views of the old country by British expatriates. Among them, notably, was Dr. Joseph Priestley, the discoverer of oxygen, who was welcomed by Democrats of Thomas Jefferson and Thomas Paine's persuasion. Cobbett came to Philadelphia in 1794 and the next year published a pamphlet anonymously excoriating Dr. Priestley. Several more of his pamphlets opposed the Democrats; he had become a bookseller with an extraordinary gift for popular expression. In 1796 he appeared as "Peter Porcupine" who defended John Jay's Treaty with Great Britain which Democrats were bitterly denouncing as a betrayal of the Revolution's goals and sacrifices.

Cobbett focused, too, on Dr. Rush's career in the earlier Yellow Fever horror. Rush's patriotic services not helping the doctor's image in Cobbett's view. It wants notice that there was no significant alternative cure for Yellow Fever known at this time; attention was all on the drastic nature of the Rush blood lettings and purges. Cobbett's inimitable prose now rang out to the people of Philadelphia and beyond, as in *Porcupine's Gazette* with his couplet:

> The times are ominous, indeed,
> When quack to quack cries purge and bleed.

Cobbett's emphasis was on Dr. Rush's vanity, as he saw it, and here he was clearly inaccurate; Philadelphians better read Rush's sincere will to serve. Cobbett's personal strictures—some so personal as to touch Dr. Rush's family itself—were beside the mark. More disturbing was his eloquence regarding the facts. Dr. Rush had claimed almost a hundred percent success, yet deaths had multiplied out of all reason. A local outbreak had become a city-wide nightmare. The implications were appalling: according to Cobbett, it was Dr. Rush, not the Yellow Fever, which had filled the Quaker City's graveyards.

Dr. Rush had no alternative but to sue. His attorneys were Joseph Hopkinson, a young man soon to be famous as author of the patriotic "Hail, Columbia"; Moses Levy, of sharp and memorable statement; and Jared Ingersoll, the Attorney General of Pennsylvania. Cobbett's defense team included Robert Goodloe Harper, a Federalist leader and Congressman from South Carolina. The Justices included Dr. William Shippen, of high standing and no friendship for Dr. Rush. It was the trial of the decade.

It proceeded with firm attention to the issues. Dr. Rush's attorneys decried libel in face of public opinion sympathetic to freedom of the press, even when libelous. At issue, too, was the reputation of Philadelphia's leading citizen. In the meantime Cobbett had moved to New York, and it was there that he received the dark news. He had been found guilty, and sentenced to pay $5,000 in damages.

Cobbett took the crushing blow well. Friends came to his aid. He issued his burning *RUSHLIGHT* papers which sold sensationally, helped pay his debt, and augmented his fame. Although Dr. Rush could claim victory, and was praised and congratulated to his face, he knew there were enemies skeptical of his Yellow Fever services who were gratified that Cobbett had voiced their doubts and resentments for them. In 1799 General George Washington died, aged sixty-seven, having been bled by one of Dr. Rush's admirers, and the shadow darkened for the moment about him.

In 1800 Cobbett returned to England where he shed his Federalism and emerged as the nation's unforgettable radical of radicals. Dr. Rush's civic services never ceased. He pioneered sensitive treatment of the mentally ill, his own *Diseases of the Mind* (1812) being a pioneer work in psychiatry. He suffered a personal tragedy when his son John, who had once sought a duel with Cobbett himself, became insane and had to be incarcerated in Dr. Rush's ground-breaking building for the insane on what would have become the University of Pennsylvania campus.

Others of distinction had erred, and many without so full a record as Dr. Rush's of civic virtue. His fault had been an unwillingness to leave so dubious a problem as the Yellow Fever open, to read what he preferred into the record, without regard for the doubts and opinions of colleagues. Posterity was generous, but it could not forget.

Rush's own *Autobiography* was published in 1948, his *Letters* in 1951. Winthrop & Frances Neilson, *Verdict for the Doctor* (1958) focuses on the trial. Nathan G. Goodman, *Benjamin Rush* (1934) is by a Philadelphian who absorbed himself in original documents. J.H. Powell, *Bring Out Your Dead* (1949) brought an analytical mind to the plague and its conditions.

Gustavus Vassa
(1745?-1797)

*"By every means
in my power"*

AFRICAN SLAVE, LITERARY FIGURE, AND TRAVELER, GUSTAVUS Vassa stood out among many whose fortunes in the eighteenth century touched American affairs. Few had the talents which made his memoirs durable. He was born Okaudah Equiano, the son of an East Nigerian tribal chief, probably near Onitsha, and enjoyed a happy childhood in his community. It was lost when he was about ten years of age and kidnapped by nearby tribesmen. Equiano passed through various hands before being brought to white slave traders on the coast. During the voyage to the West Indies he saw brutality toward slaves which molded his outlook. He was taken to Virginia where he was bought by Michael Henry Pascal, an officer in the Royal Navy, and then transported to England.

Pascal named him for the sixteenth century Swedish warrior-king, Gustavus Vasa, adding an "s" to his second name. While still at sea the boy began to learn English, thanks to a friendly young sailor. Following his master, Vassa spent a number of years on sea and in ports, and saw fighting between the British and French in the Mediterranean and in Canada. Meanwhile, during Pascal's visits to London, Vassa saw sisters of one of Pascal's friends, who grew to esteem him. They helped Vassa with his education and had him baptized in St. Margaret's Church, Westminster in early 1759. His memoirs, the main source of knowledge regarding Vassa, tell of many of his vicissitudes in service.

He had been promised freedom, and had earned it; but when he asked for it in 1762, Pascal was enraged and sent him to the West Indies to be sold. Fortune gave Vassa a good master, Robert King, a Philadelphia Quaker and merchant who taught him commercial arts and to whom he was faithful in return. He travelled between Philadelphia and the West Indies for his master, in the meantime building up savings with which to purchase his freedom through cautious trading on his own. He won his papers in 1766.

Vassa continued his association with King, and afterwards as a sailor was on voyages which took him from Turkey to Greenland, the latter during an expedition intended to open a passage to India. He returned to London, where he was a valet among educated people. Vassa was an abolitionist, and yearned to take his religious message to Africa. As he wrote:

> On my return to London in August [1786], I was very agreeably surprised to find that the benevolence of government had adopted the plan of some philanthropic individuals to send the Africans from hence to their native quarter; and that some vessels were then enlarged to carry them to Sierra Leone. . . .[Gentlemen] seemed to think me qualified to superintend part of the undertaking. . . .I expressed some difficulties on the account of the slave dealers, as I would certainly oppose their traffic in the human species by every means in my power.

Unfortunately he could not obtain the ordination deemed necessary for such a mission. He continued to hope for service in anti-slavery actions. In 1783 he made contact with the abolitionist Granville Sharp informing him of seamen on the ship *Zong* off the West African coast, who had jettisoned some 130 slaves: an atrocity which raised up Parliamentary debate and questions regarding the operations of the slave trade.In 1787 it appeared that Vassa might be able to enter into actions uniting English humanitarians and African missions. He was appointed commissary of provisions and stores for more than 700 black poor of London, who were to be sent to Sierra Leone. He could not resist, however, exposing the corruption of government agents who were buying provisions for the journey. Offended, they caused Vassa to be dismissed from the project. His petition of March 21, 1788 to Charlotte, Queen of England, begging her attention to the sufferings of West Indian slaves was kept alive in abolitionist lore and propaganda.

Vassa's 1789 book, *The Interesting Narrative of the Life of Okaudah Equiano, or Gustavus Vassa the African, Written by Himself* was recognized for its clear narrative, candor, and manifest intelligence. It was not the first such book; three others by African-born who wrote in English preceded his book, but none had his variety and talent. Notable was it that the book was instantly perceived as literary, and so recognized in America. In 1813 it was published along with the poems of the New England black Phillis Wheatley, earlier welcomed by critics. In 1792 Vassa married Susanna Cullen of Ely. Vassa travelled in England and Wales selling his book and expounding his religious and abolitionist views. Their one child Ann Marie Vassa died at age four, July 21, 1797, less than three months after her father's death. Before then Granville Sharp had heard of his last illness and visited him.

Vassa became a permanent feature in general literature, as well as in black literary annals. There were eight British editions and one American edition while he was still alive, and translations in Dutch and German. Vassa was recognized in William J. Simmons's *Men of Mark* (1887) and still later in Benjamin Brawley's *Early American Writers* (1935).

Anne Newport Royall
(1769-1854)

THE HUNTRESS.

EDITED AND PRINTED BY ANNE ROYALL.

Vol. 1.]   'NEW SERIES.   [No. 3.

WASHINGTON, D. C., JULY 24, 1854.

CONGRESS.

HOUSE OF REPRESENTATIVES.

SPEECH OF HON. JOHN J. TAYLOR,
OF NEW YORK,

A page from one of Royall's muckraking publications. There are no known sketches or photographs of Anne Newport Royall.

"Shrew"

PIONEER FEMINIST AND prototype of the muckraker for more than a century, Anne Newport Royall was notorious by having been humiliated in a Washington, D.C. court which, under an old law, found against her as a "common scold."

She was born the daughter of a farmer near Baltimore, Maryland, a Tory who may have been the illegitimate son of one of the regal Calverts. William Newport and his family being harassed by rebel patriots, they moved to the western Pennsylvania frontier where he later died, perhaps during an Indian raid. Anne's mother, following another marriage and a second death, took her children south, seeking family and aid. She finally obtained work in the household of Captain William Royall, a wealthy Revolutionary army officer and friend of George Washington.

Royall was a freethinker and admirer of Thomas Paine. Owning a fine library, he took pleasure in introducing Anne to it, and instructing her in his opinions and Masonic dedication. In 1797 he startled his family and neighbors by marrying her, and till his death in 1812 she lived as his lady and consort. She had never liked the dank and lusterless backwoods in which they had lived, and with him gone, she left the region with a carriage and three servants to enjoy the more benign regions of Alabama.

In 1823 her idyll ended when she was sued by the late Captain Royall's relatives on grounds that she had been an adulteress, had taken advantage of his drunkenness and senility, had abused him, and forged his will. A court prejudiced against Mrs. Royall and against Royall's liberal views and actions, and appealing to archaic law and custom found for the accusers, leaving her at age fifty-four stripped of her inheritance.

She now showed her metal, turning for a livelihood to travel and writing in which she probed and described a changing America of people and personalities, setting down her views and observations in hasty but communicative prose. She sought out individuals of note to fill out her picture of a vibrant democracy. Unescorted and poor, and often challenged by rude and conventional-minded persons, she was indefatigable in her search for response in a now alien world. In the course of her travels by carriage, boat, and on foot she traversed much of the habitable country, and her first publications won a tenuous status for her as author.

Although driven by need rather than literary ambitions, Mrs. Royall's explorations into personality and a significantly changing America added up to a new view of a country which had given her high opportunity and also tragically demeaned her. Her prose was not exceptional, but it came from a woman of high courage whose condition forced her to explore opportunities which made her a keen interpreter of the range of American societies and shifting values. As John Quincy Adams observed in his own famous *Dairy,* from which a single passage entered into Royall lore:

> ...[She] continues to make herself noxious to many per-
> sons, tolerated by some and feared by others, by her
> deportment and her books; treating all with a familiarity
> which often passes for impudence, insulting those who
> treat her with incivility, and then lampooning them in
> her books. Stripped of all her sex's delicacy, but unable
> to forfeit its privilege of gentle treatment from the
> other, she goes about like a visage errant in enchanted
> armor, and redeems herself from the cravings of in-
> digence by the notoriety of her eccentricities and the
> forced currency they give to her publications.

As Mrs. Royall went about her travels, she encountered many hard people who thought it proper to treat her rudely and worse, but she also met such simple humanity and intelligence as was preferred by a J. Dow, a landlord in Waterville, Maine, who refused to give her a bill: "I should be far from thinking it proper to charge a person who is rendering a benefit to the country."

She served it by making local items take on national significance, as in her Pittsburgh comment:

> All the houses are colored quite black with the smoke; the interiors of the houses are still worse; carpets, chairs, walls, furniture—all black with smoke. No such thing as wearing white; the ladies mostly dress in black, with a cap or white ruff. Put on clean in the morning, ruffs are tinged black by bed-time; the ladies are continually washing their faces. The smoke is most annoying to the eyes; and everything has a very gloomy, doleful appearance.

And in Cincinnati, where she mixed interest in notables and the churches; in the tavern at which she stayed, the cook, a mother who could not find money for shoes won her sympathy. Mrs. Royall contributed fifty cents toward the purchase of shoes:

> The poor thing burst into tears, called me an angel, and said if I had not given her the money the constable would have taken her that night. "This is just what I owe the tract society. So sure as I haven't the money to pay, the constable is sent for me. He took me away once."
>
> "But why do you subscribe?"
>
> "You are obliged to subscribe, if you work for a living, or nobody would hire you. All the servants and waiters about the tavern have to subscribe $5 a year!" Several of them were standing by and said it was true.

Sketches of History, Life and Manners in the United States, by a Traveller (1826) repaid her years of reading and thought. Later books, *The Black Book* (1828-9), *Mrs. Royall's Pennsylvania* (1829), *Mrs. Royall's Southern Tour* (1830-1), and *Letters from Alabama* (1830) continued her tale of an America which was still thinly united by sections with highly disparate ways.

Mrs. Royall followed her late husband as a freethinker and Mason, branches of the latter helping her in dire moments. She developed Jacksonian views, as in "sound money" and contempt for abolitionists, but deviated from them in her sympathy with the plight of Indians, deprived of their native soil and at the mercy of the courts. Visiting cities, she searched out institutions to determine how society dealt with orphans and old people, how the city kept its streets and public places, its memorials, and how it regarded strangers.

She gravitated toward Washington, where she tirelessly petitioned Congress for a pension, being the relict of a Revolutionary soldier. There in the Capital city she found help from John Quincy Adams, whom she personally offended with her persistence, but who saw her claims as valid. Others were increasingly more brusk toward her, as she sought to sell them her books, or to foist her anti-clerical views on them. An anti-Mason with whom she was quarrelsome threw her downstairs, breaking her leg.

In 1829 Presbyterians whose place of worship was close to her Washington house brought suit against her for public abuse, and won a judgement against her, once again based on an old law, as a "common scold." The sentence would have been ducking in a pond, but in consideration of her age, now sixty-four, the sentence was reduced to ten dollars which she was unable to pay. She was saved from prison by Jacksonian sympathies. His Secretary of War John Eaton, husband of Peggy O'Neale Eaton who was soon to precipitate a Cabinet crisis, intended to pay the fine, but before he reached the court two journalists laid down the money, for "gallantry," and freedom of the press.

In 1831 Mrs. Royall having purchased a press, and helped by a Mrs. Sarah Stack, who was to serve her to the end, she instituted the first of the two papers which were to establish her as a pioneer in journalism. Although she was not the first woman journalist—Sarah J. Buell Hale, among others, preceded her—her *Paul Pry* undertook accounts of government which no others previously touched. To be sure, accusations of malfeasance were thrown freely between partisan Democrats and Whigs, but they were recognizably self-serving.

Mrs. Royall, always hunting information, and long practiced in finding it, published hints and gossip about notables, ferreted out evidence of corruption among legislators, and in such government agencies as the Post Office. Hers was the outlook of a housewife who demanded order and respectability in society. But in assessing the changing guard in

Congress, and in her "pen portraits" of Washington figures she made a pattern in reporting which gave her precedence in "muckraking" over William Lyon Mackenzie (*q.v.*) in early social and political exposure. She published *Paul Pry* until 1836, following it with her aptly-named *The Huntress* that same year which she continued till her death.

Bleak as was her life, it was punctuated with more human contacts among legislators and journalists she sought out. The Jacksonian Major Mordecai Noah offered her respect, as did the early yellow journalist James Gordon Bennett and the somewhat more many-faceted James Watson Webb. With such as these she did what she could to gain recognition and funds. A passage in her life finds her talking with one of her "pen portraits." "Why don't you wait until we are dead?" he asked. Her reply was, "I might die myself, meantime."

That Mrs. Royall was acerbic and difficult there can be no doubt, but that she was ill-treated beyond social decency is evident. In 1849, aged seventy eight, she was finally granted a pension of $2,400 by Congress, half of which was promptly taken by William Royall's ever-alert relatives, the remainder of which went to her lawyers. Her livelihood continued to be in haunting Congressional corridors and byways for matter to be used in her newspaper columns, and for purchasers of her paper whom she could waylay.

She was not a feminist within later meanings of the word. Her cause was people like herself deprived of equity before the law, and she did break ground for women of the more industrial and impersonal post-Civil War era which lost reverence for womankind, but resented their struggles for place. Mrs. Royall's independence and pride lost her sympathy and associates in her time and after. She did not outlive her reputation as a "Common scold." She died a pauper and was buried in Washington's Congressional Cemetery.

Herbert Blankenhorn's *American Mercury* article (September 1927), "Grandma of the Muckrakers," gave perspective to other accounts of Mrs. Royall's life, which included Sarah Harvey Porter, *The Life and Times of Anne Royall* (1909), and George S. Jackson, *Uncommon Scold: the Story of Anne Royall* (1937). Best of all as following in the tracks of Mrs. Royall and reconstructing her life is Bessie Rowland James, *Anne Royall's U.S.A.* (1972).

Samuel F. B. Morse
(1791-1872)

"What Hath God Wrought!"

As an older man, Morse received world-wide acclaim as the inventor of the electromagnetic telegraph.

SAMUEL FINLEY BREESE Morse was an artist and inventor. His artistic career was notable, but aborted in full flower by native lack of support. Following some years of struggle, his work on the electromagnetic telegraph caught fire and made his name world famous. Though it took much of his energy, his political life as anti-Catholic was substantially forgotten. His several major roles in the American nineteenth century continued to want modern definition.

He was born of parents who, like many of New England birth, inherited a species of distinction by reason of their Puritan descent. His father, Jedediah Morse, a Congregationalist clergyman, earned a measure of durable fame by geography textbooks which won him the title of "father of American geography." The elder Morse also sought good relations with the Indians, his memorable *Report to the Secretary of War* (1822) further enhancing his humanistic reputation.

Finley, as he was known, was raised in an intensely orthodox home in the shadow of Breed's Hill in Charlestown, Massachusetts. He early showed artistic talent. He followed his father's footsteps in attending Yale College, having already done portraits which showed insight, balance, and a sense of nuance. It was evident that he had his vocation. With examples of Benjamin West, Copley, and the Peales behind him, there seemed no reason why he would not help build the American art establishment. With Washington Allston, whose art he admired, he went to England to study further before undertaking a career at home. In London he worked with West himself and broadened his sense of political life and society. He returned home less the rigid federalist his parents wanted him to be, but as firm as themselves in piety.

His career needed a center for marriage and security, but though he found commissions for portraits in Massachusetts and in the lower states the financial returns were seriously low. For several seasons he settled in Charleston, South Carolina, where he was better employed producing a canon of art work which would be well regarded in later years but which brought journeyman's wages then. Nevertheless he was encouraged enough to marry and, in 1823, to settle in New York as his artistic base.

Morse's labors continued to produce an erratic and insufficient income, so that his wife and child were forced to retreat to New Haven, Connecticut. There his parents, having quarrelled with Charlestown Unitarians had taken up residence. Meanwhile, their son Finley had conceived a grand project intended to appeal to nationalistic sentiments and to put his own affairs in order: a vast portrait of the United States Congress. Morse hoped several times for a Congressional subsidy for Capitol art decoration. He was constrained to finish his "Representative Hall" alone, with its eighty-eight portraits, and to hope it would bring him revenues and fame as an exhibition piece. It roused comment and some funds, but it attained no vogue and accomplished nothing for him until it became a national treasure long after Morse's death.

Morse struggled on, encouraged by young artists and such friends as James Fenimore Cooper, but vividly aware that his countrymen would not support art beyond their conventional needs. His work put him in conflict with the then dominant American Academy of Fine Arts. In 1825 he both painted one of his most distinguished works, a portrait of Lafayette, then visiting America, and initiated the revolt of New York artists against crabbed policies of the American Academy by organizing the National Academy of the Arts of Design, of which Morse was elected president.

His work continued to involve unfulfilled struggle. He lost his wife by death and required family help for his three children. He was dependent on small commissions and aid from friends and family. In 1829 he sought new inspiration in Europe with some modest commissions and hopes for a ringing success. He studied and created art in Italy, and was stirred by the revolutionary events of 1830 in Paris. There he conceived his brilliant concept of *A Gallery of the Louvre* which, in one panoramic sweep would fill the viewer's eye with Louvre masterpieces, showing their variety and significance. Morse spent three years abroad with friends and European notables.

He returned home to continuing financial failure as an artist, his *Gallery of the Louvre* accomplishing nothing for his needs. But on his voyage home he was bemused by conversation about the Frenchman Ampère's experiments with electromagnets. Experiments with electricity went back to Benjamin Franklin in America, and conjectures about it to ancient history. Morse did not then know, or realize, that the idea of electrical connection from point to point, to be monitored by code from both ends had been suggested or pursued in various places, and even at home. Professor Joseph Henry at Princeton College, just the year before, had rung a bell at a distance by means of an armature placed so as to strike the bell when attracted to an electromagnet: the principle, later, of an ordinary doorbell. Scientists in Germany, England, and France were considering ways to make the electromagnet an instrument of communication.

Morse's unique contribution, which gave him title to being the "inventor" of the telegraph was by practical refinements which took the instrument out of theory, including the finger-key transmitter and receivers, and the Morse Code. But most important was his vision of the instrument's practicality as a means of communication, once he was convinced that the electricity passed instantaneously to the receiver, no matter at what distance. This was a vision which a world of people habituated to communication by horse, runner, railroad, and boat traveling days and weeks and months could not absorb.

Morse's life was somewhat less difficult when he received a position at what became New York University as a professor of art, and his first hope for the telegraph was that its success would release him for his life as an artist. During this time he also became a major popularizer of the daguerreotype; the first photographic process, it once again eluded him as a money-getting operation, but brought in enough to encourage telegraph research. The telegraph became a matter of details of vital importance, such as the need for a continuing set of wires to continue the circuit. This required of Morse the invention of the relay. Morse at the time continued to pursue the hope of art, but his artistic production was largely finished, with some portraits left incomplete. The problem of financing never diminished. Morse acquired associates who were more or less cooperative before the telegraph won its monumental success. Morse himself struggled to find endorsement. His dream was to persuade the government of the value of the telegraph, and to sell it to its officials for $100,000. That failing—some of the people with whom he made contact thought him insane—he turned to private individuals for funds.

Meanwhile he opened another aspect of his long life—he was now in his middle years—by joining the "Know Nothings": "native" Americans who were increasingly alarmed by Irish immigrants who, they thought, could not fathom the American heritage, and needed to be curbed and controlled by those who did. Morse's piety had kept him fighting and alive in bitterest times. He now wrote passionately in defense of his country, which he equated with Protestantism, and sought office in New York as a means of controlling education in the schools and respectable people at the polls.

As a young man in London in 1814, Morse painted his self-portrait and said his face approached the "hatchet class." Morse had hoped his invention of the telegraph would give him financial security and thus free him to paint.

Morse's efforts to find funds and opportunity to prove the value of his and his partners' invention continued until 1844. Then, thanks to sympathetic contacts and his own ardent expense of energy and contrivances, he was granted $30,000 by Congress to complete a telegraph line between Washington and Baltimore which would prove or disprove his long-held claims. Building the line was a saga in itself, of interest to no one but the anxious builders. They considered a buried line, which proved impractical but consumed money. They then decided on a wire set on poles along the railroad track. There was a breath-taking moment when the builder's check on signals failed to go through, possibly revealing the line as a failure. But the defect was discovered, and the work went on.

There was actual telegraphic communication while the line to Baltimore grew, but it excited no great interest in a country which still could not assimilate its import. On May 24, 1844 the line was complete, and a young friend of Morse's was given the official right to send through a line from the Bible which was to enter textbooks for the coming century: "What hath God wrought!"

Extraordinary as the event was, it was implemented by a veritable miracle which appears to have been totally unforeseen. The Democratic Party was meeting in Baltimore to nominate a candidate for the Presidency. Morse, stationed in a room in the Capitol below the Senate Chamber was in communication with his partners, who had their sender and receiver in the Baltimore railroad depot. Morse was interested in the Presidential poll which former President Martin Van Buren was expected to win. News came to the Capitol in usual ways, by boat, horse, and railroad. Morse's interest at the time appears to have been political; he had proved his point in respect to the telegraph. He offered to set the news on a bulletin board for Congress to read. When Van Buren's drive waned at the convention and the Presidential race became open, Congressmen crowded about the telegraph to learn what was happening in Baltimore. They were electrified when word came that James K. Polk had entered the list of candidates.

Who was Polk? Congressmen now jammed the telegraph room and the corridors watching Morse as though he was a magician reading telegraphic signals. When Polk, the first "dark horse" in American political history, won the nomination, the telegraph had conquered Washington, as it quickly after did the country and beyond.

It would be difficult to say that Morse's life thereafter was anticlimax. Ahead of him was a hard fight to win all rights he could to financial returns on his great victory: against greedy partners, against claimed inventors, and, abroad, against alternative systems and pretenders. The sordid court trials had the virtue of bringing out and clarifying the sequence of events and experiments which had gone into the telegraph and its uses. A mighty saga was the laying of the Atlantic cable, which took in nations as well as entrepreneurs, in America notably Cyrus W. Field.

When nativism rose again in the 1850s, Morse, already world famous, continued his crusade against immigrants and Catholicism; though now, unknown to itself, nativism, with no future in an upwardly mobile country, gave Whigs and Democrats transitional means for sorting themselves out into proslavery and antislavery factions. Morse stood with the northern proslavery people who claimed they represented peace, in place of war. A later generation, appreciative of his genius, concluded to forget this byproduct of a towering and courageous life.

The masterpiece of Morse biography is Carleton Mabee, *The American Leonardo* (1943), with an introduction by Allan Nevins (*q.v.*). See also Harry B. Wehle, *Samuel Finley Breese Morse, American Painter* (1932) and Oliver W. Larkin, *Art & Life in America* (1960).

Sylvester Graham
(1794-1851)

"Graham's Crackers"

A HEALTH ADVOCATE, SYLVESTER Graham made regimes intended to create "symmetry" between bodily functions and religion. Entirely sincere in his findings, he advanced health measures in the face of prejudice, and survives in his discovery of unbolted, coarsely ground wheat (graham flour).

He was the grandson of a Glasgow clergyman and physician who emigrated to Connecticut, and whose son in turn replicated his career, graduating from Yale College and becoming both a preacher and doctor. At age 72 he had his son Sylvester by his second wife. He died two years later, and Sylvester was raised by relatives who neglected his education and health, so that he worked at random as farm-hand, clerk, and teacher until threatened by tuberculosis. He took himself in hand, entering Amherst College in 1823, but soon found himself at odds with its students. They resented his actor-like deportment, perhaps augmented by the solitary life he had led, and by his effort to reach them. His intense deportment was to contribute to his later success. Leaving Amherst, Graham attended to his illness, married, and pursued a clerical career. He approached health care first by becoming an agent of the temperance crusade: one of the reforms in a growing reform era. He also studied anatomy, diet, and theories of health. His own discovery of "symmetry" drew from religion and from a sense of what the body should look like, being in the image of the Creator. He denounced obesity, easily gained in a time of enormous banquets, stimulated by heavy drinking. His invention of the "graham cracker" in 1829 was to emerge as the base from which the breakfast cereal industry grew.

In 1830-31 he lectured in Philadelphia and New York on the virtues of vegetarianism, another reform cause, adding the virtues of fruit and bread, fresh air, exercise, and a cheerful outlook, all of which he found authenticated in Bible literature. His lectures drawing crowds, Graham took them up and down the Atlantic coast, winning followers and also foes who helped augment his name recognition. A striking feature of his work was his free references to parts of the body as they were affected by foods and misuse: at the time this was seen as a form of obscenity.

Honest and well-intended, Graham created followers and dissenters, some with personal stakes in his subjects. The phrenologist Orson Squire Fowler was even more successful than Graham in his pursuits, but learned from him, and added his findings to his own recommendations. Graham had his unique experiences; in Boston he was threatened by a mob of butchers and bakers, and only saved by his partisans, who reportedly poured slaked lye on the protestors from the lecture hall windows. Graham's writings, too, became part of his campaign, running from one on cholera to a controversial one on *Chastity* (1834), which favored continence. In 1836-1837, he added a lecture intended to help "colored people."

Although Graham was the subject of jokes and editorials, his work also called forth Graham bread, Graham groups, and even Graham boarding houses, where his regimes could be personalized for individuals. A *Graham Journal of Health and Longevity* ran from 1837 to 1839, and he himself furthered his own progress with *Lectures on the Science of Human Life* (1839), in two volumes, which summed up his ideas and experiences. Although his vogue passed as a working operation, it was maintained in reform circles. He had sufficient response for an earned living, while he absorbed himself in Biblical studies; a volume achieved print after his death. A sketch of his life is in his posthumously reprinted *The Science of Human Life* (1858). James H. Trumbull, ed., *The Memorial History of Hartford County, Connecticut, 1833-1883* (1886) provided further details.

William Lyon Mackenzie
(1795-1861)

*"To the Victors
Belong the Spoils"*

A FOUNDER OF CANADIAN nationalism, William Lyon Mackenzie was a leader of the 1837 uprising against the Crown which, though put down sharply, opened the way which led to independence.[1] As a fugitive from justice in the United States, he was jailed for having incited Americans to join in aggressions involving a foreign power. Released, Mackenzie found a modest "archival" job in the New York Customs House. There he discovered numerous files and papers left behind which showed deep abuse of power by Customs officials. His publication of them created a sensation with which neither historians in the United States nor Canada were able to cope, then or later. Mackenzie's return to Canada under amnesty made him a national figure, but his American career was buried in both countries.

A Scotsman of humble birth, Mackenzie had a commercial career which in 1820 took him as an immigrant to Canada. There he entered into politics. A man of tremendous energy, an idealist whose marked eloquence was expressed in his publication, *Colonial Advocate*, he made appearances as a member of the York (Toronto) provincial legislature. He developed a sense of Canadian grievances that brought him to London in

1832 to present the province's complaints to authorities. His increasing fame as a tribune made him mayor of the newly-created city of Toronto in 1834.

Mackenzie continued agitations that, by 1837, took him and his followers to the point of rebellion against imperial authority. A skirmish near the city's arsenal on December 7 costing several lives brought defiance to a head.

Mackenzie was not a gifted tactician in political or military terms. His forte was agitation and moral rectitude, both of which served the nation-to-be, but failed him in actual combat. He took his stand for independence from Great Britain at Navy Island in the Niagara River, proclaiming a republic before a horde of his own followers and others from the United States side. It was dissolved by bullets from both sides, with those from troops under the American General Winfield Scott acting against what were mainly Irish provocateurs in the United States.

Mackenzie fled Canadian troops and worked tirelessly to continue his agitation favoring Canadian independence. He had little more than his inspiring eloquence and an incredibly fluent pen to sustain him and the large family he had brought with him. His hopes now lay with Americans who had once broken with the British Empire and presumably would help neighbors to attain equal liberties; and with Democrats who might represent the greatest number of American equalitarians.

In 1839 Mackenzie was tried in court for seeking to disaffect Americans in behalf of foreign interests, and sentenced to eighteen months in prison. Undeterred, Mackenzie continued his propaganda from behind prison walls. His flow of correspondence included but did not reach President Martin Van Buren or his successor, following a brief interval, President John Tyler. Tyler's son Robert, however, gave Mackenzie encouragement and introductions following his release from prison.

Mackenzie took his family to New York City and there sought to improve his prospects. With his retentive memory and continuous reading he could furnish matter bearing on innumerable subjects. His hopes centered on the New York Customs House, a Democratic fief handling enormous inflow and outflow wealth. His sponsors, however, could only manage an "archival" position there which would sustain his family and help the busy democratic Customs entrepreneurs to manage the large amount of paper work incident to so strategic a port managing official commercial assets.

It took a Mackenzie, a stranger to American ways, to see the meaning of business transactions which affected society. His sense of social responsibility others professed publicly, but privately recognized as opportunities for favoritism, political opportunity, and simple theft. It took a Mackenzie to see immediately in the huge masses of correspondence and business documents left behind by previous incumbents a revelation of what had happened to government service. The political establishment had grown with a growing country since Thomas Jefferson's time. The New York Customs House had become a huge plum to be sucked by beneficiaries of official largesse.

The greatest beneficiary had been a Samuel Swartwout, who had served in the Revolution, been involved in the schemes of Aaron Burr, and had won the friendship of Andrew Jackson. As head of New York Customs, he was heavily involved in Texas speculations and other real estate and business schemes which made little distinction between personal and government funds[2]. In theory, Swartwout and after him, a Jesse Hoyt, were controlled by the Secretary of the Treasury's Office, to which came periodic reports of Port assets and expenditures. In fact such overseeings were shallow and subject to Democratic politics.

Thus, Swartwout was permitted to withhold payments to the Treasury that might be needed to adjust Customs import-export duties. In addition, Swartwout—and his successor Hoyt—were in position to make any variation of business deal, protected as proteges of President Andrew Jackson and of his successor Martin Van Buren. A weird aspect of then-contemporary politics was a "tradition" of betting on the outcome of local, state, and national elections, a tradition which inevitably ranged government officials like Van Buren's son John, presently Attorney General of New York, for and against politicians, in his own party and among Whigs.

Although the American political system had been building in an outpouring of lies, allegations, malice, and demagoguery, nothing like the piles of Custom House documents had ever before been made available to public scrutiny. The fascinating aspect of the book which Mackenzie hastened to assemble—an aspect which made him, with Anne Royall (*q.v.*) pioneers for the "muckraking era" yet to come— was that in addition to formal documents showing import-export transactions, he could display these public persons in their "human," that is real, personalities as irresponsibly grasping, greedy, and madly lusting for private gain at society's expense.

To be sure, they were not alone in their insatiable thirst. In fact, Swartwout had been a hero of sorts in his younger days, and his hatred of Indians, blacks, and Mexicans was shared by many passionate American patriots, as was his conviction that money filched from the Treasury of the United States was a just return to public heroes. As William L. Marcy, New York Democrat, had unforgettably said when his fellow-Democrat Martin Van Buren was made ambassador to Great Britain: "To the victors belong the spoils."

But this was also the era of reformers who were writing immortal pages in the nation's history: reformers who feared Texas as making perhaps six to eight pro-slavery American states, who thought of government service as a sacred trust, who thought business ought not to grow at the expense of the humble and needy. As Mackenzie wrote, in displaying the incessant concern of Swartwout with his grants of money to agents in Texas:

> I think there can be no doubt but that Mr. (Secretary of the Treasury Levi) Woodbury's office knew that Swartwout was a heavy defaulter long before he left for Paris—for it seems to be an object with him to remain quiet till after the elections of Nov. 1838. Mr. Hoyt and his friends could not have remained ignorant of the real state of Swartwout's affairs after June 1838 the end of his (Hoyt's) first quarter. They must have seen that Swartwout was $646,754 behind for cash paid him in bonds. Mr. Ogden, Swartwout's cashier, was Hoyt's cashier till March, 1839—he knew the whole; and yet Gilpin the Solicitor was not sent to New York till Nov. 1838. If the department received the accounts required by law, Mr. Woodbury must have known of a defalcation, even in 1837—but as he was lenient to other men who had embezzled large sums, but professed to be active (Democratic) partisans, perhaps it was his wish to be so with Swartwout and his friends. When Mr. Swartwout declined to send his last quarter's account to Washington in April, 1838, why did Woodbury not send an officer to get it till November?[3]

Swartwout fled the country, with how much money has been a matter of conjecture as he became subject to official committees in New York and Washington concerned more for Democratic public reputation than for public practice. Seen by historians as having "absconded" with over a million dollars—a staggering and almost unimaginable sum at the time—it appears possible that Swartwout may have made off with "no more" than a quarter of a million, which, indeed, he might have even made good to a degree, had his house and personal effects not been swooped up and taken away by government agents. Politicians at the same time labored to suppress discussion or to hold that Democrats were no worse than Whigs in tending to public business. Swartwout had in fact turned Whig in his last phase of connections.

Mackenzie's place in this public sensation was undefined. His book sold perhaps some 50,000 copies, before a court order shut down the press, automatically doubling the price of the outstanding copies. He himself was denounced by the Democratic papers as a "thief" of private documents, though he had sent copies of glaringly, almost innocently corrupt letters to various public personages including the newest President, James K. Polk, who had agreed that they warranted print. Mackenzie in his reformist zeal did not realize that the politicians had their own range of values, which included willingness to see competitors disgraced, but their own friends and selves kept free of scandal.

Indeed it is likely that Mackenzie himself never weighed what he was to accomplish with the book, or a second book, issued on its heels.[4] He was not so much exposing corruption to be righted, which was his dream and goal, as displaying to the general public what politics had become in an increasingly wealthy nation. Many would read his accounts of criminal theft, and wonder how they could themselves gain from the new conditions. In sum, the Mackenzie sensation was part of one of several reform eras—the Revolution itself had been a "reform era," in one perspective—with others buried in the body politic, and yet to form themselves, for outer expression.

In Mackenzie's time a separate reform drive, half separated from the country's politics, concerned itself with slaves, women's rights, religious unrest, and even health (see Graham, Sylvester *(q.v.)*). Mackenzie's unique contribution was that he observed political chicanery not through the normal spectrum of demagoguery, local interests, and national concerns, but with the scale of values of moral and unsubsidized citizens who were seeking to influence people, not votes.

In time, New York and other Customs offices would be more responsibly—or defensively—operated, and grafters and thieves would have to find new ways of obtaining quick riches through government activities. But, at the time, there was only so much that could be done to separate Democratic political habits from those of the Whigs. Ralph Waldo

Emerson's epigram, that the Democrats had the best program and Whigs the best men, meaning the most moral men, described a condition, but not a remedy. Mackenzie's description of a major Democratic chief pinpointed a common product of machine politics:

> [Jesse Hoyt] made himself...necessary to Mr. Van Buren and his son [John]...Mr. Van Buren is very penurious and covetous—Jesse would run all over New York to recover a $5 or $10, which his late employer had reluctantly lent to some poor fellow when in trouble—would hire lodgings for him on terms of economy would see to the washing of his clothes—the buying of his wines and groceries, or the stopping or getting subscriptions for his newspapers. John Van Buren bets, gambles, speculates in the stocks—in all this Jesse has been his humble slave, He electioneered, voted, betted, schemed, ran, stood, fetched, or carried, to order—was "more banks" or sub-treasury, Crawford or Jackson, Rufus King and negro freedom or "to jail with the missionaries," just as his patrons gave the signal. His object was pelf and power—patriotism, the welfare of the millions...probably never entered into their thoughts.[5]

Hoyt's methods and personality would pass quietly into history, so quietly that they could not serve the future as points of comparison and illumination. Yet they deviated by not so much as a hair's breadth from those of the later New York "philosopher" George W. Plunkitt, an illiterate grubber in political wastelands, who found his place in history with the remark: "I seen my opportunities and I took 'em."

Granted amnesty, Mackenzie returned to Toronto, and left behind his American connections, which had included service with the *New York Tribune*. He never looked back. A legislator, publicist, and printer, he was given a house by admirers, 82 Bond Street, which became a Toronto landmark. It contained not a word connecting him with his unique career in the United States.

Historians and biographers have been no more insightful into his life in America than were the Whigs and Democrats who had separate reasons for burying his achievements there. Charles Lindsay, *Life of William Lyon Mackenzie* (1862) found nothing notable to say about this "episode" in Mackenzie's career, and dictionary hacks added nothing regarding it. William Kilbourn, *The Firebrand*, showed awareness of the publications and of the sensations they created, but could not cope with their contents and did not try. Margaret Bellasis, *"Rise, Canadians!"* (1955) could not do as much. There is thus a "tradition" of sorts which requires shelving, if U.S.-Canadian relations are to deepen in this area of social interchange.

NOTES:

1   Adapted from a chapter, "William Lyon Mackenzie," in Louis Filler, *Appointment at Armageddon* (1976).

2   B.R. Brunson, *The Adventures of Samuel Swartwout in the Age of Jefferson and Jackson* (1989).

3   William L. Mackeinzie [*sic*], *The Lives and Opinions of Benj'n Franklin Butler... and Jesse Hoyt... with Anecdotes or Biographical speeches of F.P. Blair... C.C. Cambreling... W.H. Crawford... William L. Marcy... Martin Van Buren... and Their Friends and Political Associates* (Boston, 1845), 34.

4   Mackenzie, *Life and Times of Martin Van Buren* (1846).

5   Mackeinzie [*sic*], *Lives and Opinions of Benj'n Franklin Butler*, 35.

Daniel Alexander Payne
(1811-1893)

*"I shall lift up
my voice"*

Oₙ️NE OF THE GREAT MEN OF
the nineteenth century, Daniel Payne led the movement for education as a
key to Negro progress in America. Though never openly repudiated, he
was accorded moderate honor in decades following his death by those
blacks who sought more aggressive action. His basic principle was scorned
in still later decades by some black activists who taught the key to victory
was "green power," to be won by threats and terror.

Payne was born of free black parents, of English, Indian, and African
forebearers, in Charleston, South Carolina, and early showed an appetite for
learning. The historian Carter G. Woodson later observed that the South then
offered blacks a better education than the North. Payne, while still a child,
received from a private tutor a humanistic education extending from what was
always his special interest, history, to Greek, Latin, and modern languages. All
this he received while serving apprenticeships in shoemaking and tailoring.

As a boy of eighteen he opened a school for black children, free
and slave. It was so successful that the South Carolina legislature passed
a law in 1834 directly aimed at Payne's teaching, prescribing whipping
and a fine for free Negroes who taught blacks to read and write. Disheart-
ened, Payne left the South and entered the Lutheran Theological Seminary
in Gettysburg, Pennsylvania, where despite poor eyesight, he advanced his
studies while supporting himself with domestic service.

He was licensed to preach in 1837 and two years later ordained by liberal elements in the Lutheran Church. After several calls in New York and Philadelphia he joined the African Methodist Episcopal (AME) Church and engaged in preaching and organizing educational groups. He employed exhortatory tones in his sermons and speeches until his voice was affected; thereafter he adopted a more moderate intonation. He was given churches in 1845, first in Washington and then Baltimore; he roused resentment for his lack of sympathy with "cornfield ditties" and for his unswerving high cultural standards. Although he was of modest demeanor, had helped build manually the church's pews, had organized a school for pastors and an association for their elders, his own labors as pastor did not satisfy his congregation.

Asked in 1848 to prepare a history of the AME Church, he traveled widely in its behalf, as far south as New Orleans and north to Canada. Payne collected materials made invaluable by the careless way they had been kept. His work resulted in a publication basic to his church's traditions, *The Semi-Centenary and the Retrospection of the A.M.E. Church in the United States of America* (1866). He was made a bishop in 1852, and, in his continuing travels, spread his message of the need for raising the educational standards in black communities and of organizing literary societies. He refused offers to engage directly in anti-slavery work as a diversion from his own, but, as the Civil War approached and materialized, used his increasing prestige in Washington to urge emancipation.

Yet Payne did not lack eloquence, or abolitionist sentiments, in addition to his learning and material skills. As he said in an 1839 speech:

> Sir, I am opposed to slavery, not because it enslaves the black man, but because it enslaves *man*. And were all the slaveholders in this land men of color, and the slaves white men, I would be as thorough and uncompromising an abolitionist as I am now; for whatever and whenever I may see a being in the form of a man, enslaved by his fellow man, without respect to his complexion, I shall lift up my voice to plead his cause....

In 1863 Payne with great difficulty raised $10,000 and used it to take over Wilberforce, a college founded by the AME in 1856. It was situated in southwest Ohio as then part of Xenia, ten miles south of Yellow Springs where Horace Mann had set up Antioch College as a liberal arts institution. Wilberforce's mission had originally been to provide education for the illegitimate black children of southern slaveholders.

Though weighted with debt, Payne determined on high standards for the Wilberforce student body, offering it a curriculum which was comparable to that being employed in higher education elsewhere. By that time, spare, quiet-spoken, and dignified, he was noted as a minister, educator, and historian. With the war over, he returned in triumph to Charleston, and went on to create a network of AME churches and affiliates throughout the South.

He retired as president of Wilberforce in 1876, but only to continue his campaign for a literate black clergy. He had already, in 1867 visited Europe, where he was received as a distinguished American. In 1881 at a London meeting of the AME he read a paper on Methodism and temperance, expounding the view of his generation of pastors regarding its vital necessity to progress. That year he founded in Washington the Bethel Literary and Historical Association, a predecessor to that which Bishop Alexander Crummell (*q.v.*) later instituted to encourage blacks with cultural ambitions.

Payne summarized many of his views in *Treatise on Domestic Education* (1885) and his experiences in *Recollection of Seventy Years* (1888). During the World Congress of Religions, held in Chicago in its 1893 Columbian Exposition, Payne was called upon to preside over a session on American liberties. Although he had to reduce his labors to a degree in his last years—a Rev. C. S. Smith edited his *Recollections* and also his *History of the African Methodist Episcopal Church* (1891)—his interests absorbed him to the end. A young W. E. B. DuBois, whom he had tried to recruit for Wilberforce, saw Payne as saintly in appearance.[1]

NOTES:

1. For a general view of the era in which Bishop Payne and others lived and had impact, see Filler, *Crusade Against Slavery* (1986), sometimes termed the second edition, as technically it is. However, careless reviewers, some of them "specialists"—notably a Hugh Brogan, in none other than the *Times Literary Supplement*, imagined that the new edition no more than superseded the 1960 printing. In fact, its wide use required some 10 additional printings, every one of which contained numerous emendations and additions involving new books, new interpretations, and other changes, in many thousands of copies. The original publisher's unwillingness to acknowledge this fact in new printings was one reason for the author separating his book from the publisher. The new 1986 edition, of course, involves even more thorough reconsiderations and new matter.

Samuel Ringgold Ward
(1817-1866?)

"There is One Who Will Never be Taken Alive"

OUTSTANDING BLACK ORganizer and orator in the embattled pre-Civil War decades, Samuel Ward gave his career a turn which separated him from his mainstream colleagues, putting even his earlier work in the shadows. His last career was all but lost. His life helped indicate the complexities in black communal life.

Ward was born in slavery on Maryland's eastern shore; his mother hid its location from him, fearing he might accidentally refer to it and alert one of the slave-catchers in the North who sought runaways as a business. According to Ward, whose memoirs offer most of the information regarding this and related matters, his mother worked off her master's estate, paying him an annual return on her earnings. She exhibited spirit and independence which tried his temper, so that he contemplated selling the family. Young Ward's ill-health slowed this project, but his recovery threatened their safety.

Accordingly, they planned with the help of Quakers to run away, Maryland being a main road on the underground railroad. They settled in New Jersey, but feeling threatened again in 1826 made tracks for New York City. The boy attended the black school on Mulberry Street from which came such notables as Alexander Crummell (*q.v.*). Ward proved to be a quick learner. He was converted, and planned with other of his fellows for the ministry. On graduation he taught a Negro school in Newark, N.J. In 1838 he married a black New York woman by whom he had a number of children, several of whom died in childhood.

Ward early exhibited the traits and appearance of a promising leader, and won the attention of such prominent abolitionists as Lewis Tappan. Tall, personable, and eloquent, he appears to have built up a fund of knowledge largely by his own industry, though aided by a short stay at the abolition-centered Oneida Institute in Central New York. Ward developed a clear style of forceful statement and apposite reference and quotation which increasingly drew attention at public gatherings. Young Frederick Douglass whom he preceded, emerging as a Negro spokesman in the same era, considered him a comrade in arms.

Ward began his public career in 1839 as a travel agent for the American Anti-Slavery Society. In that same year he was licensed to preach by the New York Congregationalist (General) Association. He seems to have moved swiftly toward the moderate abolitionist branch in New York City, and joined with those who favored political action when the Liberty Party was formed in 1840. Although it appeared extreme to Democrats and Whigs, its aims were strictly legal: to appeal to voters in a year which all but ignored them.

In 1841 Ward became pastor of an all-white Congregationalist church in South Butler, New York, while continuing his search for further education. Although he was critical of his own pastoral abilities he yet noted that the church grew under his direction. In 1843 he resigned as pastor because of a throat condition which made him fear for his voice. Ward moved to Geneva, New York, a liberal stronghold of the time, for treatment by a doctor who also tutored him in medicine: one of the several fields he would have liked to follow.

His voice having improved, Ward joined the Liberty Party faithful the next year in agitating for its cause. The year 1844 was momentous for Liberty men. In that election year the Party's 62,300 votes, notably in New York and Michigan, lost Henry Clay the Presidency and caused consternation among abolitionists, they having inadvertently helped to elect the firmly pro-slavery Tennessean James K. Polk.

In 1846 Ward, still following opportunity and interests, became pastor of another all-white church, this time in Cortland, New York. He continued to address topics of the time, which included the admission of new slave states, efforts to disenfranchise New York blacks, and counterefforts to remove pro-slave parishioners from northern churches. He wrote in the anti-slavery press and joined with others in trying, unsuccessfully, to found black publications.

The Fugitive Slave Law in 1850 brought out Ward's matured oratory. He traveled widely to address anti-slavery audiences. In Boston, he spoke roughly of Daniel Webster, who was defending the infamous law, and won applause from whites as well as blacks. As he said:

> There is a man who sometimes lives in Marshfield [Webster's home], and also has the reputation of having an honorable dark skin. Who knows but that same postmaster may have to sit upon the very gentleman whose character you have been discussing tonight? [Hear! Hear!] "What is sauce for the goose is sauce for the gander" [Laughter.] If this bill is to relieve grievances, why not make an application to the immortal Daniel of Marshfield? [Applause.] It is not only true that the colored man of Massachusetts—it is not only true that the fifty thousand colored men of New York may be taken though I pledge you there is one, whose name is Sam Ward, who will never be taken alive. [Tremendous applause.]...

He was conspicuous in the famous Jerry Rescue of 1851. It involved the forced freeing of a runaway from prison. Fearing for his own safety he fled to Canada where his family joined him. Ward took up residence in Toronto and thereafter considered himself a British subject.

Nevertheless, joining other black immigrants, for the most part runaways from the United States, he carried on work which continued earlier labors. Ward helped organize black communities and an Anti-Slavery Society of Canada. He led the fight against anti-black prejudice. He cooperated with abolitionists and Negroes in the States in their various enterprises. In 1855 his Society asked him to visit Great Britain to raise funds. He left secretly from New York, where he took a ship. His ocean trip and two-year stay in England, Scotland, Wales, and Ireland furnished him with much of the material in his *Autobiography of a Fugitive Slave* (1855).

Ward's experiences abroad perplexed him. He was troubled in retrospect to perceive that his best experiences as an American had been with people of affluence and distinction. Harassment had come mainly from the poor and ignorant. Ward had never admitted to himself that there was a great chasm between himself and his people and others, notably the Irish, whose hatred of blacks was deep, they being competitors at the lowest levels of labor and society.

They might yet learn to respect each other, but in the meantime Ward could not but be grateful to those who had given him openings and a career. Now in the British Isles he was replicating his New World experiences, receiving cordiality and warmth from lords and ladies. Ward consistently affirmed the values of his own race, but his autobiography frankly expressed dissatisfactions which made it all but unbearable to return to the scenes of harsh reality, despite such admiration as Frederick Douglass expressed for Ward in his own *Life and Times*.

Ward's dilemmas seemed reduced by his receipt of a wealthy friend's gift of fifty acres in St. George Parish in Jamaica. Ward left, presumably with his family, for Jamaica in 1855. Thereafter, separated from black communities in the United States and Canada, news of his life dwindled from rumor to silence. He was known to have served Baptists as pastor in Kingston, and for a while at least was said to have been a person of consequence there. Evidently, his land holdings proved unfruitful; he was said to have suffered poverty in St. George Parish where he lived after 1860. Thereafter, no more than fragments of conjecture appeared. He seems to have died in or about 1866.

F. Landon's "Samuel Ringgold Ward," in the *Dictionary of American Biography* (1936) does what it can with available materials. No copies have been found of Ward's *Reflections upon the Gordon [Slave] Rebellion* (1866), which might have thrown light on his final views and circumstances. William J. Simmons's *Men of Mark, Eminent, Progressive, and Rising* (1887), a work which reached out for notable Negroes, chose not to notice Ward.

Alexander Crummell
(1819-1898)

"Hope for Africa"

Sᴄʜᴏʟᴀʀ ᴀɴᴅ ABOLITIONIST,
Alexander Crummell in his life gave
evidence of the impact of education on Negro advancement in the United
States and abroad. He was the free-born son of a former slave, Boston
Crummell, said to have himself been the son of a king in Timanee, West
Africa, adjoining Sierra Leone. The elder Crummell helped found the New
York Phoenix Society (1833) which, to commemorate the death of William
Wilberforce wore mourning for a month.

Young Crummell grew tall, straight, and "as sable as Tous-
saint" in his native New York. He attended the Mulberry Street
African School there along with such later Negro notables as James
McCune Smith, Samuel Ringgold Ward (*q.v.*), George T. Downing,
and Henry H. Garnet. In 1851 they entered the new High School in
Canal Street. Abolitionist friends then made an effort to augment the
number of Negro students at Noyes Academy in Canaan, New
Hampshire, a libertarian project. Crummell and Garnet were in 1835
assigned to the school which, according to Carter G. Woodson, in his
Education of the Negro Prior to 1861 (1919), enrolled fourteen Negro
children among the fifty-two. The boys comported themselves well,
and outstandingly as July 4 orators, observed Nathaniel P. Rogers, a
famous individualist who took them to be "*bone fide* evidence" that
colored people had talent enough to be free.

Racists in the area determined to rid themselves of the school. Following dangerous confrontations, they put together a team of oxen and dragged the school building to a swamp. Crummell and Garnet went on to Oneida Institute in Whitesboro, New York, where a sturdy abolitionist, Rev. Beriah Green administered a Manual Labor school, and where they spent three profitable years.

Meanwhile Crummell had himself begun his own career as an abolitionist, joining the long drawn out fight to remove property impediments in New York to the Negro vote. In 1821 a constitutional amendment had created disabilities in the state. In 1835 Crummell served as secretary to the New York State Anti-Slavery Society in its petition campaign for removing the statute. Crummell continued this work into 1838, when he helped set up the New York Association for the Political Improvement of the People of Color. For it he delivered speeches and organized petition drives in the city and in Utica. He later continued this campaign in Rhode Island, where help was urgently needed.

Crummell also studied theology. In 1839 he became conspicuous by asking for admission to the General Theological Seminary of the Episcopal Church in New York, which the diocese's bishop successfully opposed. Crummell was finally received in the diocese of Massachusetts and ordained a deacon, later a priest. A hard working student, Crummell augmented his training in theology while serving as priest in New York and Philadelphia.

His speech-making abilities spread his fame among sympathetic audiences, and in 1848 he was able, through philanthropic help, to visit Great Britain. William Wells Brown, a noted black American, once a slave, who saw Crummell delivering speeches in churches and elsewhere in *The Black Man* (1865) remarked his "manly figure, commanding in appearance, a full and musical voice, fluent of speech... gentlemanly in all his movements, language chaste and refined." Crummell was helped by friends to attend Queens College in Cambridge, from which he received his A.B. in classics and theology.

In 1852, Crummell preached a sermon on behalf of the Ladies' Negro Education Society in Clifton, Bristol, on "Hope for Africa." Proud of the English language and its literature, he was also proud of his Negro heritage. He left the next year as a missionary to Liberia and settled in and near the capital city of Monrovia. He was soon one of the republic's outstanding citizens, delivering anniversary orations, urging education for all including women, welcoming new immigrants, and preaching the "evangelization and enlightenment of heathen Africa" as he wrote in *The Future of Africa* (1862).

At this time immigration seemed to him a high priority. He looked forward to an increased stability in Liberian government, and never tired of recounting the promise in the land's resources. He maintained close ties with Martin R. Delaney, the American leader who visited Liberia in 1859 seeking a site for his proposed Black Israel.

Crummell worked for the American Colonization Society, though it was scorned by radical abolitionists, and was also head of the High School in Cape Palmas. He maintained a close association with Edward Wilmet Blyden, also a colonizationist, and with him visited the United States in the summer of 1861, seeking immigrants and funds for Liberian education. The next year they were in America again, but the Civil War diverted too much attention to make their hopes glow.

Before leaving Liberia, both Crummell and Blyden had been appointed professors of the new Liberian College: the first such in tropical Africa. They found themselves caught in a power fight between blacks and mulattoes, centering on college policies. In 1866 Crummell was dismissed from his professorship, Blyden being retained because his salary was being paid by the New York Colonization Society. Crummell was increasingly disappointed in his Liberian prospects under mulatto domination. In 1873 he returned to the United States, and though he may have retained a few lingering hopes for return, with Blyden secure and advancing at the College, the break proved permanent.

He settled in Washington, D. C., where he founded St. Luke's Church, which he served as pastor till 1897. He had earlier advocated agricultural and mechanical training, to be sure along with the higher branches of learning. With post-war Reconstruction creating a new type of Negro leader in politics and civil servants, Crummell became more and more protective of culture. He emphasized self-help, solidarity, race pride. Although he never minimized labor or technical crafts, he worried over Booker T. Washington's labor-centered program at Tuskegee, holding that labor was the fruit of civilization, not its basis. Crummell thus anticipated W.E.B. DuBois's later concept of the Talented Tenth to lead the Negro people.

He never neglected race pride, aiding Hampton Institute to organize materials bearing on the African heritage. In 1891 he published his *Africa and America*, a collection of sermons. Among his lectures was a memorable one, delivered in 1883: "The Black Woman of the South: Her Neglects and Her Needs."

In 1897 Crummell founded the American Negro Academy in New York, limited to forty members, to promote intellectual work among

Negroes, and to defend the race from aspersions. He himself contributed the third of its published papers, *The Attitude of the American Mind toward the Negro Intellect* (1898), which scorned the "Gradgrinds" who thought encouraging Negro education a mistake. He pointed proudly to DuBois in History and Kelly Miller in Mathematics, among others as refuting derogatory whispers about black capacities.

DuBois himself held Crummell to have been more important than the Reconstruction Negro politicians, though he received less attention (*The Souls of Black Folk* [1933 ed.]). He recalled his first meeting with Crummell at a Wilberforce University commencement. "Tall, frail, and black as he stood, with simple dignity and an unmistakable air of good breeding... Instinctively I bowed before this man, as one bows before prophets of the world."

It was evident that Crummell was likely to receive increased attention, when society settled into responsible studies of its black intellectual leaders, as in E.V. Rigsby, *Alexander Crummell: Pioneer in Nineteenth Century Pan-American Thought* (1987) and Wilson J. Moses, *Alexander Crummell: A Study of Civilization and Discontent* (1989).

William Burnham Woods
(1824-1887)

*"The Government...
In Washington is
Our Government"*

AS A JUSTICE OF THE U.S. SUPREME COURT, WOODS WAS known as the first "southern Justice" since the Civil War. This misconstruance, passed on from one writer on the Supreme court to another, gave evidence of how falsehood could be institutionalized because of bias and casual historical grasp outside fields of competence. Woods was, in fact, distinguished, but because of services in areas in which specialists lacked interest or knowledge.

Woods was born in Newark, Ohio, the son of a farmer and merchant and grew a stable and well-regarded young man who went on to three years of study at Western Reserve college and on to Yale. It was a measure of his popularity that upon short acquaintance he was chosen valedictorian of his Yale class. In 1847 he joined the Newark bar and began a career as a lawyer which revealed him as dependable in his work, and effective in court. In his presentations he was clear and logical, but also capable of a rising and impressive oratory.

Woods was made mayor of Newark in 1856, and the next year was sent as a Democratic representative to the Ohio legislature in Columbus. His reputation followed him sufficiently to make him immediately Speaker of the House. In 1859 he was reelected to the legislature.

As the nation moved toward civil war, Ohio became one of the crucial states which had to be made firm against secession. It is often forgotten how strong was sympathy with southern aims in Ohio, which had maintained Black Laws inimical to Negro rights and securities and which had to be made solidly pro-Union, if the Union was to be preserved. With Missouri, Kentucky, Tennessee, and Maryland in constant jeopardy, an irresolute or uncooperative Ohio would have been a last blow, since the South did not have to win the war to be stabilized as a nation, but only to hold off Union forces till peace was declared.

In that condition, such a force as Clement L. Vallandigham represented was crucial to Ohio's rule. Vallandigham was pro-slavery, a U.S. representative in Congress till 1863, editor of the Dayton, Ohio *Empire*, with numerous sympathizers in the state. During the 37th Congress he would offer resolutions calling for an end to war with or without Union.

It was in this situation that Woods, as Speaker of the Ohio House, and following the attack on Fort Sumter, was faced with a bill for a million dollar loan to enable Ohio to put itself in a position of military defense. He was at first on the floor opposed to the bill, along with other Democrats in the House. Secretly, however, he was contriving with other legislators for ways to further defense. With the House uncertain how to act, and with President Lincoln anxiously awaiting word from Ohio on the crucial measure, it finally rested on Woods's shoulders to break the barriers.

On April 18, 1861, he took the floor in a speech which opened the way for Unionists, confessing that he had never been against the measure, and he rejoiced to think that Union sentiment was at high. The threats against the Federal Capital had to be met:

> The Government whose seat is in Washington is our Government. The States that are loyal thereto are our country. By that Government and that Country, in sunshine or storm, in peace or war, right or wrong, we will stand.

The measure swept through the House, not to be threatened again as the war progressed, though Vallandigham was to continue his agitation until sent by Lincoln through the Union lines to the Confederacy he honored.

Woods had acted in defense of the North. Now he deemed it necessary to aid in the war itself. By November 1861 he was ready to join the 76th Ohio Volunteer Infantry in which his brother was a lieutenant colonel. With the exception of several months furlough, Woods was in action throughout the war. With his units he fought at Fort Donelson and Pittsburg Landing, among other famous points, sustained one wound, and showed sufficient competence to be given a colonelcy in 1863. His forces joining General William Tecumseh Sherman, they marched with him from Atlanta to the sea, then north to Raleigh, and on to Washington. On recommendations from Generals Grant, Sherman, and John A. Logan, Woods was finally made a brigadier general in 1865, and later when mustered out of service brevet major general.

Along the way Woods made the decision to live in Alabama, In no sense was he a carpetbagger, his plan being not exploitation of Federal funds or opportunities, but business. He set up home in Bentonville, Alabama as a cotton planter, iron works manufacturer, and lawyer. He never denied he was a Republican, and gained good will from neighbors by his deportment and equitable relations. In 1867 he was elected Chancellor of the Middle Chancery Division of Alabama, and in 1869 appointed by President U.S. Grant Judge of the Fifth United States Circuit Court.

In his usual style, Woods sought to be seen as a "working judge," and his court as not a foreign "engine of oppression," but as committed to even-handed justice. His Circuit presented difficult cases in both respects because of its background of Spanish and French, as well as American law. How conscientious he was in seeking reasonable solutions may be read in his own series of reports, generally known as *Woods Reports*, and issued in Chicago between 1876 and 1883.

Of his most famous cases, the most influential was one in which he and Justice Joseph P. Bradley, later himself also a Supreme Court Justice, made the original decision. 1 Woods 21 (C.C.D. La 1870) was best known as the Slaughter House Cases and was a landmark finding. The Louisiana legislature had granted exclusive privileges to animal slaughterers, creating a monopoly presumably barred by the Fourteenth Amendment. The judges overthrew the state law, helping the nationalistic law, though it did nothing for the Negroes the Amendment was originally thought to aid. It should be noted that Woods's finding were later those of the U.S. Supreme Court as well, and that the decision touched all states, and not only southern.

Woods himself, seeking a durable peace with the former secessionists, distinguished between their Confederate laws which had supported insurrection, and others intended to encourage law and order. In several of his cases it was not clear whether black rights generally or individual rights gained.

Woods's efforts received their greatest challenge in 1876 when national elections failed to elect as President either Democrat Samuel J. Tilden or Republican Rutherford B. Hayes, and martial law or possibly renewed civil war became imminent. Despite great pressures to involve him in Alabama electorial processes, Woods refused to help or hinder the tense state maneuvers which gave the Presidency to Hayes.

He was brought into one of the most famous cases of the period, involving a disputed will and the proponent's legitimacy. The Myra Clark Gaines suit, initiated in 1834, was to be recounted in memoirs and fiction. Woods helped further Gaines vs Lizardi as attested by 3 Woods 77 (C.C.D. La. 1877).

In 1880 a place on the Supreme Court bench was vacated and Woods's name proposed. That he was not welcomed merely as a "southern judge" is seen in the mixed motives involved in such an earlier appointment as that of the first John M. Harlan of Kentucky, later famous for his enduring vision of a color-blind Constitution. Harlan had fought for the Union in his bloody home ground, but had not been made famous by northerners. It had been *because* Harlan was southern that he had been approved for appointment by President Hayes, who sought national harmony. Similarly, Hayes showed generosity in passing over Woods's lack of action in his behalf during the 1876 crisis by respecting Wood's national perspective. Woods was endorsed in the Senate by a vote of 39 to 8.

His actual tenure on the Court was relatively brief, and in no way spectacular. A few of his 218 opinions were memorable, but none of these bore on issues which had divided the Union. He followed the Court in approving the government's right to print money in peace time as well as war (Juilliard vs Greenman, 1884), and in the Civil Rights Cases of 1883, which closed accommodations to Negroes despite the Fourteenth Amendment. History would rule against this ruling in time. But History would also recall that Harlan and Woods had vigorously rejected the view of a learned colleague, Horace Gray, that Indians were not citizens (Elk v. Wilkins, 1884). There were decisions and decisions, but in following the history of law as it affected life, it helped little to stereotype a brave Union soldier and legislator as being "southern." As a southern justice later said:

> We are proud of [Woods] because he is identified
> with us, and while serving as Judge in our midst has
> known nothing but the law, and been loyal to nothing
> but the law.

    Woods Reports reflects his steady personality and regard for the Constitution. There are scattered pages about him in specialized volumes and histories of Newark and Ohio. The one essay presently separating Woods from his stereotype is Louis Filler, "William B. Woods," in L. Friedman and F.L. Israel, eds., *Justices of the United States Supreme Court 1789-1969* (1969), vol. 2.

Frances (Watkins) Harper
(1825-1911)

Grace and Color

A POET AND REFORMER,
Frances Harper exemplified opportunities created by combinations of events and current issues. The course of her work, and public response to it, had elements in common with those which made Anna Elizabeth Dickinson (*q.v.*) a public celebrity in the same era. Differences appear, however, in their personal qualities and the purposes they served.

Watkins, as she was till her marriage, was born in Baltimore, Maryland, the daughter of free Negro parents, both of whom died while she was still a child. She was raised by an uncle, Rev. William Watkins, a self-taught man of culture who kept a school for free Negroes and who passed on to his niece ideals of freedom. At age fourteen she left his home to live with others who taught her sewing, and where she developed poetic ambitions. As early as 1845 she appears to have had printed a collection of verses and prose entitled *Forest Leaves*, of which no traces were left.

She came to Ohio in 1850 to teach in a school near Columbus sponsored by the African Methodist Episcopal Church and offering the work-study plan of the time. By then she had become increasingly aware of the growing crisis between slave states and free, and of its effect on Negro communities, free as well as slave. Abolitionists and fugitive slaves made vivid for her the challenge to freedom, as did tensions reported from her native Maryland—a major gateway for fugitives—regarding treatment given runaways and even free Negroes. The role of women in the abolitionist crusade made a particular impression on her. Encouraged by abolitionists she began to explore their campaign and consider her place in it.

Boston abolitionists, led by William Lloyd Garrison, were then particularly active in defying social repugnance to women "exposing" themselves to public eyes, and in Frances Watkins they saw a woman especially helpful in their cause. Tall, handsome, light colored, and graceful in deportment, she contradicted all the stereotypes of bigots, as did her patent culture and speech. She began her public career in 1854 under abolitionist auspices, speaking in New Bedford, Massachusetts on "Education and the Elevation of the Colored Race." In an era when public lectures were a major source of public education and entertainment, she struck an immediate chord which launched her as a speaker.

Her reputation as an effective public personality and drawing card grew rapidly, as did her confidence and poise, so that before the Civil War she was in all but constant demand as an orator and recitalist. That same year of 1854 she published her *Poems on Miscellaneous Subject*s, a volume which immediately reminded readers of the earlier pioneer of black women as poets Phillis Wheatley, and which remained Watkins's most memorable title. In 1874 it was in its twentieth printing. It also augmented her repertoire of lecture subjects, which came to consist of anti-slavery sentiments, observations of black and slave feelings and conditions, particular events, all varied with readings from her own verses. Although few were memorable in a larger sense, they reflected Watkins's and her audiences' compassionate feelings, as well as the influence of Henry Wadsworth Longfellow and the well-regarded contemporary versifier Felicia D. Hemans.

Carrying her message, Watkins ranged as lecturer from Ohio as far as Maine and into Canada, meanwhile contributing new verses and pieces of prose in anti-slavery and Negro publications. She stayed abreast of events, noting fugitive cases and black personalities, and from her earnings contributed to their causes. In 1859 she was particularly in the general news, along with others who were electrified by John Brown's raid on Harpers Ferry, and she indicted a letter to him which was widely reproduced in the North.

In 1860 an hiatus was created in her work by her marriage to a Cincinnatian, Fenton Harper. She and her husband settled on a farm near Columbus, Ohio. He died in 1864, and she moved East with her daughter Mary to resume her career as a lecturer. With new maturity and eloquence she took up the themes of war and post-war reconstruction, especially as they affected blacks. With the South in the hands of Federal troops she was able to carry her speaking engagements to black audiences in the formerly Confederate states.

In 1871 she bought a home in Philadelphia, from which she continued her work, traveling on lecture tours and writing verses and prose which were not notable in their own right, but which sometimes broke ground for others. A narrative effort in 1859 won later attention as perhaps the first short story by a Negro. *Sketches of Southern Life* (1872) attempted to individualize southern blacks in verses viewing them in plantation and post-war situations, and to employ dialect. *Iola Leroy, or Shadows Uplifted* (1892), her one novel, told of a free quadroon sold into slavery— a haunting possibility troubling too many of mixed blood, and some who were not—and of her harrowing experiences before being rescued.

Harper joined the temperance crusade of the post-war decades, and broadened her work to include Sunday Schools and delinquency among black youth. She helped organize the National Association of Colored Women. Her funeral in 1911 drew numerous distinguished women, both black and white. It brought to Philadelphia Julia Ward Howe, suffragist and author of "The Battle Hymn of the Republic," to join in the ceremonies. Burial was in Eden Cemetery of that city.

It was typical of the patriarchal circumstances of the time that Harper was not included in William J. Simmons's pioneer *Men of Mark* (1887), though she was among the most visible Negroes of the time. The Rev. George F. Bragg's *Men of Maryland* (1914), however, did memorialize her, as did Hallie Q. Brown's *Homespun Heroines* (1926), and other surveys of Negro personalities and poets.

Edwin Lawrence Godkin
(1831-1902)

*Editor of the **Nation***

ADMIRED IN HIS TIME BY THE intellectual elite as the brilliant editor of the *Nation*, E. L. Godkin was scorned by others who saw him as intolerant of human nature and blind to reality in debate. He was without peer in his examination of domestic and foreign events. Yet with his death and obsequies his influence all but disappeared. How this could be was a problem in changing social currents and events.

Born in Moyne County, Wicklow, Ireland, he came of English parents on both sides, with a name which ran directly back to the twelfth century. His father, the Reverend James Godkin, was a Gladstone liberal, warm for Home Rule. He had lost his Presbyterian pulpit for favoring it. His pen served the *London Times*, among other publications, and Gladstone himself, who gave him a literary pension. His *The Land War in Ireland* was reprinted as late as 1972.

His son Edwin showed precocity in early childhood, going to a preparatory school in Armagh and, when aged ten, being sent to an English school, then, still in England, to receive instruction from his uncle, the Reverend John Edge. Following classical study in Belfast, he in 1846 entered Queen's College there, taking his degree five years later: a well-composed, somewhat imperious young man of twenty.

Thinking to be a lawyer, Godkin went to London to study in Lincoln's Inn but found himself writing for the publisher Cassell with whom his father dealt. England was just then excited by the extended visit being paid by Louis Kossuth, the Hungarian revolutionary. It was Cassell's idea to have young Godkin write a book in Kossuth's honor. The book was published in 1853 and set Godkin on his course: *The History of Hungary and the Magyars: from the Earliest Times to the Close of the Late War*. It was a formidable production for a man aged twenty-two. Godkin later observed that it was "fearfully profound" and though well-written and factual, filled with material, irrelevant for the most part.

His book called young Godkin to the attention of the *London Daily News*, which sent him to report the Crimean War. Notable in his reports was his aplomb. It had him meeting war lords and principals without diffidence, and demanding close respect to his presence. His reports impressed London observers, and on his return to London and Belfast he was welcomed as a reporter and lecturer.

With editorships awaiting him, it is not clear why he chose to cast himself loose for a permanent stay in America. One surmise has it that he resented England's class structure as limiting his ambitions, but this does not answer ultimate questions. He once confessed that American expressions of democracy often made him appreciate more England's rigid class lines and delightful vistas. He visited the old country many times, and died there. But even his later friend William James, despite his psychology, confessed that he did not thoroughly understand Godkin's motivations.

He left for New York in November 1856 with introductions, studied law with the esteemed David Dudley Field, and won friends, notably Frederick Law Olmsted, later architect of Central Park in New York, but then best known for his books on travel through the South and reportage on its ways and attitudes. Godkin resolved to emulate this feat, and took off for southern states armed with an assignment to report his findings to the *London Daily News* readers.

Wit and sharp description suffused his correspondence. He noted that the population "seems to be composed of colonels, governors, and doctors exclusively:" an observation which defined the drift of his preferences in company. He entered one inn where he found "a large party of 'gentlemen' sitting around the stove, and amusing themselves by spitting on it." The ladies of the South were as pale as death and excessively thin, which he thought must lessen the shock of their appearance after their decease. Slavery impressed him mainly in being superior to the condition of free laborers in the American North or in England.

A curious trait of Godkin was his tendency toward error due to over-confident optimism. Eighteen hundred and fifty six was an election year, and James Buchanan, a "doughface", eager to propitiate the South became President. Godkin, still reporting to the *London Daily News*, found a public happy with the choice: "Parties are broken to pieces, and nobody is going to make war on Mr. Buchanan." The new President's program was soon to be thoroughly wrecked, but Godkin never apologized for his vain predictions. It was events which went wrong, not his assessments.

Godkin was a loyal North American during the Civil War, and after peace was declared considered establishing a paper of his own. He rejected the idea of visiting the West and, from some strategic eyrie helping it to grow. The West did not interest him. His problem was solved when a plan grew among well-to-do anti-slavery men and intellectuals to set up a paper which would help free blacks to adjust to their new condition of freedom. In 1865 Godkin was appointed the *Nation*'s first editor.

Now widely acquainted with the elite in literature and the professions, Godkin could call for contributions upon such historians as Francis Parkman, such originals as Charles S. Pierce, forerunner of John Dewey and Instrumentalism, upon Dr. Henry W. Bellows of the recent U. S. Sanitary Commission on which soldiers in the field had depended, upon editor Charles Dana, George Ripley, creator of Brook Farm, the poets William Cullen Bryant and James Russell Lowell. Cambridge, Massachusetts was an endless source of intellectual authorities for Godkin to probe for *Nation* articles, and he himself found it a joy to visit there.

It was significant that the original reason for the *Nation* was soon forgotten. The black man was on his own, and these decades during which the *Nation* reigned were a great era for strong philanthropies favoring blacks, and their own production of leaders of the stature of Frederick Douglass and Booker T. Washington, as well as Bishop Crummell and Daniel Payne (*qq.v.*). They set down bases for black advancement which fed Negro ambitions for a hundred years. Although the *Nation* did little for them, it led a powerful gentility which held an all but dissolved Union together. It maintained standards of social deportment, later to be ridiculed as artificial and unnatural.

At first, the *Nation* suffered program and financial confusion. This was quickly solved when Godkin resigned his editorship, purchased the property from its troubled trustees, and set it on a course which made it unique for peerless writing and scholarship.

Godkin's overall program was "liberal" by its meaning at the time. His Crimean experience had given him a hatred of war, but with implications which could be found in such public men as Woodrow Wilson (*q.v.*). They feared what war could do to the elite peoples, the natural rulers, of the world. Destroying each other, they could leave the world to the mercies of the black and yellow populations. In challenging outright imperialists, they wrote with apparent sympathy for Chinese, Ethiopians, and others threatened by foreign armies. On closer inspection, their concern for weak nations was no more than intellectual. Godkin favored Free Trade among nations because Protectionism was a road to war, not because it raised the price of bread. He hated unions and socialism as incubating domestic war, and covered them with barbed sarcasm and ridicule from his high perch of wit and flawless English.

These talents emerged unbridled once he became not only the editorial director of the *Nation*, but also of the *New York Evening Post*, purchased in 1881 by the industrialist Henry Villard. The *Post,* like the *Nation*, was not a popular paper, but both were read by all editors and in academic circles, and penetrated their consciousness. The *Evening Post* especially enabled Godkin to develop major campaigns against corrupt city administrations which had burgeoned while patriots were away, many of them dying in the Civil War. Godkin exposed Tammany Hall's brutal robberies and terror at the New York polls. The politicians in turn threatened Godkin with prison. True reformers called attention to the slums and exploitive factories in which their constituents suffered, and to which Godkin paid slight attention.

His public image was without warmth. It extended not only to his foes but to more gracious people of his own kind. William Roscoe Thayer, then a journalist, later a noted historian, was summoned by telegraph by Godkin to be interviewed for a possible place on the *Evening Post*. He was engaged in talk about the proposed work, and dismissed. Waiting week after week for news, it finally dawned on Thayer that silence had been Godkin's answer.

Yet William James found Godkin playful as a kitten with his children in his own family circle and among friends. Family tragedies caused Godkin to flee New York for Cambridge, and he needed Europe for summer holidays. His foes found in him weaknesses to which he could not and did not respond. Thus, among the politicians he found contemptible and warranting his cruel wit appeared Grover Cleveland, a forthright Democratic President who turned against Protection of Home Industries and went down courageously in 1888 in behalf of Free Trade. Cleveland denounced Free Silver as a defaulting maneuver by debtors, and opposed imperialism. Godkin supported Cleveland's return nomination for the Presidency in 1892, and, in order to help, omitted his usual election exposes of Tammany faithful who he regularly noted in a "Directory" as "thugs," and "murderers." Clever Republicans offered to pay for *Evening Post* insertions of the omitted "Directory," while there was general hilarity among politicians for having caught Godkin evading his own civic ideals on practical grounds.

Godkin's long services to the genteel ideal of a proper society left a trail of brilliant commentary which did not persuade fighters for more fundamental reforms. They too would have wanted to avoid the horrors of the 1871 Paris Commune. They too were sickened by the assassinations of Garfield and McKinley, and by the 1886 Chicago Haymarket Riot. They were less horrified than Godkin by the threat which William Jennings Bryan as Democratic nominee for President posed to the major parties in 1896. Yet Godkin gave them a powerful point of view from which they could deviate in ways that reached people Godkin himself scarcely noticed.

His own flesh and blood personality was nowhere on the scene. A distinguished shade while he was still on earth, Godkin suffered his final tragedy when the Spanish-American War unfolded. He opposed it, but he could find no handle for criticism, surrounded as he was by public enthusiasm and warm participation. His last years found him subdued and puzzled. His volume of essays, *Unforeseen Tendencies of Democracy* (1898) raised questions—on the brink of the Progressive era—questions of social justice and equality, with which he could not cope.

Volumes of letters and reminiscences included comment on Godkin, in many cases focusing on issues rather than on his personality. Rollo Ogden, ed., *Life and Letters of Edwin Lawrence Godkin* (1906) helped less than might have been expected to illuminate his character. William M. Armstrong, *E.L. Godkin and American Foreign Policy* (1957) made strenuous efforts to capture it, but could not find it separated from the events Godkin presumed to judge. See also Nevins, Allan (*q.v.*).

Mary Edwards Walker
(1832-1919)

"Mary"

MARY EDWARDS WALKER WAS a debatable figure in women's rights lore, but unique among individualists. She was raised in Oswego Town, in the Finger Lakes region of upper New York, an area which drew many independent-minded New Englanders. Her father was a cousin of the agnostic Robert Ingersoll. Alvah Walker was a farmer whose interest in medicine doubtless influenced his daughter in her later concerns. She learned her lessons in a schoolhouse her father built and gave the town. Both parents contributed to her women's rights principles. Mary grew a small but handsome and energetic girl. She taught school for a while, but in 1853 entered nearby Syracuse Medical College, graduating in 1855.

She began medical practice in Columbus, Ohio. Then, receiving an offer of marriage from a former fellow-medical school student, she returned to New York. She already expressed independence in several ways: she retained her maiden name, asserted abolitionist views, and wore trousers and a dress coat, at the time closer to the "Bloomer" costume popularized or made notorious by Amelia Bloomer. She and her husband were doctors in Rome, N.Y. for several years before they separated permanently. It is likely that marital incompatibility hardened in her attitudes of distaste for males, and that her claim of his unfaithfulness only partially contributed to her long efforts to obtain a divorce. She finally obtained one in 1869.

She had already hit on dress reform as a major cause; a photograph of Dr. Walker (as she became for the rest of her life) showed her in a "Bloomer" costume still graceful and attractive, and she joined a relatively few others in a National Dress Reform Association.

The Civil War turned her attention elsewhere. Like Clara Barton she went to Washington and helped with the wounded, though also agitating for a medical post. Like Barton, too, she ventured independently into battle areas in Virginia where help for the wounded was urgently needed. Late in 1863 she finally acquired a commission as a first lieutenant in the Federal Army of the Cumberland, and, as assistant surgeon wore the uniform of other officers. In April of the following year, on one of her forays away from camp, she was captured by Confederate troops and imprisoned in Richmond, Virginia. During a prisoner exchange she was returned north, made famous by journalists and not yet notorious.

She embarked on a duel program of personal demands and women's rights causes as she saw them. Her agitation for compensation to war nurses was in the mainstream of patriotic justice, and even her fight to receive a Congressional Medal of Honor for Meritorious Service, awarded in 1866, took her not far away from public good will. Her fight for the "Bloomer" costume, however, carried on in public places that same year found her embroiled with strangers, and, in New York, in controversy with police.

In September, 1866, she embarked for England on a personal tour which was the high point of her career. Civil War officer, women's rights advocate, and wearer of the Bloomer costume, she projected her viewpoint in lectures which drew excited English audiences. Her return home at the end of the year was a let-down, her services as lecturer or medical practitioner not being sought. A second tour abroad, inspired by the Paris Exposition of 1867 and rounded out in England proved equally successful, but it was evident that she had not firmly established her vocation.

She sought to enter into woman suffrage, speaking from platforms with Lucy Stone and others, and working along with Belva Lockwood on the Women's Suffrage Bureau in Washington. In 1872 Susan B. Anthony made her sensational attempt to cast a vote in the national elections.

Dr. Walker made a similar attempt to vote in her own Oswego Town, but was prevented without incident.

1872 was a significant year in her career, for it marked her effort to create a woman's suffrage program of her own: one which was sweepingly repudiated by her former colleagues, leaving her alone in the field. She scorned the constitutional amendment the women offered intended to give them the vote as "amendment trash," an awkward phrase which exhibited her charmless approach. Dr. Walker argued that the Constitution having established a republic, there was no need for an amendment giving women the vote. This approach would have choked off debate at their conventions, and dampened related issues useful to the general cause. Also, her increasingly insistent demands for more time to be devoted to dress reform lost her so much sympathy that organizers finally debarred her from attending their meetings.

Her writings, too, showed her compulsion to foist opinions on readers rather than win them by discussion. *Hit* (1871) offered a sampling of women's causes, but also such irrelevancies as her own phrenological chart. *Unmasked, or the Science of Immortality* (1888) protested the rude treatment of men toward women in marital relations, presented her often dubious conjecture as facts, and included an uncalled-for chapter on hermaphrodites. The latter may have thrown some light on her own psychic development.

The 1880's saw her total transformation into the Dr. Walker of legend, about whom rumor flourished. She divested herself of every article of female attire, going clothed in men's coat and trousers, shirt, stiff collar and tie, and high hat. A contemporary photograph of her, apparently taken unasked, showed her walking a street in Washington. It caught also a woman looking at her from a distance with frank repugnance. Since Dr. Walker practiced little medicine then or later, she may have been in Washington on one of her missions before Congressional committees in which she appeared alone to express views. As significant was her willingness in 1887 to appear on several Midwestern dime museum sideshows.

After 1890 she retired increasingly to her Oswego Town homestead which had come down to her. Her offer in 1895 to open a "new wives' training school" was reported to the press, but drew no students. The final drive for woman's suffrage in the 1910's involved her not at all. She was mainly active in interminable law suits of no general concern. Isolated from events and in poverty, she was all but alone following a fall from the Capitol steps in Washington in 1917. She died two years later at a neighbor's house, and was buried in the family plot wearing the black frock suit with which she was identified. A simple stone over her grave was marked with the word "Mary."

She appears briefly in a number of period pieces, notably Helen B. Woodward's *The Bold Women* (1953). Charles McCool Snyder, *Dr. Mary Walker: The Little Lady in Pants* (1962) is sufficiently definitive.

A strangely prophetic view of Mary, since it was drawn by a J.B. Hudson in 1859, before she revealed herself in full transvestite personality and clothing.

Hazen Stuart Pingree
(1840-1901)

Potato Patch Mayor

HE WAS A PIONEER PROGRES-
sive whose reform achievements in
Detroit inspired emulation beyond
Michigan and all but nationally. Although often seen as "forgotten," his
career was so deeply imbedded in
urban history as to rouse recollection
whenever the prospects for cities became moot.

He was born in Maine, the son of a farmer of old New England
family, and went to work early in a shoe factory. When the Civil War
began he enlisted in what became the 1st Massachusetts Heavy Artillery,
served continuously until captured, then served the time in the notorious
Andersonville Prison, from which he escaped and was able to rejoin his
regiment. He continued in service till the war ended.

Having heard that there were opportunities in Detroit, he decamped
for that city. It bustled with new enterprises of every kind, and drew new
residents from all parts of the settled country, as well as from Canada and
abroad. The city was helped by access to the Detroit River, which lead
into the northern reaches of Michigan and the Great Lakes. In Detroit
Pingree found a congenial partner with whom he rapidly expanded their
shoe factory. As they moved toward affluence Pingree himself was seen

as a popular employer and business man, well liked by his employees: one whose eye for precision in work and quality production was outstanding. By the time Pingree became interested in public service his firm, employing some seven hundred workers, was the largest such business in the Midwest.

Detroit was a mainly Catholic city with high percentages of foreign workers, including Irish and Germans, a large Polish community, with incoming Italians and others. Those of Anglo-Saxon stock ruled state-wide with their "native" constituency of farmers, as by political sharpness exerted on the 200,000 citizens of Detroit. Pingree, though of the rich Detroiters, remembered his youth and war experiences and had a strong empathy for the poor, a keen sense of the wrongs they suffered through ignorance and exploitation. When he ran for mayor in 1890 he had a general idea of their basic needs: an honest administration, an eight-hour day, and ethnic respect. This was inadequately realized by political bosses, headed by the Democratic saloon-keeper Chris Jacob, and including Republican manipulators who spoke for Detroit's elite. Because of restlessness among the poor and the need for a reform front to appease city discontent, the attractive Pingree was offered by Republicans and won the mayorship for their party.

In time, forces for reform, in Detroit as elsewhere, would be depreciated as "genteel," over-concerned for political corruption and vice, and legally punctilious: qualities such people as E.L. Godkin (*q.v.*) emphasized. In fact, Pingree did scandalize some of his own people, who took to freezing his family out of social invitations and criticizing him bluntly. They disliked his spirited campaigns for office, his drinking with the Irish, his showing little reverence toward genteel ministers and charity givers. There were, however, there as elsewhere, well-educated and conscientious people in local government and business who approved his basic program, his emphasis on equity, and who joined him in developing it. Pingree was many times to be accused of demagoguery, but he employed it only because he was unwilling to lose points in his fight to modernize Detroit.

He learned quickly and expanded his program, as did opposition to him. At bottom of their differences were city franchises and lucrative contracts intended to benefit businesses before citizens. Some obsolete systems gave way readily. Wooden-block paving, carried over from the past, rooted and crumbled faster in rain and cold under the tramp of pedestrians and horses and iron-wheeled wagons. Such paving was replaced by asphalt, though often mixed excessively with water. Favoritism ruled in sewer construction as in the purchase of school books. Most vital were the meager wages and the miserly street railway services which discriminated against the neighborhoods of the poor.

Pingree learned quickly that the horse-drawn cars and the streets the horses trod were in poor repair, though the fare was kept at five cents. Electric trains on grooved streets with tracks were necessary, which the traction magnates were unwilling to build. Yet they held to franchises and wanted them extended.

The Depression of 1893 struck hard at Detroit as elsewhere, not only increasing despair but turning workers against each other. "Chase the Dagos back to Italy," circled readily among the native-born, some members of the American Protective Association, dedicated to clearing the land whenever they could of Catholics. For all Detroit's religious persuasions Poles too joined in baiting the Italians, though the city council tried to eliminate both from the city work-pool. Pingree labored to find work for aliens, and, losing ground with his own people, drove deeper roots among those of larger mind.

The secret of his growing popularity, at a time when former associates were ignoring him in the street and his own Republican Party was conspiring to cast him out was shown in the act which continued memorable beyond his lifetime. Pingree had made contact with Henry George's Single Tax panacea—essentially the idea that ground belonged to all, that only *improvements* should redound to the business man's benefit—and pondered its practical use. Although he found little, it did suggest that unused land—vacant lots—which the city had in abundance could be used by the unemployed for raising food. His idea caught on, could not be stopped, and resulted in "Pingree Potato Patches," an inspirational concept which actually flourished, and was borrowed by city administrators elsewhere.

Pingree's popularity continued to grow, despite his loss of influential Detroit elements, because of his evident compassion, his genuine concern for the needy. Nonetheless, his causes could not have advanced without his overcoming serious legal and economic problems. Streetcar, electric, and gas corporations were powerful in the city and in Michigan's capital in Lansing. Pingree had a choice of several approaches, and he chose among them for strength and tactical purposes. For labor-capital relations he urged arbitration, and used it when possible to cool down tempers and win time. For

One of Pingree's "potato patches."

bringing executives to the bargaining table he turned to combinations of law, public agitation, and threats.

All the utilities sought long-term franchises, with stipulations which could keep them in the courts while they maintained their original charges. Pingree learned that the street car franchise was invalid, and used this as a weapon to have the fare lowered to three cents. He forced improvements in service, won electric lines, solicited competition to force down ticket pre-charges. His foes were not without arguments and threats of their own, in their street railway duals, and in their gas and electric quarrels. Pingree succeeded in building a municipal electric plant from which utility-users gained. Pingree won followers and lost others in the power struggle. As one council member said openly: "[I]t is only too plain that if I want to keep up my business I cannot remain with council and support [Pingree]."

The Republican Party had been unable to stop his re-election in 1894. He was now so well admired that they needed another strategy. City watchers everywhere kept eyes on his adventures. The major Standard Oil Company critic of the time, Henry Demarest Lloyd, urged Pingree to come to Chicago to help break boss rule. Frank Parsons (*q.v.*) in Boston was inspired to run for mayor. James Couzens, soon to be famous as Henry Ford's associate and himself later mayor of Detroit and United States Senator, dreamed early of emulating Pingree. It was a sign of Pingree's solid status that the Republican leaders concluded to back him in his 1896 run for governor in order to get him out of Detroit.

Before that occurred, he fought one last battle which pitted him against none other than Tom L. Johnson, later to be a darling of the Progressives, and even earlier a professed follower of Henry George. Johnson was a complex man who as a young man had invented the fare-collection box, and grown rich by bribing councilmen in various cities to deliver to him franchises for strategic city lines, then selling his franchises to street railway builders. In Pingree's last period as Detroit mayor, Johnson was brought in to their city by the street railway interests to fight their battles with Pingree for them.

In his last years as a freebooter, working for himself as well as his financiers, and before himself becoming the reform mayor of Cleveland, Tom Johnson fought Pingree with cunning and partial results. He stymied some of the mayor's plans and bewildered the Pingree forces regarding their private-ownership efforts. Pingree went to Lansing as governor with his work unfinished.

He found that, deprived of his base in Detroit, he could not use its power to move the state legislature. His main target was the state railroads, which offered on a larger scale the problems he had encountered with the local street car magnates of Detroit. His attempts to make the railroads subject to equal tax laws were rejected by his legislature during his first term, and stopped by the coming of the war with Spain when all attention focussed on its progress. Pingree had no choice but to go along with popular sentiment in order to retain the good will of his constituents. He won his second term handily, and returned to his fight for tax equity for railroads with better success, so much so as to inspire Robert M. LaFollette (*q.v.*) in Wisconsin in his own battle with railroad interests.

Pingree was in poor health, and felt the need for perspective. He was evidently something of a sportsman, since his post-political plans included a Theodore Roosevelt-type of project involving elephant hunting in Africa. He was also interested, from his early army experience, in the Boer War, and planned to write an account of English-South African differences and their engagements. His death while in England put an end to all projects, which had included a return to Detroit, where he was buried, but where he had hoped to serve again as mayor.

Pingree's own book, *Facts and Opinions, or Dangers that Beset Us* (1895) gives a good sense of his style as agitator and reformer. M.G. Holli, *Reform in Detroit: Hazen S. Pingree and Urban Politics* (1969) is an academic study of his Detroit political career.

Anna Elizabeth Dickinson
(1842-1932)

Histrionics

O**RATOR**, LECTURER, AND stage performer, Anna Dickinson ex- emplified the mixture of liberalism and social entertainment which accompanied the reform era of the pre-Civil War period through the War and post-War decades. Less substantial a per- son than Frances Harper (*q.v.*), Dickinson pioneered excitement to middle- class auditors who were affirmative toward the women's drive for self-expression in that period. Her turn toward the stage made a proper coda to her career.

She was born in Philadelphia in a Quaker household. Her father's death when she was two years old left the family destitute. She received some instruction at home, and a few years of attendance at the noted Friend's Select School, but by 1857 was put out to work as a copyist. She then turned to school teaching in Philadelphia and towns about. Already long suppressed in her social circumstances, she found emotional release in Methodist churches and in the furor created by abolitionists. In a time during which followers of William Lloyd Garrison had opened platforms to women agitators for his message, and in Philadelphia where Lucretia Mott had more decorously addressed Quaker assemblies on like topics, Dickinson found opportunities for emotional release.

In 1860, aged eighteen, she began to address antislavery and other gatherings on abolitionist and women's causes. Possessed of a clear and vibrant voice, youthfully attractive, and rousing rather than informative, she struck a note which was suited to a period which was unconsciously mobilizing forces for war more than for debate.

Garrison had earlier sponsored such women for his cause as the Grimké sisters, Abby Kelley, and Lucy Stone. He now sponsored Dickinson, arranging a meeting for her at Boston's famous Music Hall in 1862. Her success was so startling as to raise calls from New York and elsewhere for her presence. Meanwhile she had found employment at the United States Mint in Philadelphia, but her passionate declarations regarding "The Rights and Wrongs of Women," and similar appeals were so effective as to raise questions about her vocation. With war on, Dickinson had broadened her repertoire to take in a whole radical program. Her sweeping charges, which included upbraiding General George B. McClellan as serving treason came to the attention of Mint officials. She was discharged from her work, and fairly launched on the celebrated portion of her career.

Having as yet no regular schedule, Dickinson, like Clara Barton in the war's earlier stages, looked about Washington for themes to further. She visited troop hospitals and took to New England forums an appeal for the Union cause which the wounded had served. It proved insufficiently dramatic. Help came from New Hampshire where Republicans faced with an election looked for inspirational help. Dickinson furnished speeches so successfully in that state and in Connecticut that her presence caught new fire. Brought back to New York, and in the same Cooper Union which had earlier responded to Abraham Lincoln's more staid appeals, Dickinson captured her thousands of listeners with her invective and scorn of Democrats and disunionists.

Dickinson now had her cause, victory in the war, and her technique, which brought out emotional female presence and sensibility, free movement on platform, and personal indulgence which enabled her to exchange insults and charges with hecklers and opponents. Her fame mounted rapidly as she followed radical changes in government support and criticism. Her first approach found her a defender of Lincoln's leadership, and brought her before Congress itself, January 16, 1864, with Lincoln in attendance. Demanding direct action against the South and slavery, she then voiced radical impatience with Lincoln's conservative program; but in the fall elections she closed ranks with the Republicans against McClellan and the Democrats.

The end of the war saw Dickinson a ripe performer for the lecture circuit, and highly paid for her services. At her best as a critic and radical she rode the wave of pro-Negro sympathy. In the first of her two books, *What Answer?* (1868) she approved intermarriage. Though never a regular partisan of suffrage politics in the fashion of Susan B. Anthony, she exploited the movement's demand for women's vote. For more formal audiences she offered her speech on Joan of Arc, she herself having been graced with the comparison by lecture circuit organizers.

Dickinson fared well in postwar years and into the 1870s, drawing as much as $20,000 in high years. She acquired a variety of associations and contacts among serious figures like the journalist and later diplomat Whitclaw Rcid, whose long term attention she could not hold. The political demagogue and blusterer in war, General Benjamin F. Butler (he had ruled in New Orleans that ladies discourteous to Union soldiers would be treated as women of the streets) granted Dickinson better regard as her vogue faded. Changing times were indicated by her having as lecture manager James Redpath, previously known as an abolitionist, now no more than a businessman exploiting opportunities. Her fame was such that as late as 1886 it would inspire Henry James's *The Bostonians,* in which the novelist fancied her as the daughter of the Transcendentalist Bronson Alcott, whom he portrayed as a vain exploiter of her talents.

Although Dickinson had lost her early bloom of youth which had first given aura to her histories, she for several years in the 1870s held her stature in public. She was generous to family and friends even to improvidence. By 1876, still no more than thirty years old, she had to reassess her public status. She tried for a career as playwright and actress, but her appearance in her own play, *A Crown of Thorns* was catastrophic. Still, Dickinson persisted in trying to reach the new public in unwanted plays while spending her substance. As late as 1882 she tried playing Hamlet himself as a woman. It was a novel idea, but it brought her ridicule.

Such had been her early impress as public personality that as late as 1888, Republicans, remembering her old services to their party, attempted to utilize her in their Presidential campaign against the incumbent Grover Cleveland. Although she was as free with her invective as in long-ago times, her performance was such as to cause the politicos to drop her from the campaign.

The rest was a long silence, equal in length to her time of prominence, punctuated by a bout with insanity, with court cases, meager living, and final decades of public forgetfulness softened by a kindly couple who took her in after her hospital commitment and were family to her in their Goshen, New York home. There she lived with her memories and illusory hopes. She died and was buried there.

Dickinson wrote part of her story in *A Ragged Register* (1879), but with little insight into her celibacy which fed only on the impersonal attention of others. Giraud Chester, *Embattled Maiden* (1951) emphasized the rhetoric which affected her public success. She is treated in numerous books dealing with women of the Civil War and post-Civil War periods; see for example *Eminent Women of the Age* (1872), "Anna Elizabeth Dickinson," by Elizabeth Cady Stanton.

Josephine Shaw Lowell
(1843-1905)

A Measure of Women

PIONEER SOCIAL WORKER AND inadvertent feminist, she set up women's needs of her time on the public agenda. Appreciation of her services was later dimmed by the horde of women whom, into the Progressive era, she set to work building on that agenda.

"Effie," as she was known in childhood, came of distinguished Boston-area forebearers of merchant family and training for civic duty. Her father, Francis George Shaw, was active in Brook Farm progressive projects; later, in support of Civil War aims, he headed the Freedman's Bureau. Josephine was raised in an atmosphere of culture and enterprise. In 1847 the family moved to Staten Island, New York. Her father, already retired, considered plans for the family, and in 1851 moved them to Europe where they steeped themselves in Old World lore. "Josephine," her mother wrote when she was ten, "is the genius of the family. She can cook, cut out things, trim hats and caps, speak French, German, and Italian, and write poetry."

They returned home in 1855, thereafter a time of gathering crisis. Her elder brother, Robert Gould Shaw, left Harvard College to begin a business career; but then early in 1861 concluded to enter the army as a soldier, rising from second lieutenant to colonel of the first Massachusetts Negro regiment, the 54th. His death before his troops at the violent assault on Fort Wagner, Charleston, South Carolina, July 18, 1863, was the first of the sorrows which determined Josephine's life. Her brother's body was said to have been bitterly thrown into a trench among those black comrades by the embattled Confederates. He was later memorialized in a sculpted plaque on Boston Common by Augustus Saint Gaudens; in a poem by William Vaughn Moody, "Ode in Time of Hesitation" (1900); and most recently by the movie *Glory.*

That same fall Josephine, aged twenty, married Charles Russell Lowell, a nephew of the poet, and himself already a veteran of the war and colonel of cavalry. As he wrote at the time: "I am going to marry upon nothing; I am going to make my wife as happy upon nothing as if I could give her a fortune. ...I know now that it would be unwise to allow a possible want of 'daily bread' in the future to prevent the certainty of even a month's happiness in the present." Josephine spent the winter with him in the field in Virginia, attending to his and other soldier's wants, which included writing letters for the wounded in foreign languages. Colonel Lowell had survived twelve horses being shot from under him, and met formidable adversaries including Con-federate guerrilla John Singleton Mosby of "Mosby's Rangers." Lowell's for-tunes ran out at the battle of Cedar Creek, where he suffered wounds, but refused to leave his command. Additional wounds the next day, October 20, 1864, killed him. Six weeks later his wife delivered a daughter, whom she named Carlotta Russell.

Josephine returned to New York where, accompanied by her daughter, she took up life with work for Negro relief and education, and raised money for the National Freedman's Relief Association. She then broadened her outlook in work for the New York Charities Aid Association which acquainted her with poverty, vagrancy, crime, prisons, and institu-tions, and the dire treatment of pauperized and criminal women and children. A striking, handsome figure with all but marble-like beauty, al-ways in black, yet always feminine and gracious, and, in her writing, with clear prose and an unswerving concern for facts, she was wholly separate from traditional charity givers. Legislators immediately saw the difference. Her first targets were almshouses and jails run by time-servers and ex-ploiters, where children and women were intermixed with men in hopeless squalor. Her reports, written for a more impersonal time, were colder than Dorothea Dix's older appeals to the social conscience.

In 1875 Josephine was asked to prepare a state-wide study of the New York poor. She had a horror of aimless charity as no more than maintaining dependency, and grimly accepted that Draconian measures to avoid such repulsive conditions might cause pitiful suffering. But she emphasized the inhuman conditions in her report in which the poor were asked to improve their lot, particularly helpless children and women. Josephine's impressive findings won over Governor Samuel J. Tilden. In 1876 he appointed her to the State Board of Charities, the first woman to be so selected. Josephine now expanded her operations. Although her career was confined to New York State, her superior findings and results increasingly affected the entire nation. Her innumerable visits to idiot asylums, jails, hospitals, orphanages exposed social evil and indifference. But it was her powerful reports and increasingly strong contacts, as with young Theodore Roosevelt, which drew serious young men and women to her, taking in the wants of the destitute and despairing without regard to race or sex. Her private appeals, too, were forged in the same cold steel. As she wrote to a legislator who had ignored a previous request for a copy of a law forbidding the imprisonment of witnesses in New York:

> This does not deter me, however, from asking again, if you can help me to find the law in question, for I have just heard of a most flagrant case, that of a Norwegian sailor, whose pocket was picked by a companion, and who has consequently been already imprisoned in the Richmond County Jail, which is a filthy hole, full of criminals and vagrants, for thirty days, and unless something can be done about him, he is to stay there another month. If he should turn anarchist, or nihilist, and murder everybody connected with the law or government when he gets out, it would not be a surprising result!

Josephine's campaign to house women in separate prisons, to provide matrons for them in public situations, and to recognize other conditions separating sex and youth drew together the best of new social workers. In 1882 she brought about organization of the New York Charity Organization Society, which she led for the next quarter century. Her writing, too, reached beyond her profession. In 1884 her *Public Relief and Private Charities* spelled out her program of relief which was not charity but rehabilitation. She was now famous to many of the younger women who came to her office or were invited in gatherings to her and her daughter's home to discuss strategy in reaching legislators and the public. Josephine was increasingly aware of the affect of politics on action. In 1889 she left the Board of Charities to direct wider campaigns. In 1890 she founded with others the Consumer's League of New York: a model for many customers organizations intended to influence work conditions, the quality of products, and women's place in industry, and bringing cruel and unscrupulous men in commerce and industry to heel.

Meanwhile she had become aware of the larger battles between labor and capital, threatening the peace of the nation. She was a pioneer in seeking solutions to debilitating strikes, shut-downs, and violence. Her *Industrial Arbitration and Conciliation* (1893) led the way to ideas and techniques promising mediation.

In the last phase of her life she was a mentor to women anxious to engage in civil and political affairs. She fought Tammany's insidious system of bribes and favors, led the state's Civil Service Reform Association, and stayed abreast of Progressive developments till her death by cancer in 1905. Her passing brought together the flower of her associates to honor her career. She herself was put to rest beside her husband in Mount Auburn Cemetery, Cambridge, Massachusetts. See *In Memoriam: Josephine Shaw Lowell* (1906); W.R. Stewart, *The Philanthropic Work of Josephine Shaw Lowell* (1911).

Anthony Comstock
(1844-1915)

"Comstockery"

AN ANTI-VICE REFORMER, Anthony Comstock, in long and arbitrary pursuit of allegedly immoral and obscene publications, became notorious to those concerned for civil rights and artistic values.

He was born in New Canaan, Connecticut, and raised by well established farm people. To his "mother fixation" and her life values have been ascribed his extreme views and his persistence in maintaining them under duress. He received only a public school education. As a sturdy young man he served in the Civil War, where he first saw much to disapprove in the conduct of his fellow-soldiers. On his return to civil life, he entered business as a clerk, but found outlet for his energies in subscribing to the Young Men's Christian Association program, for which he made his first arrests. These involved two men who were circulating what he took to be obscene reading matter. The event was not without incident. One of the accused struck him with a bowie knife, leaving a permanent scar which he hid behind whiskers.

The Y.M.C.A. continued to help Comstock formulate his crusade. He clarified enough of it to launch a successful campaign in Congress for what became, March 3, 1873 the "Comstock Law." This made the passage of obscene writings through the U.S. mail illegal. Comstock himself was approved as a postal inspector, serving without salary. That same year he organized the New York Society for the Prevention of Vice, of which he became secretary. He was now famous for his fearlessness in ferreting out matter he deemed pornographic at whatever cost to his own personal security or personal prestige.

Outstanding in the 1870s was his persecution of Virginia S. Woodhull, whose life was a combination of manifest chicanery and blackmail succeeded, in a turbulent social era, by a bold identification with women's rights. She won the support of suffragists, and herself became a partisan of "free love" as part of the program of civil liberties on which she "ran" for the Presidency between 1870 and 1874. Her exploitation of the gaudy issues of spiritualism, sexual hypocrisy, and freedom of speech drew in such notables as Susan B. Anthony, Isabelle Beecher Hooker, sister of Rev. Henry Ward Beecher, and Beecher himself. Woodhull flung charges about which brought on the great court case of Beecher *vs* Tilton, involving charges of adultery. Woodhull's published views led not only to her arrest by Comstock, but itself became a legal issue in free speech which brought to her defense reputable people. Her vindication in court won her status in history as well as notoriety. It gave her, however, no such status as Belva Lockwood would win as an advocate and as the first woman to run legitimately for the Presidency.

Much of Comstock's crusade against pornographers and frauds was valid in an era which matched ill, pregnant, and otherwise distraught people against cyclical cheats and quacks who promised aid to ignorant sufferers. Comstock's *Traps for the Young* (1883) was largely a record of useful work on behalf of deceived and even endangered individuals. His annual reports described in 1914 state and federal court actions touching some 3,697 accused persons, 2,740 of them pleading guilty to charges or having been convicted of crimes.

Unfortunately, Comstock could not distinguish between false nostrums and valid experiences in the arts. His drive against the Art Students League in New York in 1906 was badly aimed and inspired Bernard Shaw's long remembered denunciation of "Comstockery." Erratic, too, was Comstock's later campaign against the painter Paul Chabas, whose "September Morn" was innocence itself, made memorable only because of Comstock's persecution. It was one of the first of such harassments to cause artists and writers to hope to be cited by Comstock and his successors as pornographic or obscene as a step toward affluence.

Comstock by the time of his death had premonitions of having lost his cause, and even that he might lose his official post as inspector of mails. Charles G. Gallaudet, *Anthony Comstock, Fighter* (1913) was an attempt to justify his long campaign, but the study by the great journalist Heywood Broun and Margaret Leech, *Anthony Comstock, Roundsman of the Lord* (1927) felt free to patronize him with good humor and even a measure of understanding.

John Boyle O'Reilly
(1844-1890)

Patriot and Journalist

An IRISH-AMERICAN PATRIOT and journalist, and acknowledged leader of his people in post-Civil War New England, John O'Reilly had youthful adventures that made him a legend to the Irish.

He was born into an old and cultured family at Dowth Castle near Drogheda, Ireland, the O'Reillys going back a thousand years and with innumerable descendants. At age nine he was apprenticed to the Drogheda *Argus*, then sent to the Preston *Guardian* in England to prepare for a newspaper career. In 1860, however, he chose to join the 11th Lancashire rifle volunteers as a private.

In 1863 he was back again in Ireland, and taken with the Fenian cause, advocating home rule by revolutionary means, if necessary. He joined the 10th Hussars, which drew many Irish youth, his purpose clearly being to persuade them of the justice of Fenianism. His undercover work was discovered in 1866, and he was tried for inciting to mutiny and sentenced to be shot. This decision was altered to that of twenty years imprisonment. He attempted to escape from several English prisons, and as a result suffered solitary confinement and hard labor. In 1867 he was transported with others deemed hardened offenders, and set down in western Australia. The young, attractive Irishman's desperate escape the next year in an American whaling vessel became an often-recounted adventure.

O'Reilly finally landed at Philadelphia, Pennsylvania late in 1869, where he promptly took out naturalization papers. He began his American career by lecturing to Irish audiences, then moved north to join the Boston *Pilot* as journalist, and to begin the writing career which contributed so much to his fame. As a poet O'Reilly voiced generous sentiments more than original thought, but his ballads contained a genuine ring and on occasion rose to full expression, as in his poem "Dukite Snake," which caught an Australian spirit. His writing so sufficiently impressed Horace Greeley as to bring the offer of a position on the *New York Tribune*, but O'Reilly concluded to stay in Boston.

It was his honesty of expression and generous regard for others which singled him out from many other Irish spokesmen. His criticism of the poorly planned 1870 attempt of Irish patriots to seize Canada and hold it as hostage till Ireland was freed roused bitter retorts, but O'Reilly stood his ground and gained respect from more reasonable people among his own and outside. O'Reilly, of sturdy middle height, round face, and curly black hair and moustache, gained public stature. In 1876 he bought the *Pilot* with the help of Boston's Catholic Archbishop and ran it till he died. Married and the father of four daughters, he was a mediating figure who, for example, deplored the riots which defaced Orangemen and Irish Catholic relations. He praised such Protestants as John Mitchel, for having helped the Irish cause. Mitchel was an Irish revolutionary who had suffered transportation and escape much like O'Reilly, but he had been a bitter Confederate sympathizer in America.

Notable among the controversies which embroiled O'Reilly was that during the heated presidential election of 1888. By trickery he was able to obtain a letter from the British Ambassador, Lionel Sackville-West, to the United States that suggested intervention in American domestic affairs. O'Reilly's prompt publication of the letter forced Sackville-West's recall and angered the British press.

O'Reilly as a public figure received so many calls for addressing assemblies that he was forced to put limits on the number of engagements he could accept. Especially noted were his speeches during celebrations of Daniel O'Connell and the Irish poet Thomas Moore. Defying Irish prejudice he spoke in praise of Negro Americans, before them in 1885, and at the dedication of a monument to the black martyr of the Boston Massacre, Crispus Attucks in 1888. One of his more felicitous poems had an Indian, a Yankee, and a black honoring a deceased, heroic trapper, and commenting separately that he had had a red, white, and black heart.

His books included volumes of verse, a novel, *Moondyne* (1880), which voiced generous hopes for better prison conditions, and a book on *Athletics and Manly Sport* (1888). Of special interest was a "prophetic" novel of England in the twentieth century which reflected his ecumenical status in the community, having been written with Robert Grant, himself a well-esteemed jurist and fiction-writer, Fred J. Stimson ("J.S. Dale"), and John T. Wheelwright.

O'Reilly was cut off by an accident, he having in the night taken from a cabinet the wrong bottle, deadly chloral, rather than his medication for tension and tired nerves. His memorial stone in Holywood Cemetery was only a huge boulder with his name on a plaque. A public subscription raised $18,000 for a Boston statue. A bust of O'Reilly was installed in the new Catholic University in Washington. His friend of many years, James Jeffrey Roche, aided by O'Reilly's widow, prepared a life, and published it along with his poems and speeches (New York, 1891). William G. Schofield, *Seek for a Hero* (1956) was fictionalized, but drawn from full records.

Jacob A. Riis
(1849-1914)

The Other Half

J ACOB A. RIIS WAS A SOCIAL REFORMER AND ACCORDING TO his friend Theodore Roosevelt "the most useful citizen in New York." His fame declined in post-World War I decades, which wanted more radical views of urban unrest than Riis offered. He later regained partial status, mainly as a photographer of realistic scenes of poverty and deprivation.

Riis was born in Denmark, the son of a school teacher. Raised to be a carpenter, he came to New York in 1870. There he suffered extreme need which tested his endurance, and which he never forgot. In 1874 he gained editorship on a political sheet, the *South Brooklyn News*, and began his career as a reporter. He rose to the staff of the *New York Tribune* where he was given the often onerous job of police reporter on the lower East Side.

Riis had an innocent streak in his make up which enabled him to report conditions which turned many of his fellows into bitter cynics. He looked for human interest stories capable of touching and rousing the less disillusioned citizens to the shabby state of the slums. His articles for the *Tribune*, then the *Sun* after 1890 probed circumstances which had proliferated following the Civil War, at the expense of the new immigration, exploited by uncaring house builders and industrialists. Bewildered men, women, and children, often with limited language and organization, were condemned to penury and prostitution. Riis's articles and photographs turned light on dark tenements and fire-traps. *How the Other Half Lives* (1890) made Riis famous.

Riis, buoyed by his native optimism, was never like the succeeding muckrakers able to follow through to the causes of social disorder, but his revelations of urban infamy spoke for his deepest feelings. *Out of Mulberry Street* (1898), *The Battle with the Slum* (1902), and *Children of the Tenement* (1903) laid ground for later, more penetrating exposes, but made Riis an influence in cities throughout the land as writer and lecturer. Mulberry Bend, notorious for its crime and decay, came to symbolize his work. As a park and with its Jacob A. Riis Neighborhood House, it flourished for several generations as a memorial to him.

Riis's autobiography, *The Making of an American* (1901), was one of the folk memoirs, like those of S.S. McClure and Edward Bok, which took on classic status. It included, coincidentally as in the great editor S.S. McClure's autobiography, a remarkable chapter of faithfulness to an ideal which triumphed against high odds, and spoke positively for their generation. Riis had left Denmark with an image in his mind of unqualified love for a particular girl: one who not only did not love him, but loved another. He corresponded ardently with her, though she tried to discourage his hopes. The death of her beloved left her free for Riis, and she became his wife. In his autobiography he gave her a chapter to write which she filled largely with memories of her past love.

Riis travelled across country in behalf of his anti-slum cause at the expense of his health, which finally failed him entirely. In the 1920's, thirties, and beyond he was mainly recalled in the lower schools as author of *The Making of an American*, inspiring to children of minority groups. The rise of photography, seen as art, finally led to his rediscovery, less as a reformer than as a pioneer photographer. Many of his camera shots were made famous by repeated reproductions, much in the manner of the artist-photographer Edward Steichen. See Peter Hale, *Silver Cities: the Photography of American Urbanization* (1984); James B. Lane, *Jacob A. Riis: the American City* (1974); *The Complete Photographs of Jacob Riis* (1981), 8 microfiches.

New York's East Side conditions before the Progressives improved them.

Anna Carpenter Garlin Spencer
(1851-1931)

Defense of the Family

SHE WAS NOTED IN HER TIME as a pioneer for woman's rights and as a suffragist. To the end of her life as a scholar and activist Spencer favored expanded women's opportunities and academic study of family and sex. She was evidently a transitional figure in a time when social problems changed to undercut her perception of what society needed or cared to maintain.

She was born of old New England family in Attleboro, Massachusetts, her father's name having been originally Garland, and raised in Providence, Rhode Island. Her mother was a spirited abolitionist who passed her reform impulses on to her daughter. Her father served in the Navy during the Civil War.

Anna attended public schools and also received "private collegiate" instruction which prepared her for the public school teaching she pursued for several years, while she also began her writing career with the *Providence Daily Journal*. In that era of public appearances by such women suffragists and cultural speakers as Frances Harper and the orator Anna Dickinson (*qq.v.*), there were many who sought to follow their example. It proved natural for an energetic girl like Anna with religious beliefs which wanted sharing, and aspirations for womanhood, to speak at meetings and be well received. Anna Garland was tiny and quietly dressed. Yet she had presence and a vibrant voice. She won a growing reputation.

In 1876 she left the Congregational church, beginning a process of change which drew her deeper into religious liberalism. She married a Unitarian minister two years later, William Henry Spencer, older than herself by eleven years. Although she still gave occasional sermons in Providence and in the pulpits her husband filled in several cities her main concern over the next decade was her home and family life. She had lost one child soon after birth, but her daughter Lucy survived.

The family returned to Providence in 1891, where Mrs. Spencer was ordained a minister, the first such appointment in the state, and where she was given charge of the Bell Street Chapel, liberal and non-denominational. It had been initiated two years earlier by a James Eddy, whose life she later memorialized. Her ascent to the pulpit was cordially received in Providence and elsewhere, as were her sermons and discourses calling for active faith and social concern. Her husband retired from his own church work in 1893, and later as an invalid required her care.

Mrs. Spencer became increasingly more involved with such causes as Florence Kelley (*q.v.*) and others were in the cities making better known than religious questions. The base of her thinking, however, was not the child labor and factory inspection issues which absorbed many social workers. She was a suffragist, and later a pacifist, and lent her fluent pen to these and other subjects. But her main concern increasingly became the family itself, and the behavior of its individual members. She was also drawn to the role of women, historically and in the present: an interest which would later give her a place on campuses as a teacher.

Meanwhile, she resigned from the Bell Street Chapel "movement," as she termed it, in 1902, and moved with her family to New York to join the New York Society for Ethical Culture, the associate director of which she became in 1904. Its director Felix Adler's less activist emphasis, however, conflicted with her need to move in what she saw as critical directions, and she left him to direct and then lecture at the New York School of Philanthropy. She retained nominal connections with liberal religious sects, but her main career grew elsewhere.

She was now aware that the traditional family was being challenged by pragmatists and libertarians, and looked for evidence that the family was the hard base of civilized living, and necessary to advanced causes. She learned from history that women had advanced from sale, capture, and enslavement to higher forms of consequence, all leading to the suffrage and workplace opportunity. But the family remained the core of life, and, as her own life gave evidence, that the man must be the breadwinner: "Two firsts there cannot be unless you have a large fortune." Home needed tending, and children fostering.

The world of prostitution fascinated her. She followed its historic course and intended controls for it in the reform era. She saw economics as a limited solution. Involved was the nature of women, and social competence to address it. As early as 1890 she had written in *Century* of the need for a "moral chemistry." In *Forum* of 1913 she held venereal disease "the unique menace to race integrity."

She took such views on travels to the University of Wisconsin, where she lectured in its Milwaukee extension service, and elsewhere, and continued to write in general and women's publications. She closed in, however, on professional magazines, such as the *American Journal of Sociology* and the *International Journal of Ethics*. Her book *Woman's Share in Social Culture* (1913) was well received, as was a second edition in 1925. *The Family and Its Members* (1923), emphasizing "individualization," appealed to its middle-class readers.

She taught sociology and ethics at the Meadville Theological School in Pennsylvania (1913-1918), and at the University of Chicago in 1918 and from 1920 till her death. She also helped set up a consultation center at Teachers College, Columbia University, where she lectured on social science. During World War I she stayed abreast of peace actions, and persuaded Jane Addams not to join Henry Ford's fantastic effort unilaterally by way of a "Peace Ship" to mediate between the warring nations.

Her basic cause continued to seem valid to auditors and readers. But though she was a friend of Charlotte Perkins Gilman, known for her *Women and Economics* (1898), of Susan B. Anthony, and of Jane Addams, and although she served on numerous boards and at innumerable conferences, she did not note that her role was almost entirely peripheral to the causes they served.

The one cause which was truly her own was that of ending prostitution as a threat to family, and she made much of the citizens committees of the 1900s which hoped to bring down the law on pimps, corrupt politicians, and other exploiters of vice. An apparent victory of the time was the passage of the federal Mann Act which made it a crime to transport females across state lines for immoral purposes. Mrs. Spencer pushed this aspect of family preservation farther than anyone else in her time. She was a leader in the American Purity Alliance which aimed to rouse the family itself in self-defense.

The Alliance intended to reach prostitutes and rehabilitate them for social life, by way of counseling, material aid, legal and medical measures, and moral inducements. Had she reached her goal, society would have proliferated a network of committees and specialists which and who would have outlawed brothels, and associated drinking and gambling places. She was sufficiently acute to change the Alliance's name to American Social Hygiene Association, and she herself directed its Division of Family Relations.

She was active and sought after into her eightieth year: a small, bright-eyed, white haired lady, always in grey. *Survey* assessed her as a "World ambassador from the court of good will." The liberal minister John Haynes Holmes saw her as a manifest leader in her several fields. She was stricken with a heart attack while attending a dinner for world peace, following a full day's work, and died two days later.

Although world peace, like her other causes, was as necessary in 1931 as at any other time, it is evident that her experience with the cause and other of her causes, including social hygiene, did not take into full account the causes which militated against them. Mrs. Spencer was not so naive as the popular versifier of World War I who, during American intervention, urged the soldiers to "come back clean." Mrs. Spencer's approach to prostitution was helpful and informative. In the glare of wars, poverty, and human compulsions, it was pitched too high, at least for the times. Times, however, did change. The apprehension caused by the spread of the dread disease of Acquired Immune Deficiency Syndrome (AIDS) did appear to soften attitudes toward the more intransigent partisans of family. Whether this crisis would redound to the honor of such pioneers as Mrs. Spencer could not be known.

Although Mrs. Spencer received warm and respectful obituaries, there was no follow up of interest in her career. It is scattered in books dealing with her many causes. A chapter about her appears in Winifred and Frances Kirkland, *Girls Who Became Leaders* (1932). See also David J. Pivar, *Purity Crusade* (1973).

Edwin Markham
(1852-1940)

"Hoe Man" in the Making

Markham at age sixteen.

Born CHARLES EDWARD ANSON Markham, poet and public figure, he was in the general consciousness from 1899, when his poem, "The Man with the Hoe," was first published in the *San Francisco Examiner* till his death at home forty-one years later in Staten Island, New York. Yet his passing also signalled the complete collapse of his reputation.

He was a long time reaching recognition. His parents, Samuel and Elizabeth (Winchell) Markham, moved in 1847 from Michigan to Oregon. Edwin (known as Charles) was born in Oregon and could claim notable English ancestors and a large family of siblings and half-brothers and sisters. His father, however, a forthright woodsman, came to suspect his humorless, neurotic wife of infidelity, and divorced her shortly after Charles's birth. She took him and a daughter north of San Francisco where she began a long, gloomy odyssey which shadowed her son's life from babyhood to fame, and beyond.

Young Charlie was raised with blows, exhortations, religious strictures from the age of seven. He rode horse and tended flocks in deep loneliness, and grew a sturdy outdoor youth who had picked up a love of romantic poetry and Victor Hugo writings from found books, and a hunger for education which was given direction by a sympathetic schoolmaster. His struggle for learning was resisted by his mother, who feared his leaving her. His learning was earned by hard labor, first by farm and ranch.

In the midst of these lone efforts he may have briefly joined with a highwayman in undefined adventures. They coincided with his alleged "miracle" of having found buried money which enabled him to continue his education. He later identified his wayward companion, perhaps wrongly, as the notorious "Black Bart" of California notoriety. Markham told contradictory tales of having nobly repudiated the outlaw's offers of a life of crime, but also of having engaged in strange, unspecified adventures in his early years.

His mother on many occasions darkened his youth and impeded his growth; it is evident that theirs was a love-hate relation which kept him returning to her while he worked to realize his dreams and tie them with more gracious women. His first marriage, to Annie Cox of Coloma, where gold had first been discovered, and where he taught, came to an end by divorce in 1884. It had him dreaming fitfully while he looked half-unconsciously for a way out. His liaison with Dr. Elizabeth Sentor, whom he hoped to marry, and for whom he obtained a divorce, was frustrated by her death in 1885. He married Caroline Bailey in 1887. Meanwhile he made attempts at poetry publication. They took him two ways, one, of a socialist who heard the tramp of workers' feet foretelling a better world, in somber and threatening verses, and, secondly, as an idealist who sought "beauty" such as was considered distinguished in *Century*, *Scribner's*, and other eastern magazines.

A middle way made him a follower of Thomas Lake Harris, whose most faithful attendants saw him as a prophet and seer, literally able to read the future as well as interpret the past. Harris also raised communes in which he was "Father" Harris, and which fed on his revelations and freer man-woman relations than the world generally tolerated. Although Markham never gave up his infatuation with Harris's Swedenborgian visions, he never publicly acknowledged them: one of the compromises which in time defined his life.

A few of Markham's "working-class" verses appeared in malcontent publications, notably William Morris's *Commonweal*, published in London, and some of his verses had a power which was never given free play or notice. But Markham was more encouraged by the approval and acceptance which came to him in modest proportion from more conventional editors and writers, in Boston as well as his own Bay Area. In 1890 he won appointment as principal of the experimental Tompkins Observation

School in Oakland, across the bay from San Francisco, and so was finally established. He brought his mother to live with him, while exploring relations with such exotic writers as the poet Joaquin Miller and the more notable Ambrose Bierce.

The next year Markham's mother died; his second wife died two years later. In 1895, following experiments, he settled on Edwin Markham as his name. In 1896 he met a school teacher, Anna Catherine Murphy, of modest family, but sharing with Markham a dedication to verse, and wholly submissive to his wants. They married in 1898, and a child Virgil was born the next year

How slowly Markham's maturation proceeded can be seen in his having made acquaintance with Jean François Millet's painting "The Man with the Hoe" as early as 1886. His numerous notes contained many references to it, as well as tentative lines of verse commenting on the bowed French laborer of the painting. It was not till New Year's Eve 1898 that Markham, at a literary gathering in San Francisco, read his completed poem to the assembled guests. Its impression among them was overwhelming. Bailey Millard, editor of the *San Francisco Examiner*, and himself destined to be a notable editor of muckrakers, was so deeply moved that he featured "The Man with the Hoe" in his paper January 15, 1899. Its success throughout the country and then beyond was unprecedented. Overnight, Markham found himself universally known and sought.

His was a best-seller, and with offers of all kinds for writing as he chose, he elected to become an easterner, setting up home in Brooklyn, New York, then finally across Manhattan Bay in Staten Island. He also publicly arranged his past and present as he thought fit. Handsome, graying, with compassionate yet good-humored features, he appeared as a humanistic, more civilized Walt Whitman. His mother became in his account a long benign, helpful companion. There was no divorce in her past, or his, and few distressing details aside from acceptable poverty and hard labor for an education.

Markham's second volume promised to maintain him as a national figure and poet, and social conscience. It contained a poem which rode the tide of contemporary feeling: "Lincoln," filled with memorable phrases and metaphors. Unfortunately, Markham felt compelled to surround it with fanciful details of occasion and composition. The poem's own triumphal career culminated in a 1922 reading by Markham at the dedication of the Lincoln Memorial in Washington before a hundred thousand spectators.

Although a more than modest income was available to Markham, he felt it necessary to seek it out and augment it through ephemeral journalism and public appearances, finally almost entirely before women's clubs, chamber of commerce assemblies, and other such gatherings. They required travel, set talks, and innumerable readings of his own verse, often composed for the occasion. Markham was aware that he was being taken from large-scale and ambitious ventures. He developed an outlook which justified him as an evangelist of beauty, or, for more discriminating critics, as one needing to labor for bread. A third posture made of him during the Progressive era a spokesman of the people. This actually resulted in some valid writing on issues of the day, notable articles on child labor. These, supplemented with essays by Benjamin B. Lindsey and George Creel, became *Children in Bondage* (1914).

However, the era's intellectuals became conscious of Markham's lack of solid literary productivity, and, more obscurely, that much of his life was facade. Despite innumerable cheerful letters between Markham and his wife, she was left increasingly alone. His own suppressed passionate nature, fed by the many women who attended clubs and poetry assemblies, sometimes with unfulfilled demands, qualified the heartiness of his public appearances and made for a shallow picture of his crusade for beauty which newspapers and club minutes reported.

The rise of new and fresher poets in the 1910s still found him respectable among them. Markham was a founder of the Poetry Society of America, and reigned among its figures, though seen ironically by such talents as Robert Frost and William Carlos Williams. Although Markham's birthdays became an annual tradition, and despite huge celebrations for him in the East and in the West, which he visited as a native son, it was evident that the new literary scenes and the more formidable talents increasingly obscured his tangible production.

Nevertheless in 1926 he completed a work which, like so much of his writing, had matured from long processes of thought and effort. *The Ballad of the Gallows Bird* drew together his long sense of folk forms of verse, his faith in the Harris-Swedenborg visions of life and death, as well as his sense of fantasy which had too long served complacent interests. In his poem a hanged murderer, using hard words and precise adjectives, having thought he had cheated the gallows, wanders in ugly ways seeking his home, before he finds himself once more before a remembered site. There are ravens "making mirth" with the brains and eyes of a dead man swinging from a rope:

> A sudden gust, and the strangled shape,
>> That humped and dangling thing
> Wheeled round its face, with holes for eyes...
> 'Twas *I* that hung against the skies:
>> 'Twas *I* on the rope a-swing!....
>
> Then a sudden shout crasht into my brain,
>> The truth on my spirit fell...
> God of my soul! I was *dead*....and damned...
>> And trampt the roads of hell!

Charles Angoff (*q.v.*) who served H. L. Mencken on the *American Mercury,* saw the poem which Markham had sent to Mencken, argued for it despite its length, and it appeared in the magazine in August, 1926. Markham continued in astonishingly good health almost to the end. He made strenuous trips often organized by mercenaries who humiliated him with rude demands and with no concern for his comfort or purposes. In 1938 Markham's wife died, and he, finally exhausted, expired two years later. He was buried beside her in Calvary Cemetery, Los Angeles.

It is evident that not a little of his career did not add to his distinctions, but explained them. There was much that was false in the praise he received as "Dean of American poets." But those who held that his talent had not survived "The Man with the Hoe" were themselves limited in vision. They did not notice that poetry had, at best, a hard row to hoe in America. The constant harping on the Millet painting and poem did not permit an intelligent assessment of Markham's other poems, thus implicating the critics themselves in unsatisfactory overviews.

As for Markham's distortion of his life's realities, it derived in part from his need to live it among people who were uninterested in the truth. His sexual troubles, too, were no more than the obverse of later poets's sexual excesses, which often resulted in no more valid artistic transmutation than his, and no better adjustment to time. Upton Sinclair, for example, held that his Progressive comrades who died before encountering the times of Harding and Coolidge were lucky not having had to adjust to the vagaries of Sinclair Lewis's fictional Babbitts and Elmer Gantrys. Also, America was notorious for producing artists whose first distinguished acts were not followed by notable seconds and thirds.

There were lessons in Markham's odyssey which were more true than the easy praise he had first received or the easy disdain which followed. Frost was many times the poet that Markham had been, but his life, too, had been marred by malice and distortions. Not only was Markham's poetry too carelessly set aside. Poetry itself suffered from popular lack of interest, with many poets following assembly lines of grants, gifts, and academic appointments in order to function at all. If Markham was part of the problem, he was also part of the solution. See Louis Filler, *The Unknown Edwin Markham* (1966).

Left: Markham and his wife, Anna, circa 1935.
*Below: Markam reads his poem **Lincoln** at the 1922 dedication of the Lincoln Memorial.*

Edward Willis Scripps
(1854-1926)

"Damned Old Crank"

ADMIRED AS AN INDIVIDUALIST and builder in journalism, Edward Willis Scripps furthered freedom of the press. He exemplified the workings of popular communication in his time. Lincoln Steffens (*q.v.*) thought him a great man, but his success rather illustrated popular efforts to build democracy. He created the first chain of newspapers.

Scripps was born obliquely into a newspaper tradition. His grandfather, William Armiger Scripps, had edited *The True Briton* and published the *London Daily Sun.* A cousin, John Locke Scripps, helped found the *Chicago Tribune.* Scripps's father, a failed London bookseller came to America to run a farm in Rushville, Illinois which his father had bought. His own most memorable achievement was fathering thirteen children by three wives. The third picked up their farm from his incompetent hands and worked it for the family benefit. Other relatives also created opportunities for Edward: tall, sickly, with dreamer-like tendencies, much lost in books.

He yearned for a career in "literature," but had no way for advancing this fantasy. At fifteen he would have liked to join James E. Scripps, editor of the *Detroit Advertiser and Tribune*, but this half-brother, nineteen years older than Edward, saw no profit in him, though his sister Ellen was employed on the paper and would later be a source of strength to him. An English cousin who had opened a drugstore in Detroit brought Edward to Detroit as a clerk. He was able to move over to the *Advertiser and Tribune* as an office boy. In 1873 the *Tribune* building burned. James used his insurance money to reestablish it as the *Detroit Evening News*, with Edward as the delivery boy.

Here he showed his genius talent for organization. He put others to work while he systematized deliveries of the new, two-cent paper. He helped the paper compete further with the more elite five-cent publications by extending deliveries to Detroit suburbs. The great depression of 1873 was a mighty opportunity for the Scrippses. A financially hardpressed public gratefully received the more modestly-priced *News*.

Eddie Scripps's talents for advancing the *News* now appreciated, he moved into editorial work, then persuaded his half-brother to make him an editor. He showed a basic grasp of the public's wants at the time by urging his reporters to make spirited reports, critical of corruption and civic slackness. This perception of the uses of popular unrest and indignation—for he also curbed them, when it was expedient to do so—helped him through subsequent decades when outmoded buccaneer business practices were put under fire by reformers and muckrakers, and when journalists like William Randolph Hearst and Joseph Pulitzer spelled out catchy slogans to the general public.

Scripps rarely tried to compete with these giants. Nor could he compete with the long-established papers of the East. His audience was the Midwest, where new cities and populations struggled to build civic systems, using older strains of American and new immigrants.

Scripps now went through a hectic time during which he raised himself to be a force in journalism. He drank and smoked heavily, and fell into sexual adventures, his own upbringing found repulsive. At several points he was all but prostrated by excessive indulgence and had to rest and recuperate abroad.

His brother James developed the original idea which was to make the young man a tycoon: of purchasing a number of papers to be run as one enterprise. Young Scripps became editor then owner of the *Cleveland Penny Press*, and there developed another of his key principles: to make the editor the sole dominating figure of the paper. This meant that news could be made according to local interest, rather than advertisers' preference. As a result readers were drawn into the newspaper's program, and circulation flourished. It was Scripps, too, who discovered that a commonplace event, like a marriage between insignificant persons, could become a matter of general interest when it was highlighted with intimate detail and so became everybody's experience.

Scripps took these guiding ideas to St. Louis, where his *Chronicle* tried to compete with Joseph Pulitzer's *Dispatch*, then to Cincinnati where he acquired fifty-five percent of a local paper's stock and also a business manager, Milton A. McRae, who was to serve him for over two decades. In Cincinnati, too, he overcame a personal crisis when a woman with whom he had consorted attempted blackmail. Scripps boldly called in reporters and related the facts of their relationship, and their agreement to part company. To his relief the public proved indifferent, a fact which added to his understanding of public opinion, as well as his cynicism.

Scripps—or E.W. Scripps as he became for the rest of his life—now had his program for reaching toward a life of affluence and power. He would buy, or begin, newspapers for small amounts, always holding on to a commanding percentage of the paper's ownership. He would find promising editors, also for small amounts. If their paper succeeded, he would lead it on his populist program. If it failed he closed its offices and looked elsewhere for promising opportunities. He sealed another part of his career in 1885 by marrying a minister's daughter, Nackie Holtsinger, and thereby closing forever his dissipations in sex. Several children were to grow into his business and inherit it.

Scripps now enjoyed a comfortable and secure income from his holdings in Cleveland and Cincinnati, though the St. Louis venture had not proved profitable. It took several years before he could push his larger plans. His brother James had been in control of the family papers. In 1887 an ill man, James needed rest. He and other family members including E.W. Scripps signed an agreement not to sell their stock outside their family circle. While James was abroad, E.W. Scripps pushed for more centralized control of the several papers, and, with advertising and other expenditures boldly expanded circulation.

On James's return an open quarrel over E.W Scripps'policies dissolved the agreement and left him free to follow his own plans, using his Cincinnati and St. Louis papers as a base. Later mediation and arrangements gave him the Cleveland paper, and others with variant fortunes in Kansas City, Akron, and Chicago, with still others in prospect. In time he had a controlling interest in twenty-eight daily papers in fifteen states.

Two of his exploits became famous. In 1891 he bought 400 acres above San Diego, California, and there began building Miramar, his regal estate with all but innumerable rooms and services. His newspaper chain he made firmer in 1902 by setting up his Newspaper Enterprise Association to feed his papers news, features, and specialty items. Scripps's papers were rarely distinguished and famous in their own right. They were serviceable. They entertained and informed a local citizenry. but in their number they constituted a formidable social force.

In 1907 Scripps challenged the Associated Press, then exercising a brutal authority in the control of news and its presentation; Upton Sinclair (*q.v.*) was later to riddle its handling and manipulation of the news in his *The Brass Check.* By creating the United Press as competition, Scripps forced the A.P to pay better regard to the views and editors of the numerous papers it influenced.

Miramar and the UP kept Scripps visible during the Progressive era, especially as he began his long practice of setting down what he called his "Disquisitions." He invited noted contemporaries to Miramar, to trips on his ninety-six foot yacht, and elsewhere for conversation.

Roughly dressed in casual trousers and boots, with a cap of some sort to deter colds—Scripps was a crank about health—he seemed picturesque and unusual to his admirers. They savored his cynicism as real wisdom. He expressed lack of respect for humanity, and even, he wrote, for himself.

How useful his "disquisitions" were was debatable, proceeding as they did from his own experience, with little concern for the validity of the larger social factors of the time. Thus, Scripps calculated that one native white was a better prospect for his readership than two or three Negroes or "recent" immigrants. This may have been accurate at the time, but offered no dynamic for social change. His attacks on department stores in order to reduce their advertisements and increase readers was original, but gained as much from reform pressure of the period as it contributed to it.

Scripps subscribed to Woodrow Wilson's (*q.v.*) war in 1917 because he imagined war was good for humanity by relieving itself of excess population. Such fancies did little for understanding the war itself, or its aftermath. His life as a semi-recluse did not deprive society of a vibrant spirit.

His anti-monopoly services were real, though made for selfish reasons. His best memorial was the Scripps Institution for Biological Research, founded in 1912 with the aid of his sister Ellen Browning Scripps, best known by its later name, the Scripps Institution of Oceanography. His own fame as, using his own terms, a "damned old crank" was less likely to interest posterity. In his yacht he cruised about the world, and on one of those cruises while entertaining people off Monrovia, Liberia in March 1926, he died, and in accordance with his instructions, was buried at sea.

Gilson Gardner, *Lusty Scripps* (1932) and Negley D. Cochran, *E.W. Scripps* (1933) set down the basic facts of his life as journalist and per-sonality. The family-sponsored Charles R. McCabe, ed., *Damned Old Crank* (1951) used some of his "disquisitions;" the inaccurately titled Oliver Knight, ed., *I Protest* (1966) more amply drew from them.

Frank Parsons
(1854-1908)

Martyr to Reform

FRANK PARSONS LIVED A
career that forecast the Progressive era
and was part of it. His short life, filled
with ardor and achievement, was part of a time and movement which
could not understand short-sighted goals. It was a sign of shaken
faith that he should be remembered as "father of vocational education," which indeed he was, but which would have seemed to him
the least of his accomplishments.

Parsons was born in Mount Holly, New Jersey, of Scotch-Irish
and English parents of little status or means. Precocious and intense
in his hunger for achievement, he put high school behind him at age
fifteen, and Cornell University in three years, graduating first with a
degree in civil engineering. A humanist as well as capable in technical
matters, he seems to have been uncertain where to put his energies.
He began as an engineer with a railroad, then taught school in Massachusetts. In the "Gilded Age" of affluence and speculation he concluded that a degree in law would help him define his goals. He
completed three years of study in a year and won his degree in 1881.
The effort was too much for his physique, which broke down, forcing
him to spend several years recuperating in New Mexico.

Parsons opened a law office in Boston, but found law practice
distasteful. He undertook the preparation of law books for a living, but his

interests were elsewhere, in literature and education, and also in social tendencies at home and abroad which were creating "Christian socialism," soon to be found at home in the work of Edward Bellamy and the Populist movement. For several years Parsons lectured on literature at the Young Men's Christian Association in Boston. In 1889 he published *The World's Best Books* which gained him status in academe. Parsons assumed a lectureship at Boston University in 1892. It gave him a base from which he expanded in ways which influenced the reforms of his time.

With railroads spread over the country, and exercising a powerful force on the nation, and other monopolies forming in vital areas, it was evident to many that a people's movement favoring individual initiative and basic freedoms must rise in response. The need called forth a host of politicians like Robert M. LaFollette and journalists of the stripe of E.W. Scripps (*qq.v.*). Parsons undertook to help by clarifying issues and the detail behind them. He wrote numerous articles, notably for the *Arena*, and in time helped create or headed such organizations as the National League for Promoting Public Ownership of Monopolies. His voracious reading and ability to formulate issues found first expression in *Our Country's Need* (1894), a plea for "mutualism," a cooperative concept which also called for individual initiative.

Rational Money (1898) undertook to explain the effects of free market manipulations which had fostered panic-catastrophes in 1873, again in 1883, and still again ten years later. *The Telegraph Monopoly* (1899) was the first of his books to put his phenomenal reading into vital motion; it entered into legislative and reform activities, and was part of the anti-monopoly drive of the next years. In *The City for the People* (1899) Parsons finally clarified his goal: to build an educated public which would control its increasingly complex social structure. His *Direct Legislation* (1900) provided the means by which control could be won.

During the next years Parsons gave himself wholly to his cause. In 1897 he accepted a professorship at Kansas State Agricultural College while maintaining his Boston connections. Kansas politics had been upset by Populist triumphs which affected the institution. Parsons, along with other idealists on the faculty, worked to adapt its curriculum to their democratic purposes. A radical conservative change in the administration cost them their places on campus, and they moved on to Trenton, Missouri, where they founded Ruskin College of Social Science, with Parsons as dean and professor. When this experiment failed, he returned to Boston. There he became an advisor to E.A. Filene (*q.v.*) and also cooperated in an effort to create a settlement house, the Civic Service Home, organized to help immigrants to adjust to their new environment: part of a national reform movement in New York, Chicago, and elsewhere. Parsons also helped set up a Breadwinner's Institute. It not only offered education to ambitious people too poor to enter Boston's regular colleges and institutes, but encouraged their hopes with diplomas. Meanwhile Parsons's activities took him not only about the country, gathering and imparting information, but abroad as well.

With the Progressive era now in full swing, Parsons was able to offer it his most mature works. *The Story of New Zealand* (1904) in its more than ample account, detailed the country's experiments with expanded suffrage and social security, and inspired Charles Edward Russell's visit there to see and report for himself. *The Trusts, the Railroads, and the People* (1906) and *The Heart of the Railroad Problem* (1906) joined the paramount issues of the time, and called Parsons himself to Washington to help legislators with the various laws they were debating to curb monopoly. Once more, however, as in his youth, Parsons fell physically behind with overwork. The rewards for the Progressive drive seemed too close at hand for judicious living. His death found him with two books still unpublished. *Choosing a Vocation* (1909) indeed broke ground for an increasingly necessary means for preparing to work in the world, and *Legal Doctrine and Social Progress* (1911) spelled out one of his earliest concerns.

Howard V. Davis, *Frank Parsons* (1969) was written with a narrow interest in vocational education. W.D.P. Bliss's edited *The New Encyclopedia of Social Reform* (1910) was a massive compilation of causes and personalities, including Parsons briefly, which and who dominated the period. Parsons receives a chapter in Arthur Mann, *Yankee Reformers in the Urban Age* (1954).

Harry Thurston Peck
(1856-1914)

Cultural Marvel

A PHENOMENAL SCHOLAR AND
popular litterateur, Harry Thurston
Peck, in life, reflected the double
standard of the academic and public
establishments of his time. On one hand Progressive writers demanded a
more open and forthright intellectual climate appreciative of public needs.
On the other hand the academic world held to rigid standards of scholarship
and social deportment. Peck, son of a Connecticut schoolmaster, was able
to meet standards in both fields, for a long while. His unique mind easily
made configurations of persons, events, languages, and histories as they
came before him.

Known as brilliant during his student days at Columbia College,
he went on to classical philology, and studied in Paris, Berlin, and Rome.
He spent some years as a writer in the Latin field, his *Students' Series of
Latin Classics* being outstanding at the time. Peck then returned to Columbia in 1890 as Professor of Latin, but with a difference. He emerged as
the wonder of his department. Students were mesmerized by his apparent
knowledge of everything, his Latin and Roman explanations being interlarded with comparisons linking them with French, English, German, and
other matters and occasions.

Peck's need for expressing and augmenting his strange talent for
paradigm soon took him out of the classrooms and halls he had in hand

to the scholarly and popular fields in downtown New York. He became editor of the multi-volumed *International Encyclopedia*. At the same time, he served as literary editor of the highly intelligent *Commercial Advertiser* (1897-1901) and also of the much less substantial *Munsey's Magazine* (1907-1911). He edited the formidable *Bookman* (1895-1902): the best such publication promoting books and authors in its time.

Meanwhile, he issued as editor, and in large part as writer his 1700-page *Harper's Dictionary of Classical Literature* (1896), double-columned, small type, a compilation of some 10,000 items, many like those on Athens, Caesar, Sulla, Rome, Scipio Africanus filling many columns and pages, and involving etymology, interpretations, dates, bibliography in never-ending round: a book to stir wonder.

Peck wrote other books, including *The Personal Equation* (1897); *What Is Good English? and Other Essays* (1899); *William Hickling Prescott* (1905); *Studies in Several Literatures* (1909); and, most original, *The New Baedeker* (1910), which found American Cities as worth visiting as those abroad. Peck's *Twenty Years of the Republic* (1906) was impressive in its own right, showing a detailed sense of the passing years, from 1886 to 1896, from President Grover Cleveland to President Grover Cleveland again a sense of its personalities, modes of speech, issues of war and peace which, considering its author and circumstances provides double meanings on many pages.

Especially as one sees Peck as he was then, a nattily dressed man about town in cream-colored derby hat, spats, and carnation, attending to his several offices, taking in all the Broadway plays and writing immediate commentary on them, staying abreast of current fiction in his own *Bookman,* and dazing with his comments a constant stream of friends and acquaintances. In the din of the New York of the time, he was another of its natural marvels. Yet such was its society that he could be struck down in a moment, as by a passing car, as he was.

Peck seems to have found no median for the several civilizations in his head. His *Twenty Years of the Republic* accepted the democratic tenets of the time, but did not perceive the strong underlying premises, those of his Connecticut forebears, which still held society together. Peck had lived spiritually too long in patriarchal Athens and Rome to realize that masters like Plato and Cicero, and others who filled the pages of *Plutarch's Lives,* did not comport with New York's particular rounds and expectations.

He seems to have experienced a change of life impulse which directed him toward new personal desires. He divorced his wife and married again. In June 1910 a former secretary sued him for breach of promise, producing letters which revealed Peck as a naive would-be philanderer. The letters, reproduced in the local press, destroyed him. He was stripped of his Columbia position. His editorships disappeared. Peck suffered collapse. Taken in by his former wife, he tired of her company and moved into a lodging house. He lost all his friends and connections.

He attempted to make a living by writing articles for what had been his own *International Encyclopedia*, but evidently concluded that time lay too heavy on his hands. Borrowing money from his former wife, he bought a gun, crossed the river to Jersey City, and there in another lodging house, March 23, 1914 took his life. His former president at Columbia University, Nicholas Murray Butler, thought he had inherited lunacy; Butler could not imagine anyone not crazy putting in jeopardy such emoluments as Peck had possessed. An academic, Thomas A. Bailey, thought himself witty by referring to Harry *Thirsty* Peck, but this was mere campus heartlessness. Peck had lived in the wrong age at the wrong time.

A curiosity was it that another Peck—no connection—Walter E. Peck, brilliant too, but in the more specialized area of nineteenth century English literature, author of the massive, two-volume *Shelley: His Life and Work* (1927) also fell catastrophically, having made uncalculated passes at a Hunter College student. This Peck, however, was a drunkard who survived for many years in the New York Bowery, dying at last on an exceptionally cold night while huddled in a driveway. He had told a *New Yorker* reporter that he had preferred drink to academic status and rewards, though why the two pursuits could not have been more comfortably synchronized was a question he apparently could not face.

Woodrow Wilson
(1856-1924)

"Golden, Glowing Words"

WOODROW WILSON WAS THE first President of the United States from the South since Andrew Johnson; he was noted as an advocate for peace, and also as the President who won his country to intervention in World War I. His world-wide fame diminished as succeeding decades raised questions regarding the wisdom of his course, but contained enough enigma to assure continuing interest in him as a person and national phenomenon. ˉ

The son of a Presbyterian minister and southern patriot, he enjoyed a happy childhood in his Staunton, Virginia birthplace, where he played the violin and often entertained with a good singing voice. He grew up infused with the southern viewpoint on national affairs, attended Presbyterian Davidson College in North Carolina, then went on, as had many promising southern youth since before James Madison, to the College of New Jersey, later Princeton University. There he made his mark mainly in oratory.

A significant episode in his senior year saw him expected to win a favored prize in debate. He would not conform to contest stipulations, however, when instructed to defend "Protectionism," even as an exercise in oratory. The South then devoutly favored "Free Trade." In a campaign biography issued in 1912, this event was cited as an early example of Wilson's integrity. In fact, the subject stipulated had been woman suffrage, which young Wilson then firmly opposed; but 1912, a year of insurgence in the women's fight for the national vote would have been a poor time for recalling the fact.

With his South still in the hands of Federal reconstructionists, Wilson thought his entry into the national politics—he intensely followed politics—lay through law. Accordingly, he entered the University of Virginia law school, graduating and receiving admission to the bar in 1881. It quickly became evident that he had no talent for seeking and finding legal business. His main social interest outside of politics had become English literature, a pursuit he had picked up from his Georgia fiancée, later his first wife, Ellen Louise Axson. He had also developed a passion for the work of the English litterateur and banker Walter Bagehot, who seemed to him an ideal commentator on life and letters and whose clarity and realism he sought to emulate. Meanwhile, he had no vocation at age twenty seven, and a loving but somewhat anxious family agreed to his entry into the Johns Hopkins history department, then developing its "German" tradition of hard facts and research.

Although Wilson had no stomach for extended research, he gave off an attractive sense of dignity and distinction. He had developed a communicative style of writing that suggested thoughtful surveillance in the history field and adequate knowledge; he himself believed he could be an influential commentator on social concerns.

In 1885 he published *Congressional Government,* which finally gave him public exposure and success. It was an attack, couched in learned phrases, on Reconstruction in the South as a threat to democracy and impugning of the presidency. The crucial fact was that it received praise from northern commentators as well as southern, and established Wilson in scholarly circles. His book, an essay at bottom, used opinion rather that facts, exploited dissatisfaction with Reconstruction politics, but hid its southern bias effectively in the process.

Although *Congressional Government* did not meet standards of the "new history," Johns Hopkins administrators stretched considerations for Wilson and granted him his Ph.D. Wilson was on his way. In the next years he taught successfully at Bryn Mawr and Wesleyan, and developed lecturing skills which made him a favorite on the academic circuit where he emphasized good humor and cultural grace, then in short supply in the academe of the time. His publications were all essays, even his *Division and Reunion*, which honored General Robert E. Lee and also an idealized

Abraham Lincoln. *An Old Master, and Other Political Essays*, and *Mere Literature and Other Essays* all contributed to his visibility.

Wilson learned German and developed grandiose plans for courses and writings in political science and the new field of Administration—plans which his increasing public presence did not require him to consummate. In 1890 he returned home to Princeton as professor of jurisprudence and political economics, and proved ingratiating to students and admired by his peers. In 1902 he became the first layman to be made president of Princeton, and thereafter assumed a greater dignity and personal reserve than before.

In the next decade while the Progressives enjoyed eminence, he termed himself a Democrat of the conservative wing of the Party. He won recognition among influential journalists and party leaders who sought an answer to Theodore Roosevelt's charisma and Progressive programs and who needed to separate the Democratic party from taints associated with big city Democratic bosses and southern rebels. In time, they were successful in blurring the memory of Wilson's consummate southernness—several generations of students imagined he was from New Jersey—but it was the political bosses of the state who gave him his opportunity to break strongly into politics, and that because they fancied him a political innocent who could be a front for them against over-aggressive Progressives.

Wilson had received national notice in instituting a system of colleges at Princeton in the care of tutors, little more than England's system at its major universities, but, in the American setting, giving a tone of democracy and comradery. His reputation had bloomed as he fought to make Princeton's new Graduate School part of the liberal arts setting, rather than separated from the main campus and fostering an elite. This fight separated old guard alumni from more modern elements among faculty and administration. Wilson's tenure as president was threatened, and he seized the offer of the New Jersey Democrats to run for governor in 1910.

That historic fight drew to his side the state Progressives and others outside the state. It wants notice that Wilson's new Progressivism did not contradict the views inherent in his southern upbringing. Southerners before the Civil War had denounced northern industry as crueler in practice than their slave system. Wilson sincerely feared trusts and wanted them curbed. And he saw in big city northern political machines the friendliness and compassion of which they boasted. The 1910 run put Wilson into the governor's seat in Trenton and exposed him as a hidden Progressive. It made him a contender for the presidential race two years later. In the meantime a series of Progressive laws had come from him and over his desk, and the image of an upright scholar and successful administrator deepened. The vital split among Republicans, conservative and Progressive, widened as President Taft and former President Theodore Roosevelt buried each other in recriminations, enabling Wilson at election to assume presidential office with a minority vote.

Wilson was now a figure of the highest general interest, with facets of personality—reserved, introspective, academic in experience—unusual in a President. The public responded according to its instincts. During the campaign, Wilson had thought it would advance his cause to be popularly called "Woody," but the nickname did not catch on. There was interest in his wife and three daughters, and the marriage of one of them to his Secretary of the Treasury William G. McAdoo was a public event. Wilson was always dependent on the company and sympathy of the women close to him, and his wife's death in the White House in 1914 roused great sympathy, as his marriage in 1915 to Edith Bolling Galt stirred interest.

Between these two events, however, Wilson consummated a friendship with Mary Allen Hulbert which, if made public at the time, would have had unforeseeable consequences. Some of Wilson's contemporaries knew of the event but there was no public exposure. Wilson's panic and fear for his reputation contrasted negatively with the dignity with which Mrs. Hulbert refused shoddy offers intended to ensure her silence.

The first Wilson term was to be hailed as the greatest reform era since that of Andrew Jackson. On sober review, it summed up in executive terms the efforts of the preceding reform era proper. Its highly touted Free Trade Underwood Tariff did not function, as English warships and German submarines diminished Atlantic trade. The Clayton Act, proclaiming labor's freedom from the Sherman Anti-Trust Act ("labor is not a commodity") did little to limit war between the corporations and organized labor. The Federal Reserve System, intended to make economic panics and depressions obsolete, failed to control runaway credit and financial adventureism, and brought on ghastly results in time. The LaFollette (*q.v.*) Seaman's Act, and similar legislation obviously showed the nation as a whole, rather than the Wilson Democrats, clearing up archaic and cruel naval conditions. Nevertheless, Wilson gained regard as a result of the legislative march, and further gained by the Democratic slogan of 1916: "He kept us out of war."

In fact, the British Cabinet was sharper than Wilson in watching American public opinion, for Wilson would have called earlier for war with Germany, had it not been for clear domestic and Congressional opinion favoring non-intervention. Wilson had been of two minds regarding war, fearing that major carnage among the most civilized nations would enervate them and offer opportunities for authority spreading to racially inferior people and nations; and harboring attachments to the British Isles—the old home for Wilsons—which left him open to their ambassadors.

Wilson had made a fateful alliance with an unelected southern political advisor, "Col." E.M. House, whose quality could be measured by his anonymously published novel, *Phillip Dru: Administrator* (1912). It carved the image of an American paternalist who, following a great military victory over Latin American forces, "gave" them democracy under the strict guidance of superior American educators and politicians. House, thought of as Wilson's "other self," in fact acted as all but President, while heaping praise on his chief. The lack of public analysis of House through this momentous era, permitting him to have secret meetings with the European heads of state like a visiting potentate was to embarrass historians from that time on.

Wilson went to bed on the night of the 1916 presidential election day thinking that he had lost the office to Republican Charles Evans Hughes. He woke President again by a hair's breadth, thanks to a vagary in California's electoral vote. But once again Wilson was able to utter the "golden, glowing words" which permitted such dedicated pacifists as Upton Sinclair (*q.v.*) to dream of permanent peace under his leadership—a peace promised by the British chiefs and furthered by the British scholar G. Lowes Dickinson, thanks to a coming League of Nations. Wilson offered his famous "Fourteen Points" as conditions for peace, eliciting the atheist Premier Georges Clemenceau's scornful comment that God himself had only stipulated ten.

Wilson took his entourage to Paris for peace talks, astonishing and alarming J.M. Keynes, soon author of the famous *Economic Consequences of the Peace*, by "Doctor Wilson's" feeble knowledge of European affairs and even geography. Wilson and House imagined themselves objective in their private discussions, able to discuss even such possible eventualities as war with Great Britain. House setting down the details for posterity did not realize how their unconscious presumptions—such as black and Jewish inferiorities—marked their thoughts and judgments.

What Keynes did not grasp was Wilson's extreme faith in the League of Nations idea. It would bind the major powers in the world and, by democratic fiat, force recalcitrant or outlaw powers to accept their find-ings. Peace was inevitable, given the League of Nations.

Wilson returned home to find that Americans, who had freely given their sons to the war, now wanted nothing more than to have the survivors home. They had permitted a crushing of pacifist forces at home, a quelling of dissidents, an unleashing of vigilante forces. And now they gave ear to such distinguished figures as Robert LaFollette, Sr. , who warned that join-ing Wilson's League of Nations would no more than put Americans at the mercy of conniving foreigners.

Wilson embarked on a body-straining tour of the country pleading with the people who had so much admired his eloquence that only the League stood between new marshalling of economic and military might, and peace. On September 26, 1919, he collapsed while speaking at Pueblo, Colorado, suffering disabilities which effectively ended his premier role as President.

His wife's dominance in their household ensured that government administrators, Democratic Party leaders, friends, petitioners in the public interest would have no access to her ailing husband. Essentially, the presidential office was held vacant, awaiting a new incumbent. The Democratic national convention the next year chose as his successor for presidential candidate a second Ohio journalist and politician, James M. Cox, to match against Warren G. Harding, the Republican candidate.

Wilson, using apocalyptical language in his speaking tour, had warned that if America refused leadership to the League, it would have to face an even more devastating war than the one just concluded. This made him for many a modern prophet. Others wondered ironically whether the Almighty had chosen the Presbyterian denomination to lead the world to eternal peace. Wilson was interred in the Episcopalian Washington Cathedral, far from the parochial considerations which had contributed to his national ascent, though only a short distance from the White House. His errors, such as could be clearly discerned, he shared with an indeter-minate percentage of his fellow citizens.

Ray Stannard Baker (*q.v.*), Wilson's designated biographer, issued a multi-volumed *Life and Letters* (1927-1939) of his wartime chief. These were in time superseded by the vastly more scholarly Arthur Link, (*Life*) (1947-1965) in five volumes, and Link *et al.*, editors, *The Wilson Papers*, begun in 1966, and in 64 volumes in 1991, with others in prospect. There were in addi-tion innumerable lives, recollections, and materials issued over the years. Wilson's life, nevertheless, remains open to further interpretations as events unfold at home and in the world.

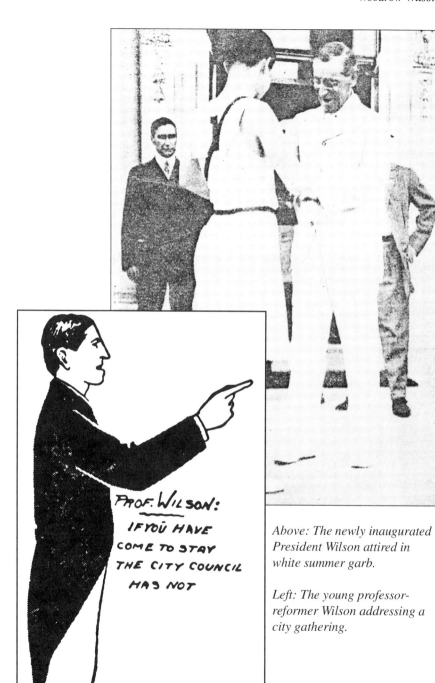

Above: The newly inaugurated President Wilson attired in white summer garb.

Left: The young professor-reformer Wilson addressing a city gathering.

Frank Harris
(1856-1931)

Romantic Scoundrel

BORN JAMES THOMAS HARRIS in Galway, Ireland, Frank Harris was a picturesque adventurer and writer with controversial impact on his generation. Although most notoriously known for his *My Life and Loves* (1925-1929), which detailed innumerable fornications and alleged affairs in cities and places around the world, his was a literary scandal which won its modicum of defense, but also dimmed appreciation of earlier writings and actions which had once seemed more seriously memorable even when debatable.

A small, homely, aggressive boy, he won a Cambridge University scholarship at fifteen, but impatient of delay because of his youth, he accepted a small gratuity instead and ran away to America. He worked at odd jobs in New York and Chicago, and probably Texas: *My Reminiscences as a Cowboy* (1930) is shadowed by his life-long tendency to fabricating adventures. Yet Harris's book, despite excessive elaboration, may have deserved better that J. Frank Dobie's complete skepticism as expressed in his *Guide to Life and Literature of the Southwest* (1952).

He did attend the University of Kansas, where he mixed study with precocious sensuality and romantic aspiration. Kate Stephen's *Lies and Libels of Frank Harris* (1929) provides corrective to his tales. It does not explain the ambition which sent him off to Germany seeking further intelligence and access to famous men, whom he sought to impress with his ardor, his rich voice, and idealism. Studied seriously, his years in America were probably deeper and made more of an impression on him than his surface recollections indicate. A young, constantly alert and undoubtedly talented boy, basically alone, his responses to environment and individuals took in language, types of personality, and occupations which influenced the directions he took.

His siege of London in the late 1880s and 1890s made him both famous and of questionable status. Bold and unscrupulous he succeeded as editor of the *Evening News* and the *Fortnightly* while furthering sexual liaisons which defied Victorian standards.

As editor of the *Saturday Review* he reached the apogee of his editorial career, while also seeking out literary lions of the quality of Thomas Carlyle and the novelist George Meredith. Harris did not so much "discover" rising stars like George Bernard Shaw and H. G. Wells as give them ample room to display their talents; in any event, he was identified with a distinguished publication.

He also began his career as writer, his *Elder Conklin and Other Stories* (1894) won over Meredith who affirmed that Harris's was the best hand writing in English. For those seeking to understand Harris those once famous stories warrant close reading. Harris yearned for greatness. He was already bemused by his readings in Shakespeare and the life and words of Jesus Christ. He was influenced, too, by the new realism sought and labored over by such writers as Thomas Hardy and George Gissing in England, and Stephen Crane and Harold Frederic in the United States. Harris suppressed his truculence and self-serving prose to set down tales which caught some of the actual life and inflexions of the frontier he had known. Such stories in his collection as the title-piece, "Elder Conklin," and "Gulmore, the Boss" attained an objectivity which was in direct contrast with the Romantic tradition in which Bret Harte and Owen Wister wrote.

Such distinction as Harris's stories might have received was marred by aspects of his London career. His foes read with approval Frederic Carrel's portrait of a conceited fraud, *The Adventures of John Johns* (1897). It failed to notice Harris's genuine regard for true talent, and that he stood by Oscar Wilde when others had scurried from his side.

Harris left the *Saturday Review* in 1898. His subsequent editorships ranged from the shabby to the questionable. He turned increasingly to his own writing. His most famous story was "Montes the Matador" in which he strove to match Prosper Mérimée's *Carmen*. Because so much of his writing has become a matter of titles, rather than reading and expert comment, it seems relevant to set down an excerpt from this story. It tells of an almost legendary bull fighter, whose achievements in the ring were all but unbelievable. Montes, a small, limping man—there is psychology in Harris's narrative—falls in love, and becomes engaged to ironically-named Clemencia, who, however, is infatuated with and secretly gives herself to a secondary bull-ring figure, Juan. Montes discovers this and plans his revenge, once he has innocently given in to Clemencia's urgings that he give Juan his chance as a matador. In the ring, Juan nervously eyes a malignant bull, and expresses relief that Montes will stand by him. Montes assures him he will stand by Juan as Juan has stood by him. Juan suffers a horrible death. Montes then makes his last visit to Clemencia's home:

> I went upstairs and entered the room. There she sat with her elbows on the table and her hair all round her face and down her back, and her fixed eyes stared at me. As I closed the door and folded my arms and looked at her, she rose, and her stare grew wild with surprise and horror, and then, almost without moving her lips, she said:
>
> "Holy Virgin! You did it! I see it in your face!"
>
> And my heart jumped against my arms for joy, and I said in the same slow whisper, imitating her:
>
> " Yes, I did it."
>
> As I spoke she sprang forward with hate in her face, and poured out a stream of loathing and contempt on me. She vomited abuse as from her very soul: I was low and base and cowardly; I was—God knows what all. And he was handsome and kind, with a face like a king... And I had thought she could love me, me, the ugly, little, lame cur, while he was there. And she laughed. She'd never have let my lips touch her if it hadn't been that her mother liked me and to please him. And now I had killed him, the best friend I had. Oh, 'twas horrible. Then she struck her head with her fists and asked how God, God, God, could allow me to kill a man whose finger was worth a thousand lives such as mine!
>
> Then I laughed and said:
>
> "You mistake. You killed him. You made him an *espada*—you!"

As I spoke her eyes grew fixed and her mouth opened, and she seemed to struggle to speak, but she only groaned—and fell face forward on the floor.

I heard afterwards that she died next morning in premature childbirth. I left Madrid that night and came here, where I have lived ever since, if this can be called living....Yet at times, now fairly content, save for one thing—"Remorse?"

"Yes!"—and the old man rose to his feet, while his great eyes blazing with passion held me. "Remorse! That I let the bull kill him. I should have torn his throat out with my own hands."

The Bomb (1908) showed Harris's curious sympathy with anarchists. His *The Man Shakespeare* (1909) and *The Women of Shakespeare* (1911) were scorned by academics, but won such generous intellectual appreciation as that given him by the novelist Arnold Bennett.

Cold shouldered in England, Harris took up life in America, where he was welcomed by dissident youth and socialists. His love life continued indiscriminate and ample. A striking vignette culled by researchers involved one representative New Yorker who served his sexual needs, whom he showered with apparently vital anecdotes. In retrospect the relationship seemed to her inconsequential and unmemorable. Harris's *England or Germany?* committed him against the Allies, and, in 1917, the American censorship looked askance at his *Pearson's Magazine*, the last of the "muckraking" periodicals.

Meanwhile he scored a sensation with his *Oscar Wilde* (1916), and published the first of his volumes of *Contemporary Portraits* (1915), vivid sketches and alleged reminiscences about the famous persons he had known or claimed to know.

Now thoroughly on his own, he matched conventional contempt for him with followers and admirers who held him to be a forerunner of a freer life and expression. His *My Life and Loves* circulated under the counters of book dealers in several countries. The volume seemed to defenders to portray an open, honest nature in a hypocritical world. In the meantime, too, he seemed to preserve his youthful appearance in marked degree, though furthered by dyes and other cosmetic aid. He had married for money in his London period. He retired to Nice, France, with his gracious and forbearing wife Nellie, who, with friends, helped to sustain his actual decrepitude.

Even while he lived, new writings about sex and sexual adventures put his increasingly in the shade. Still later literary developments would all but obliterate them. His reminiscent writings increasingly showed their patently self-serving character. Much of the literature about him ranged from negative to disillusioned. The responses of his contemporaries to his personality and goals were more dependable, and illuminating of their times. Some of his stories projected a view of life which gained by being separated from his personality. Although his Shakespeare books were patently flawed, they embodied an independence of spirit and technique which were evocative.

He died in Nice, August 26, 1931, following an attack of bronchitis which had plagued him for years. Among other ailments, his last attack was accompanied by hiccoughs which went on for nine days. He had stubbornly refused aid intended to relieve his sufferings, but finally accepted an injection of morphine. Services were conducted for him at the local Episcopal Church. After a raising of funds, he was buried in the British cemetery at Cancade.

A manuscript on Bernard Shaw, mainly the work of others, was given a splendid launching, thanks to the generosity of Shaw, who remembered him with kindness and perhaps envied him his swashbuckling ways, and whose lengthy introduction called the book to the attention of critics and readers. I.A. Tobin and Elmer Gertz, *Frank Harris: a Study in Black and White* (1931) broke ground in following Harris's career in some detail, discovering lies as well as some surprising truth. Philippe Pullar, *Frank Harris* (1975) gained from the passage of time and releasing of old secrets and facts: as "definitive" as could be expected, except for judgment of Harris's writings. Gertz's *The Short Stories of Frank Harris: A Selection* (1975) offered controversial choices.

Alfred Henry Lewis
(1857-1914)

Creator of "Wolfville"

AUTHOR OF THE FIRST LITERARY Western fiction, Lewis was so popular in the period from 1890 to the 1910s as to have been read to pieces in original and reprint editions. This vast approval rating did not move the literary establishment of the time, which all but ignored Lewis, despite the admiration voiced by such of his friends as Theodore Roosevelt and Charles Edward Russell, and, later, the highly admired author of western lore, J. Frank Dobie. Lewis's public image was complicated by his high visibility as a contemporary journalist and author of patent ephemera.

Like many westerners, he was born in the East. Many "westerners" were ex-Confederate soldiers who could not face their ruined homelands and turned their horses' heads west. They helped give the cowboy country's speech its southern flavor. The outlaw, William H. Bonney, better known as Billy the Kid, began life in Brooklyn, New York. A. H. Lewis originated in Cleveland, Ohio as a precocious youngster who read law, passed the bar requirements at age nineteen, and served as prosecuting attorney for the city in 1880, four years later.

In 1881 he left with his family for Kansas City, Missouri, where his father planned to continue his trade as a carpenter. Lewis became a cowboy, herding cattle to Dodge City and becoming a figure from New Mexico to Nevada. He edited several papers for intermittent periods in that large area. With Tombstone, Arizona, having been made a crossroads by its silver strikes—at one time having a larger population than San Francisco—it drew Lewis's particular regard and became the original of his later "Wolfville" stories.

Lewis returned to Kansas City in 1885. He settled down and married, engaging in law and real estate. As he later told it, he had the habit of meeting with a friend for purposes of "drinking and telling lies." On one occasion he told his story of what became "Wolfville's First Funeral," and was urged to publish it. Lewis followed this advice, but fearing it would hurt his business to be associated with such pursuits as story-telling, had it printed as by "Dan Quin." It struck an immediate chord. Lewis then began expanding that side of his concerns, but slowly. He entered into journalism as a full-time occupation, first for William Rockhill Nelson's famous *Kansas City Star*, later for the Washington Bureau of William Randolph Hearst's *New York Journal*. He saw his West as being supplanted by sullen farmers who stretched barbed wire along the vast spaces he had once ranged freely with hardy and interesting people.

He created in his mind the image of an "Old Cattleman"—based on an actual character he had known—whose endless tales and Scheherezade-like anecdotes built up a panoply of individuals, some of whom he had known in Tombstone and elsewhere, others whom he created out of known characters or to exemplify types of good or evil, or simple variety inhabiting a West turned brighter in his memory.

Lewis was never entirely happy with the East which was now his home. He sported clothes with western flair and flowing ties. Like residents of the Great Plains he judged people as individuals, and for key qualities of courage, forthrightness, and honesty as he saw them. In his journalism, this seemed to shallow critics to place him among "reformers," but his rapid-firing abuse of people who offended his sensibilities added up to long years of journalism which was not memorable or worth detailing.

The other Lewis, the Lewis of the "Old Cattleman," was a calmer and more philosophical person with a deep sense of humor, endless recollections of things witnessed or heard, and with a realistic sense of life's vagaries. Lewis's "Wolfville," and other scenes made up a microcosm of the cowboy West. It included a base of solid citizens—marshals, natural leaders, doctors, ministers, and barkeeps, and their ladies, as well as adventurers, male and female. It included, too, ugly characters, some as notorious as Billy the Kid, whose tale he told under another name, who cut down harmless or helpless people, but whose excesses as often caused them to conclude with bullets in front or back, or at the end of a rope.

Lewis in the course of his work moved between Chicago, Washington, and New York, and was a friend of such diverse people as William Randolph Hearst himself, Theodore Roosevelt, who had had a western period, Charles Edward Russell, who, beginning in Iowa, became a leader in journalism, then in reform; and others, including Bat Masterson, a legend from the West who had become a United States marshal, then a sports writer in New York, and for whom Lewis had a special admiration and respect.

It was Roosevelt who urged Lewis to publish his first Wolfville stories, and helped him to put them in order. In 1897 *Wolfville* was a sensation, selling and continuing to sell, as readers responded to Lewis's pungent prose, reminiscent of hard, western need for information—Who are you? What's your game? Is that horse yours?—or softer, with western courtesy, and the circumlocution due half-acquaintances with the privacy everyone needed. There were no policemen on the frontier, only marshals and citizens who often had to improvise an informal law which made for routine and somewhat predictable days.

There were times, many times, when ordinary intercourse failed, and the church social or ladies sewing club, or the men's endless congregations in taverns, did not hold the town together. The shootings at the O. K. Corral in Tombstone, when the Earps met with the Clantons and the McLowrys was the kind of event which did not fit with ordinary law, and almost certainly resulted in a legend which, though immortal, was as mythical as that of Achilles at Troy. In fact, Lewis, nursing his own prejudices, could not handle it in factual terms. It was not by local accuracy that Lewis made his mark in literature.

His weapons were language and plot, and not plot in the ordinary sense, but as a function of character and situation. Thus, he had a marshal searching for a law-breaker, finding him, and levelling his gun at him:

> "See yere, Harris!" says East, "that a-way."
> Tom wheels, an' is lookin' into the mouth of East's six-shooter not a yard off.
> "Put up your hands!" says East.
> But Tom don't. He looks over the gun into East's eye; an' he freezes him. Then slow an' delib'rate, an' glarin' like a mountain lion at East, Tom goes back after his

Colt's an' pulls it. He lays her along side of East's with the muzzle p'inting' at East's eye. An' thar they stands.

"You don't dar' shoot!" says Tom; an' East don't.

They break away an' no powder burned; Tom stands East off.

"Warrant or no warrant," says Tom, "all the sheriffs that ever jingles a spur in the Panhandle country, can't take me! Nor all the rangers neither!" An' they shore couldn't.

The present writer once talked to an old man, an editor of culture, whose life in the Southwest had not been too distant from what Lewis remembered. He averred that he had never heard language such as Lewis had used. Certainly, anyone attempting conversation in the area today, and employing Lewis's vernacular as communication, would cause blank stares. But that would be the case if one attempted to do the same using Charles Dickens's and that of his friends as models. For involved was not only vernacular, but individuality and time and place factors. Ordinary readers of the late nineteenth and early twentieth century understood that instinctively, and translated easily in their minds from the western, as from the dialects in the East.

Lewis's "Old Cattleman" was superficially "racist," in modern parlance, and freely employed words of his time. Yet a number of his tales were penetrating in appreciation of Spanish, Indian, and black dignity, courage, and even grandeur. "How the Raven Died" was written with deep feeling for the Indian in liquid-words translation. With its "Story-that-Never-Ends" it literally borrowed from Scheherezade of the *Arabian Nights' Entertainments*. "Death, and the Donna Anna," an unforgettable tale, reproduced Spanish nuances of thought and feeling, surrounding it with tragic art. "Long Ago on the Rio Grande" mixed humor and war, a strange echo from the *Charge of the Light Brigade*, and a coda of personal honor.

Lewis was a good friend, and a man of sensibilities. He needed company to be able to bear seeing David Graham Phillips (*q.v.*), who had been shot and was dying in a hospital. From time to time Lewis indicted prose which merited saving beside his *Wolfville* books. This was notably the case with *Human Life*, the publication he edited in which he included personal biography. It went down in 1911 with others which offended conservative opinion and ended the Progressive era. Lewis's death in 1914 was unheralded as the nation moved on to other things.

Lewis contributed his own "Confessions of a Newspaperman" in *Human Life* (1905-1906). His valuable essay, "Some Cowboy Facts," drawn from *Wolfville Nights* (1902) is reproduced in Louis Filler, ed., *Old Wolfville: Chapters from the Fiction of Alfred Henry Lewis* (1968) which also includes an introduction regarding him.

Florence Kelley
(1859-1932)

The "Kelley Brief"

FEMINIST AND REFORMER, Florence Kelley fought for laws touching women and children at work and elsewhere affecting public policy. Born in Philadelphia, of a Quaker mother and an assertive ironmaster father of old Scotch-Irish descent, she showed qualities of both. "Pig Iron" William Darrah Kelley gained fame as a congressman for his protectionist fight against foreign iron products. His daughter learned legal ways to curb the greed of employers in behalf of workers and families which were easily exploited.

A good student, Florence overcame early physical illness sufficiently to enter Cornell University with an interest in social studies. Recurring sickness kept her from graduating until 1882, though then with a Phi Beta Kappa and a thesis, "Law and the Child," which foreshadowed her later career. Since no university in the country would permit her to enter law school, she went on to the University of Zurich where she studied Marxism and translated into English Friedrich Engels's *The Condition of the Working-class in England in 1844* (1877). Engels himself wrote a preface to the second edition of the book in 1892.

In 1884 she married Lazare Wischnewetzky and settled with him in New York. They had three children. Disagreements and incompatibility grew between them and she left him for Chicago in 1889, divorcing him, but maintaining the "Mrs." along with her maiden name. She left her children in the home of the quasi-socialist Henry Demarest Lloyd in nearby Winnetka, and herself entered into the work of Jane Addams's Hull House. She soon set up her own apartment close by. She and Julia Lathrop, a social worker, explored the living and working conditions of women and children in Chicago. They risked their lives entering into rooms and tenements in sweatshop districts where disease caught on quickly and germs could even be embedded in the garments being made.

Mrs. Kelley was helped by work she performed under Carroll D. Wright, first Commissioner of Labor in the U.S. Department of the Interior. Wright pioneered the gathering of statistics which helped focus actions in labor's behalf, as later shown in his *Some Ethical Phases of the Labor Question* (1902). Mrs. Kelley's strenuous efforts to uncover malignant work conditions, and a smallpox epidemic that alarmed Chicago, caused liberal Governor John P. Altgeld to commission her to gather data on the exploitation of children in slums. Largely because of the report she brought back, Altgeld forced a child labor law through the legislature controlling child employment and carrying with it the appointment of a factory inspector. Upon the bill's passage Altgeld gave the post to Mrs. Kelley.

She quickly learned that the law, specifying humane and equitable conditions, would not be honored. The young district attorney of Cook County was astonished at her calling to his attention the case of an abused eleven year old. If he assumed the case, he told her, there would be cases quickly following against such businessmen as Marshall Field. Mrs. Kelley saw it was necessary for her to fight her own court battles, and took the law course at nearby Northwestern University. It had gained receptivity to women's wants from Frances Willard's educational work. In 1894 Mrs. Kelley was granted her LL.B.

Her reports as state inspector were now so formidable and insistent that she was able to gain a new child labor law that laid more responsibility on law-enforcement officers. Her work continued to make her a leading light to others elsewhere concerned for the well-being of women and children. Her *Hull House Maps and Papers* (1895) were a landmark of guidance to women in reform. In 1897 when Governor Altgeld's term of office expired under storms of conservative disapproval, she lost her position, but stayed on at Hull House.

In 1899 Kelley returned to New York to be secretary of the National Consumers' League. She had helped to build it up, a growth from and successor to Josephine Shaw Lowell's (*q.v.*) Consumer League of New

York. This became the base from which she agitated for women's rights as workers and for child protection. She lived at the Henry Street Settlement, New York's equivalent of Hull House. With numerous male and female reformers she fought for minimum wage laws, woman suffrage, educational and work place standards, and a U.S. Children's Bureau, later established in 1912.

Mrs. Kelley agreed with socialist perspectives and helped found the Intercollegiate Socialist Society (later the League for Industrial Democracy). However, she also retained her Quaker viewpoint, which kept her from joining the then active Socialist Party.

Her book *Some Ethical Gains through Legislation* (1905), which spelled out Progressive goals, was influential. Her unique achievement, however, came from her long experience in gathering materials to make vivid the plight of women and children caught in onerous labors. She persuaded Louis D. Brandeis, widely known as "attorney for the people," to defend before the Supreme Court an Oregon statute prescribing a maximum of ten hours work for women per day. Mrs. Kelley herself gathered piles of evidence that labor affected women differently from men, and it was this raw evidence that made the difference. It broke away from the rule that the validity of law depended upon its universal application. It introduced gender differences as making good law. This movement away from simple precedent and abstract equity in the interest of facts was to be known as "the Brandeis Brief." It could just a rightly have been "the Kelley Brief," though Brandeis's presence and style were doubtless vital to the event.

Formidable in deportment, quick with evidence and in debate, with excellent voice and appearance, Mrs. Kelley put her mark on the era. She was a prolific writer as well as aggressive persuader. The manner in which she linked her causes added strength to them individually. She wrote *Modern Industry* (1913), was associate editor of the influential *Charities*, and contributed to many other reform publications. She edited for publication Edmond Kelly's *Twentieth Century Socialism* (1910). In furthering her legal career in reform she compiled *The Supreme Court and Minimum Wage Legislation* and *Comment of the Legal Profession on the District of Columbia Minimum Wage Case* (1925), and drew on legal support for her eloquence in causes ranging from woman's suffrage to pacifism. The death of her own daughter in 1905 had added intensity to her pleas for child protection at all ages. In 1905, too, she had found a haven for periodic rest in a cottage near Brooklin, Maine, and it was there that following her death from anemia in Philadelphia she was buried.

Mrs. Kelley was well remembered by her friends and co-workers, who memorialized her in Josephine Goldmark, *Impatient Crusader* (1953) and Dorothy Rose Blumberg, *Florence Kelley: the Making of a Social Pioneer* (1966). She looms large in such works as Maud Nathan, *The Story of an Epoch-Making Movement* (1926) (the National Consumers' League) and Jane Addams's *My Friend, Julia Lathrop* (1935).

Bolton Hall
(1854-1938)

"Three Acres and Liberty"

A LAND REFORMER AND businessman, Bolton Hall was among those of the well-to-do whose concern for the poor and un-successful helped keep fluid the nation's mainstreams. Hall was born in Armagh, Northern Ireland, the son of a distinguished minister, the Reverend John Hall. Bolton Hall found inspiration in his younger brother Thomas Cuming Hall who was also destined for distinction in the pulpit before taking the chair of Christian Ethics at Union Theological Seminar.

Bolton Hall was raised in Dublin until 1867 when the family fol-lowed their father to New York, where he had been offered the Fifth Avenue Presbyterian Church. Hall himself entered the College of New Jersey (later Princeton University), from which he received an A.B., then an M.A. In 1888 he was granted an LL.B. from Columbia University.

A big, hearty, and capable man—he had been an oarsman on Princeton's competitive crew—Hall first practiced law, but was also strongly drawn toward books and public issues. He took easily to real estate dealings, in which he gained sufficient funds to enable him to devote himself increas-ingly to the social crisis of the late nineteenth century.

Henry George's *Progress and Poverty* (1879) was Hall's major revelation. It explained to him why he himself had advanced so readily by buying strategic parcels of land, and how it was that land values did not accrue to the benefit of the great masses of his fellow New Yorkers. According to Georgian theory, it was the presence and work of people which created land value, and thus the value of the land should be theirs. Hall was a major figure in organizing the New York Tax Reform Association, and he propounded elsewhere the Single Tax solution of the George followers.

Hall wrote well and with clarity, qualities which won him a prize offered by the magazine *Popular Opinion* for an essay on taxation. His work in the field was comparable to that done in monopoly by Judge James B. Dill, an organizer of monopolies under convenient New Jersey laws. Dill held that monopolies were inevitable under current commercial dynamics, and that the sooner this economic inevitability was completed, the sooner would come the solution to the social dangers it created: government regulation. Hall, however, was an activist in behalf of those who suffered in housing and commerce under land monopoly, and though he advocated Georgian economics in the volume he edited, *Who Pays Your Taxes?* (1892), he was not satisfied to wait for time to right the wrongs of excessive taxation.

A good speaker and advocate, he helped to organize the American Longshoreman's Union in 1896, undoubtedly helped in his appeal to the workingmen by the Irish brogue he had not lost. According to Hall, he was offered the Democratic Party nomination for governor of New York in 1900 but refused it because he feared it might leave him a front man for policies he opposed.

Hall involved himself deeper in reform issues after 1900 at the expense of business ventures. He commented in articles on various issues, and also pursued a religious thread in his discourse mainly influenced by Leo Tolstoi's outlook. Hall's books reflected Tolstoi's religious views as well as their personal correspondence, in particular his *Even as You and I* (1896) and *What Tolstoi Taught* (1911). Hall's *Free America* (1904) appeared in several editions, one with an introduction by Tom L. Johnson, another businessman turned Georgian and reformer. Johnson had made his fortune by buying street car franchises before becoming Cleveland's controversial mayor. "Free America" was for many years a slogan of land reformers.

Nineteen hundred and seven was the year of the money-market crash, instigated by warring financiers, and causing the historic fall of the

Knickerbocker Trust Company of New York. It brought on institutional bankruptcies across the country, deprived many people of their savings, and ruined others. Hall had been a director of the Knickerbocker, but withdrawn earlier as part of his general diminishing of business interests. By coincidence he had ready and published that year his *Three Acres and Liberty*, at a time when disillusioned people were seeking a living beyond currency investments and other urban concerns. Hall's book, describing the durability and gains in farming, turned many people "back to the land" in significant numbers.

His panacea against poverty harkened back to that proposed by the famed reform mayor of Detroit during the Panic of 1893. Hazen S. Pingree (*q.v.*) had invited desperate workers to utilize vacant lots belonging to the city for growing needed vegetables, notably potatoes. Hall's book was filled with practical suggestions as well as information from his store of experience. He implemented his major work with others, *A Little Land and a Living* (1908) and *The Garden Yard: A Handbook of Intensive Farming* (1909).

That same year of 1909 Hall undertook to direct a practical example of cooperative living, in an era which also produced other such quasi-socialistic efforts, often in the agricultural areas of New Jersey, and notably *Helicon Hall*, as erected by Upton Sinclair (*q.v.*). Hall's project, "Free Acres," was composed of some seventy acres near Summit, N.J. It was realistically conceived and trimmed of special fancies. Lots at Free Acres were not sold, but rented. They were administered by a central body, democratically instituted but unreceptive to irrelevant social enthusiasms. Some forty families occupied the holdings. Free Acres flourished, and attracted public interest and visitors. It continued to flourish successfully after Hall had left the fold, and even after his death.

Hall's religious views found elaborated expression in his *The Living Bible —the Whole Bible in Its Fewest Words* (1928), and though less influential as a message, undoubtedly contributed to the welcome he received from many George followers and others socially inclined. It has been noted that *Progress and Poverty* was unique as a major economic tract in concluding with a chapter on religion. George himself believed he had discovered a universal law. Nevertheless it was George's character and social concern—and the practical extrapolations of a Bolton Hall—which made them durable guides.

The Georgian analysis itself had patent limitations for later decades. The rise of technology, for example, made land values less fundamental than they had earlier seemed. Hall's work was thus closer to such earlier experiments as Brook Farm than it could ever be to such places as Oak Ridge or Cape Canaveral, which also affected social economics.

The Georgian literature includes writings which bear on Hall's activities, for example, A. N. Young, *The Single Tax Movement in the United States* (1916). Charles B. Barnes, *The Longshoreman* (1915) deals with the conditions which inspired Hall's influence. Hall's own books contain information regarding his activities. His *Who's Who* entry provides some personal details, as does his brother's biography of their father, *John Hall—Pastor and Preacher* (1901).

Edward Albert Filene
(1860-1937)

Economics and Human Nature

THE SOCIAL REFORMER AND theorist of capitalism, he was born in Salem, Massachusetts, the son of German businessman William Filene (originally "Filehne"). Filene left Europe in 1848, aged eighteen, was a merchant tailor in Boston, and in 1856 opened a store in Salem. Married to a Bavarian, like himself of Jewish background, he raised a family which made morality, rather than religion, the basis of living. The elder Filene made several moves while raising his sons for business. The future weighed heavily on Edward, a small child troubled by a sense of insignificance, and with no enthusiasm for his father's absorption in buying and selling, mainly women's clothes and related merchandise. Of a near-scholarly bent, he looked forward to study at Harvard College, where he had been accepted.

In 1881 his father, who felt age approaching, sold off several of his ventures in order to open a store in Boston, named William Filene's Sons Company. Anticipating retirement, he recruited Edward and his younger brother Lincoln to take it over, which Edward did without complaint, though disappointed by his loss of higher education. He soon turned necessity into a way of life which was to affect commercial thinking and much more.

E. A. Filene as he became for the rest of his life, as president of the landmark Filene's, and as a civic personage, turned attention on business generally as a public concern. He undertook a series of innovations which were intended not so much to aggrandize himself, though he thought it appropriate for himself to prosper, as to extend the benefits of capitalism to others. Lewis Tappan had earlier helped create the idea of a one-price system, as opposed to haggling. Filene made customer-satisfaction a first priority, even, as he explained to his sales people, if it meant sending customers to a competitor. Most famous became his Automatic Bargain Basement which set prices for a limited time, to be lowered as the merchandise failed to sell out. Filene insisted that the stock not be inferior to comparable stock on other floors, but as good, thanks to the superior purchasing ability of his buyers.

Under the slogan of "permanency, profit, and service," Filene's grew in fame and prosperity, though E. A. Filene was personally disappointed that new partners in his firm did not help him further his quality-and-low-prices program, or his Filene's Cooperative Association intended to augment employee participation, and ending in employee ownership and administration of the department store. For that matter, it turned out that employees were not themselves interested in owning and operating Filene's. They preferred benefits to responsibility. By 1928 Filene's board of directors were thoroughly fed up with Filene's experiments, and drew up a plan which kept E. A. president for life, but unable to interfere with their more traditional modes of operation.

In the meantime, Filene had extended his interests into Boston and beyond. Exploring organizations of all kinds for their direct social potential, he hit on the idea of a chamber of commerce which would involve his business peers in larger affairs. First a Boston Chamber of Commerce, then one for the state, for the nation, and finally the International Chamber of Commerce became objects of his solicitude.

He himself, helped by talented young secretaries and aides, took to writing and publishing articles on public affairs. Lincoln Steffens (*q.v.*), made famous by his "muckraking" exploits concerning corrupt municipal governments was called by Filene in 1909 to prepare what became "Boston 1915" which was to involve such worthies as Louis D. Brandeis, "the people's attorney," A. Lawrence Lowell, president of Harvard University, and even Martin Lomasney, political boss of Boston. "Boston 1915" itself did not advance as a Steffens and Filene project, but it did introduce the idea of city planning, as compared with routine and even innovative administration, and in George Kibbe Turner's (*q.v.*) commission form of government. In 1912 it enabled Filene to present to his State Legislature a pioneer report on city planning.

Peace was a long-time concern of Filene, involving America's connection with the Philippines, the increased deadliness of war instruments, and the possibility that the European War, as it was called in 1914, might draw in the United States. Unlike Grenville Clark (*q.v.*) Filene was unable to act as both a patriot and a peace advocate, at least directly. He did join former President William Howard Taft and others in organizing their League to Enforce Peace which had the potential as it proved to enforce it mainly against Germany. He did, however, maintain peace as a separate cause, though his achievements in the field were moot. Steffens was to conclude that Filene created agencies which helped his foes rather than his friends.

Thus Filene approved of the Dawes Plan for helping a defeated Germany to regain social and economic life and helped reassure French authorities that this was no threat to their security. Obviously the purpose of the Dawes Plan was at least in part to strengthen the Germans against the military threat of Bolshevik Russia and their own communists. But whether Steffens was more correct in his famous phrase to say of the U.S.S.R. that he had seen the future and it works would become debatable.

Capitalism continued for Filene to be the basis for prosperity and therefore peace, and in the 1920s he expanded his efforts to improve its operations. In doing so he created a theory of manufacture and distribution which questioned the simple supply-and-demand premises of earlier economists. Filene was first and foremost an enemy of waste, and even compulsive in the matter. He once said that he was always careful, before leaving home perhaps to attend a concert to be certain that he had turned off all the lights. For he knew that if he came to doubt that he had he would feel compelled to return home to reassure himself. He never tired of saying that we had not so much as begun to examine the possibilities for saving, as in packaging. Pursuing rationality, he could not assume that people might, for whatever reason, endorse and prefer the less good. It certainly, in his Progressive psychology, never occurred to him that packaging could become a species of racket, with the package becoming not a means but an end, or stronger than the packaging materials it was supposed to protect in transportation. Yet rationality was the hope of civilized living.

Although Filene's was essentially a merchant's view of the economy, it had universal aspects in capitalist theory. For example, he recommended the best for workers: high wages and minimum wages, un-employment insurance, medical care. All this would put money in workers's purses, and their families, which could be spent on merchandise, permitting high turnover and lower prices. He saw the market possibilities as bottomless; there were whole continents which had not yet been reached as consumers. He admired Herbert Hoover's work as United States Secretary of Commerce and Henry Ford's initiatives in the mass production of automobiles.

Filene's ability to attract talented aides was all but unique. Among them were not only Steffens, but such others as Glenn Frank, who became president of the University of Wisconsin, and Charles Merz, later editor of the *New York Times*. Moreover, Filene's associations with famous states-men and publicists were all but universal. Their thoughts and direct help entered into his books influencing 1920s and Thirties actions, such as *The Way Out: a Forecast of Coming Changes in American Business and In-dustry* (1942), which failed however to see how so legitimate a prosperity as that of the Twenties could be interrupted, and *Successful Living in the Machine Age* (1932) which heralded in part the coming New Deal. Filene himself had endorsed installment buying as complementing legitimate in-dustrial ventures. His failure to foresee the torment it might cause people over their heads in debt, and to businesses which lost anticipated funds derived from Filene's limited grasp of human nature, despite his rigid con-cern for facts and dislike of charity and even philanthropy.

Rounding out Filene's theory were his projects, which affected the nation's economic and social structure. Though he did not create the idea of a credit union, he was mainly responsible for its American development. The credit union promised social responsibility and human values, low interest rates and cooperative action. Filene chose Roy F. Bergengren to carry the credit union message beyond Massachusetts, which he success-fully did. Filene's Credit Union National Extension Bureau carried on such effective lobbying and advertising services as finally to win a Federal Credit Union Act from Congress.

Also, as part of his program for leavening capitalist operations with popular participation, Filene granted funds which set up the Coopera-tive League in 1919. This was supplemented by the Consumer Distribution Corporation which was responsible for encouraging the building of con-sumer cooperatives, helped out further by Filene's Good Will Fund. These enterprises failed to change the nature of free enterprise, and, to Filene's disappointment, did too little to influence capitalist thought and action.

Nevertheless, Filene's was a formidable achievement. It was crowned by his establishment of a Twentieth Century Fund, which received from him an endowment he himself could not withdraw or influence. He later willed the Fund which became a unique fact-finding organization, the major portion of his legacy.

Filene hailed the advent of the New Deal, and was among the first of his wealth to do so. His bitterness at being unsupported in his act by his business colleagues was shown in his repudiation of the U. S. Chamber of Commerce in 1936. A dapper man, short in stature, who took pride in his accomplishments, as seen in the care he gave his *Who's Who* entry and personal appearance, he continued serious about his projects to the end. Always concerned for peace, he urged mutual assistance pacts which would be more effective than the League of Nations had proved to be, and which would include Soviet Russia in negotiations. A considerable traveler, he contracted fatal pneumonia during a European trip. His ashes were brought from Paris to Boston and strewn in the Charles River Basin. A collection, *Speaking of Change: a Selection of Speeches and Articles* (1939), gave a sense of his presence and views, and *Liberal's Progress* (1948) by the well-regarded Gerald W. Johnson surveyed Filene's career. His place in a changing world, however, was yet to be defined.

Ernest Lacy
(1864-1916)

"A Golden Debt to Nature"

A POET AND DRAMATIST, Ernest Lacy had a modest and largely frustrated career that threw light on twentieth century cultural changes. An excellent student in a talented family made tragic by their lawyer-father's alcoholism and financial irresponsibility, young Lacy became one of those who, like poets Sidney Lanier in the South and George Henry Boker and George Cabot Lodge in the North, rejected "materialism" in favor of the "classic" ideal. In Lacy's case that meant following the iambic pentameter of the Elizabethans.

He wrote sonnets and plays. In the 1890s with a "romantic" theater drawing audiences, he appeared to have a good chance for success. Julia Marlowe played his one-act *Chatterton,* with its intimate grasp of the boy-genius's ill-starred dream of success and suicide, and took it on tour. The popular actor Joseph Haworth played Lacy's *Rinaldo, the Doctor of Florence,* patently Shakespearian with its Iago-like villain and Hamletesque hero. Lacy's sonnets, too, had a freedom and range which went beyond imitation, but rejected the tumult and reality of the post-Civil War world about him.

Lacy was born in Warren, Pennsylvania, but was raised in Philadelphia and trained as a lawyer and litterateur. He taught English literature in the famous Central High School of Philadelphia, the second high school in the country, Boston Latin being the first. Theodore Roosevelt as President of the United States was present to help dedicate the third Central High School building, and uttered once-famous words, urging the boys to fight fair and "hit the line hard." The school drew notable leaders and professors, as they were called, and also scores of notable students, from Henry George and the Populist-author Ignatius Donnelly to, in Lacy's time, Alexander Woolcott and Gilbert Seldes, noted critics in popular culture.[1] Lacy's own colleagues included John Duncan Spaeth and Christian Gauss, who moved on to Princeton University as part of its now president Woodrow Wilson's (*q v*) determination to get stimulating younger men for his semi-tutorial studies based on the English model. Lacy possibly hoped to be so called as well. If so, he was not called. Instead he became a somewhat awesome and admired professor for his talented Central High youngsters and continued to dream of status among poetry fanciers and theatergoers.

His hopes were badly based, poetry being a secondary pursuit in his America, and the theater then a rigidly entertainment vehicle, producing excellent vaudeville and little else. Not until the 1920s would it become more. A major factor in his life was the loss in 1892 of his keenly intelligent brother

President Theodore Roosevelt addressing the students at CHS Dedication ceremonies. He advised them: "Don't flinch, don't foul, and hit the line hard!"

William who, in his twenties, wrote a devastating book-length rebuttal to Herbert Spencer's *The Unknowable*, part I of his *First Principles* (1862). Also trained for the law and with a philosophic bent, the young man gave ordered evidence that Spencer had not proved his case. To his dead brother Ernest Lacy wrote several of his poignant sonnets, remembering: "that white face Time never will restore!" and "A chair with waiting arms, a likeness sweet,/ The markers left within a favorite book,/ The half-worn shoes that cased those weary feet."

Lacy never recovered from his great loss. It did inspire him to continue his poetic pursuit of Thomas Chatterton, whom Wordsworth had seen as "the marvelous boy who perished in his pride," and whom Coleridge, Shelley, de Vigny, and others up to the present memorialized. Lacy visited Bristol and London where Chatterton's tragedy took place, and recreated in his mind the England of their late eighteenth century.

JOSEPH HAWORTH

In ERNEST LACY'S GREAT PLAY

RINALDO

Under the Direction of GEORGE H. BRENNAN

CASTLE SQUARE THEATRE.
COMMENCING MONDAY FEBRUARY 25 TH

Meanwhile Lacy pursued more earthy theater in Philadelphia playhouses and wrote poems and literary essays. He was inadvertently a pioneer figure in cinema, delivering a lecture in 1897 to accompany a film on the Höritz Passion Play. One of his own rough prose comedies, *The Ragged Earl,* found its way to the screen.

In 1900 he published *Plays and Sonnets*, which was well received, but ineffective in terms of sales and visibility. His sonnets touched some contemporary themes, as in "To an Ape," with its stoic final line: "We shall be one, proud ape, when we are dust." And its ironic "Siege of Malaga," suggesting little choice between Christian charity and Moslem:

> Fair Malaga reduced—behold the scene:
> Triumphal entry, gold from captives wrung,

> A tilt of torture with bamboos made keen,
> Arabian maidens to her favorites flung
> Through courtly bounty of a Christian queen;
> And hark! the *Gloria in Excelsis* sung.

Perhaps his most perfect sonnet "Newport at Noon" was written with total objectivity, contrasting the colors of life with those of death, and hiding his personal sorrow:

> The sunbeams glinted from empurpled cloak
> Like burning glances from a mantled love;
> A wind blew seaward, and loose sand above
> Swept down the hardened beach in lines of smoke;
> With misted edge the claret billows broke,
> Spilled on the marble ebb, and spreading drove
> The piping snipe that on the wave-ware throve
> Toward carrion crow, which rose with boding croak.
>
> On shadowed waters lit with streaks of green
> And fringed around the cliffs with breakers hoar,
> A cutter, keeling in each gust, was seen;
> While through impenetrable blue there wore,
> From straining eyes, a spectral ship serene
> On a landless voyage to an alien shore.

Lacy's life was no sadder than anyone's, and his occasional passion resulted in poems, rather than actions reaching 1900 audiences. Would, he wrote, in "A Storm:"

> Would that I could on warlike field contend
> With lance and sword for native right to think,
> And conquering live, or meet a knightly end;
> But I am locked in dungeon, where the clink
> Of griding chains and noisome things offend,
> And when I thirst they give me gall to drink.

Nevertheless in his pessimism he pursued his Chatterton theme, and finally completed *The Bard of Mary Redcliff*, in five acts. It was thoroughly immersed in its times and capable of taking audiences with it there. "It will live," Lacy wrote to a friend. E. H. Sothern, Julia Marlowe's husband, was supposed to give the work on stage, but thought better of the venture. Such friends as Spaeth praised the poem-play, and are part of the lost record. They had their own lives to live, and could do no more for their late friend.

There is all but no bibliography on Lacy. He was praised by Arthur Hobson Quinn, the theater historian, but buried in the long lists of theater favorites and stage carpenters. An academic work, Robert A. Walker, *The Poet in the Gilded Age*, did not run across Lacy, though it ran across scores of versifiers. Spaeth wrote a *Dictionary of American Biography* piece about Lacy. Accounts of Marlowe carry photographs of her as Chatterton.

Yet there are surprises: unconscious sensitivities hidden in apparently dormant topics which raise eyebrows when they suddenly emerge. The present writer's *Dictionary of American Conservatism* drew a "review" among a range of others which was all but a comment on conservative contemporary culture. A George W. Carey, professor of political science at Georgetown University, wrote in a publication, *The World & I*. His review chose from the book's 1500 entries none other than that on Lacy, "inter alia," which included such other patent conservatives as Emily Dickinson who coped unsuccessfully with their times. Wrote the professor, meaning to show Lacy's irrelevance to more momentous matters:

> [We] are informed that [Lacy's] "masterpiece," *The Bard of Mary Redcliffe* (1910) was to star a well-known actor of the time, but new tendencies created by the Progressive era and the rising youth movement...sank this enterprise.

What the professor was careful not to say was that there was a wee bibliography attached to the passage: the present writer's edition of *Chatterton*. This would have required the professor to read and comment upon the poem-play, something the professor was evidently reluctant to do, time being money, and life complicated enough. So readers could, instead, follow the professor's code-message to its unspoken conclusion: that nothing had been said which need befuddle a doctrinaire conservative. As the professor added: "And so it goes throughout the volume." Several others in conservative stalls said right out that Emily Dickinson was not a conservative, apparently meaning, without realizing it, that good poets could not be conservatives.

A sample of Lacy's verse in *The Bard of Mary Redcliffe* suffices to reveal Chatterton's end, toward which all the action moves:

> This mirror gleams
> A crystal lake in which my wraith appears
> With Orkney seaweed spread upon its head
> Foreshadowing my doom. I shall not live
> To hold a candle nightly to the glass
> And watch my face grow old: to see the lines
> Deepen to ditches round the eyes and mouth
> When Time besieges Beauty; to make that fight,
> Which must be lost, against the first gray hairs—
> Plucking them out lest winged Love espy
> The ghostly vanguard of advancing years.
> Nor last, with taper held in palsied clutch,
> To view the muddy orbs, the lips caved in,
> The visage rutted, as if a thousand cares,
> After long rains, had driven their heavy wains,
> With iron-bound wheels, across the features—No!
> The spirit of my youth shall never peer
> Through age's hideous mask.

Lacy himself was spared this scene, dying at fifty-two of cancer. Many of his poems expressed more serene sentiments, like "A Prayer," which asked for strength, not light, and accepted that, like rustling maple leaves, he would pay "a golden debt to nature." He was grateful for love, for awe of Pike's Peak and Westminster Abbey. He found devotion to country, and was angry that Henry James had disavowed citizenship, even if he intended to clasp hands with England, beleaguered by war.

Yet, at bottom, there was resentment in Lacy for the lack of honor and advancement he had experienced. Even the hope—the expectation—of posthumous appreciation only moderately helped. "It will live," he had said of *The Bard*. But in that post-Darwinian age, this gave only a modicum of satisfaction, at best. His last word to robust America showed spirit of his own:

FAME

> What matter if no living soul be stirred
> By aught these artful cells of verse contain?

The rhythmic clanking of a minstrel's chain,
The outcast years that huddle in each word.
The breathing present will be sepulchred,
And from these tower walls deviced with pain,
A voice unheeded through a jealous reign
In Time's impartial session shall be heard.

Pah! Why should Fancy feed on juiceless lies?
Come, Fame, when life in spicy breeze can scud
Past singing islands, under amorous skies;
For who, to drift upon a century's flood
That will its own song-laden barks disprize,
Would sit in hell and dip his pen in blood?

NOTES:

1. See   D.F. Labaree, *The Making of an American High School* (1988). See also Albert Mordell (*q.v.*).

The faculty of Central High School in 1912 included Ernest Lacy (first row seated fifth from left) and his brother Benjamin (first row seated second from left).

Robert M. LaFollette
(1855-1925)

"Fighting Bob"

WISCONSIN GOVERNOR AND
United States Senator, Robert M.
LaFollette was the prototype of the
dedicated and courageous public official at home, whose stand against
American intervention abroad in the first World War was judged a model of
dissidence. As an aspect of the Sixties youth revolt against American achievement, he was subjected to academic skepticism in an interpretation yet to be
linked with academic conditions and especially the history discipline.

A Wisconsin farmer's son, LaFollette was born poor and raised to
hard farm labor. He worked his way through the University of Wisconsin in
fashion traditional to great numbers of ambitious midwestern youth who carried memories of regal American statesmen, notable in law and state houses.
To support himself while studying LaFollette taught school. On campus he
made himself known by issuing and editing his *University Press,* and being
interested in campus theatricals. Oratory, too, was highly regarded, offering
memory of Clay, Webster, and Calhoun, and public service. Like Albert J.
Beveridge in Indiana, at DePauw University (then Asbury College), La-
Follette competed in oratorical exercises, and like him won a highly prized
interstate contest in the field. He received his B.S. in 1879.

LaFollette entered law practice, and, backed by trophies and local
Madison acclaim felt able to marry his college mate Belle Case, the first
woman in Wisconsin to win a law degree and herself highly regarded for

mind and ability. She was to serve beside him and to augment her own issues and concerns for almost half a century. LaFollette moved directly into Republican politics, entering in 1880 into the race for attorney general of Dane County and opposing the routine selection process which the party elders favored. Though only twenty-five years of age, he was considered mature by the time's standards, midwestern children having been immersed in political lore since early childhood. By exhausting labors he made himself a familiar face to the county citizens and won nomination and election. At this stage of his career he was a traditional Republican even in the rhetoric he employed.

Short, sturdy, wearing a moustache (later a beard) and with the upflaring head of hair, then black, which was to be his trademark through life, LaFollette never flagged at enunciating principles to his constituents and making their needs a first priority in his speeches. He continued to defy official Republican counsel in his state, winning election a second time, then moving on toward a Congressional seat. In 1884, not yet thirty years old, he contested and won it, and went on to Washington for what became the first of three terms.

At first glance, LaFollette was a loyal Republican, known as upright rather than Populist, a representative chiefly identified with the Party's major concern, Protectionism, which discriminated with high tariff's against foreign imports. But LaFollette's principles went further. He would not enter into the game of drawing as much federal funds as possible into his state merely because they were allocated to Wisconsin. "Pork-barrel" projects, when they fed special interests, did little for LaFollette's constituents. Projects for extending railroads, laying waste wilderness, dredging waterfronts too often built facilities at the expense of more socially-directed enterprises, and only strengthened the hold of politicians over the needy. Philetus Sawyer, a Wisconsin millionaire lumberman and railroad entrepreneur, dictated the state's policies often at the expense of farmers and others who suffered by them.

Sawyer, as United States senator and head of Wisconsin's congressional group, of Republicans as well as of those in the Madison state house, soon discovered LaFollette's pertinency in judging government bills on their own merit. Sawyer attempted to instruct LaFollette regarding particular bills he fancied, bills drawn up by corporation executives and their lawyers. LaFollette's refusal to cooperate astounded the senator, who denounced him to his face as a "bolter."

In 1890 McKinley's tariff schedule, the most firmly protectionist bill till that time, won Republican and LaFollette's endorsement. Wisconsin Democrats seized on citizen dissatisfaction with the schedule's effect on prices, as well as on notorious state legislation that hit at schools conducted in foreign languages. The Democrats turned the Republicans out of office, and with them went LaFollette, who returned to Madison to practice law and denounce his Republican bosses, including Sawyer, for skulduggery and fraudulent practices.

LaFollette's tireless appeal to farmers in particular became legendary as he drove his horse and buggy from farm to farm, but it was an incident in 1891 which became not only famous in Wisconsin, but symbolic of what the young Progressives of his generation stood and fought for. It is fair to say that Sawyer, exchanging favors with other politicians and businessmen, simply did not understand that more than ambition prompted such of his opponents as LaFollette. Boss-rule and favoritism seemed to Sawyer the reasonable rule in public behavior. He could not perceive that an expanding country made such direct controls untenable in the long run and must give way to better systems. The change, however, required principled LaFollettes to put themselves forward in opposition and live with the consequences.

When an old habit of Republican treasurers of skimming state funds for personal use was uncovered, and the treasurers set up for court trial, Sawyer looked about for friendly assistance. He later professed not to have known that the trial judge was to have been Robert G. Siebecker, LaFollette's brother-in-law. Why, however, he would have thought of La-Follette at all to be a "consultant" in the cases, considering that LaFollette was notorious to him and other Republican leaders because of independence and haranguing of constituents is unclear, unless one assumes that money habitually entered into Sawyer's thinking and negotiating. Asking LaFollette to see him on "some matters of importance," he clearly offered money. LaFollette reported himself as having said: "Senator Sawyer, you can't know what you are saying to me. If you struck me in the face you could not insult me as you insult me now."

Much later academic commentators would wonder aloud whether Sawyer actually used language indicating a bribe offer, and if LaFollette, considering his early "dramatic" interests, in fact used such language as he reported. But given cultural insight, they could have noted that LaFollette's language comported with his known speeches and standards of right and wrong, as compared with Sawyer's. What is certain is that the less learned constituents to whom LaFollette carried the message of the offered bribe, used as they were to rhetoric from candidates, saw virtue and accuracy in LaFollette's account, and began to perceive that all the emoluments offered by the machine politicians—loans, sympathy, nationalistic Protection, porkbarrel projects—did not compensate for behind-the-scene deals which kept them divided and weak.

The machine was far from crushed by the LaFollette scandal, and though LaFollette fought throughout the 1890s for status, a direct primary which would force democracy in nominee selection, and railroad legislation regulating charges made on helpless farmers, he was rejected for the gubernatorial candidacy at Republican conventions. In 1900 he finally overcame opposition and won the governorship: a significant step toward rising national Progressive hopes.

As governor LaFollette had first to battle for control of the legislature in Madison, and it was only following a second two-year victory, and a third that he was able to win new laws: a direct-primary law, one regulating railroad rates, and then further controls, backed with advice and research by informed pundits of the University of Wisconsin in Madison, who worked with enthusiasm to further what became known as "the Wisconsin Idea," that is, of informed responsible government.

LaFollette came to the Senate in 1906 as a Progressive favorite but alien to the "millionaires's club" which then controlled that body. There senators received the crusader with disdain. In one historic Senate session, "Fighting Bob" faced a languid senatorial assembly with his intense display of facts, and, observing that many seats were vacant, remarked that seats temporarily vacant might in time be permanently so.

Muckrakers honored LaFollette, and an increasing number of Progressives joined him. From 1906 onward he worked to build them into a political force. His fame increased with his Senate filibuster against a weak railroad legislation. He met with Progressives and with them planned strategy. In a new departure on the speech-making circuit, he made calling the roll of votes on key legislation part of tactics for alerting his auditors to the tricks and schemes many legislators tried to keep hidden and obscure.

As Theodore Roosevelt and his designated successor William Howard Taft continued their tenure in the White House, LaFollette was the tried and acknowledged leader of the Progressive movement, in 1908 receiving twenty-five votes for the presidential nomination at the Republican national convention, with much more anticipated as the 1912 elections loomed. He began *LaFollette's Weekly*, which attracted the contributions of eminent muckrakers and politicians, including Ray Stannard Baker (*q.v.*) who was to help him prepare his *Autobiography*, published in 1913. LaFollette was no favorite with his divided party or leading press figures who, on the independent side, hungered for another turn with Roosevelt as leader. In effect they permitted LaFollette to draw together Progressive forces while considering by what strategy they could turn them over to Roosevelt as Presidential candidate.

An opportunity presented itself February 2, 1912, at the annual meeting of the Periodical Publishers Association in Philadelphia, with LaFollette invited to speak both as Presidential aspirant and publisher. A sick, overworked man, anxious about a family trouble of the time. LaFollette took the assembly aback with an hysterical attack on the formal journalism of the time, which offended participants in the meeting took as signalling a physical breakdown.

Although this was clearly false, it did enable the journalists to close ranks against LaFollette, and to open the way for Roosevelt's presidential bid, when the Republican machine asserted itself in Taft's behalf. A split Republican alliance enabled Woodrow Wilson to ascend to the White House.

LaFollette lost no distinction by this defeat, but new forces of government and public opinion were turning against the previous Progressivism. New alliances called for efficiency rather than further popular democracy, which overturned the older boss system. LaFollette even gained by it in the sympathy he won for oppressed seamen. LaFollette's Seamen's Act of 1915 culminated a fight in Congress waged since 1909, in which he fought side by side with the unionist Andrew Furuseth: a "Magna Carta" for a long enslaved class of workers. It was one of the wars carried on by LaFollette during Wilson's first term in office.

The Wisconsin statesman was not lulled by Wilson's alleged "neutrality" policy, as the European War continued. Early in 1917 he led the "little group of wilful men," as Wilson phrased it, who prevented passage of Wilson's armed merchant ship bill. LaFollette fought passionately against Wilson's declaration of war against Germany, though after it was accepted he felt duty-bound to support with necessary measures the soldiers who bore the burden of war. He resisted Wilson's arguments for the League of Nations as no more than further implicating the American nation in European intrigues, and the World Court as helping.

In the new world of the 1920s, LaFollette picked up his old crusade for honest government, and, anticipating the increased importance of oil, drew up the resolution calling for a Senate probe in what became the Teapot Dome and related scandals. Facing Twenties prosperity he made his last presidential stand in the elections of 1924, gathering five million votes from the electorate. After his death his sons picked up his political challenge with distinction, and his wife began his biography before her own death in 1931. It was completed by their daughter.

Although times and trends changed in the next three decades, LaFollette's virtues shone, if anything, more unwaveringly than ever. He endured in the wistful memory of the 1920s, the anxious memories of the 1930s, as the ideal legislator: one with the people still requiring justice, firm in his dedication to American traditions, even more than to constituents. It was only when the ideals themselves came under corrosive attack from dissident youth and revolutionaries, in LaFollette's own Madison raising up alienated youth and empathetic academic instructors, that history itself began to blur and diminish him. Negative generalizations began to appear, not only in anti-American views, but in classes seeking skeptical student approval. All this culminated in a distant view of what had once been "the Wisconsin Idea."

What was the issue? It drew from a larger rationalization for revisionist history. There had been a fight "against monopoly," yes. But it hid a fight for government intervention in favor of the corporations. The Progressives in 1912 had been endorsed by none other than J.P. Morgan's partner George W. Perkins. Government "regulation" of railroads saved them from public ownership; they had briefly belonged to the government during World War I. Government "regulation" elsewhere endorsed private ownership but with only limited power to control corporate chicanery and worse in the private sector.

And LaFollette—who had he been and what had he achieved? He had, with his "theatrical" impulse, been dramatic, yes, even melodramatic. But had he really been tempted with a bribe, or had he made up a rigamarole to help him assume heroic postures? He had risen on a tide of "insurgency," but fallen as it failed to serve "consumers"—the bottom line of popular controllers. LaFollette had to work between government and corporations, and fell between them.

So Progressivism had after all been a hollow facade, not worth a serious rebel's time, or a student's. This was the message bruited among a section of historians. It was a puzzling account to a newer generation of students exposed to what was touted as "new history," which, as students, they were willing to credit, but which strangely did not comport with versions of LaFollette assumed by the uninitiated and their journalists. To them, LaFollette was still "Fighting Bob," a man of rectitude and achievement—no one out of academe thought of him otherwise. Even academic textbooks did not attempt to brave their readers with exotic accounts of LaFollette, but presented the classic tale of his human greatness and democratic achievement.

What remained undefined and yet to be spelled out was what the newer generation had in hand and mind with which to carry on the eternal war against new evils and world challenges. These required new practices, but for old ends: control of decayed social sectors needing modern adjustment. These required, for perspective, a fresh sense of such protagonists as LaFollette, and the means by which they had attained their ends.

The family memoir, *Robert M. LaFollette* (1953), in two volumes, is filled with details affecting judgment, for example, of the 1912 elections. LaFollette's own *Autobiography* (1913) adds a dimension, as do Patrick J. Maney, *"Young Bob" LaFollette* (1978), a study of LaFollette's older son, and D. Young, ed., *Adventure in Politics* (1970), the memoirs of the younger son Philip. Robert S. Maxwell, *LaFollette and the Rise of Progressivism in Wisconsin* (1956)—written before the youth uprising in academe—offers an objective view. See also H.M. Hooker, ed., *History of the Progressive Party*, by Amos Pinchot (1958). R. N. Current, *Pine Logs and Politics: a Life of Philetus Sawyer* (1950) is written with the skepticism fostered at the University of Wisconsin, which opened the way to more serious revisionist accounts, such as D. P. Thelen, *The Early Life of Robert M. LaFollette* (1966), which portrayed a shrewd, "self-righteous" actor who knew when to ignore needy movements, and when to make deals: a man on the make. See also by the same author, *Robert LaFollette and the Insurgent Spirit* (1976). *Belle* (1986), by LaFollette's granddaughter Sherry LaFollette and collaborators L. Freeman and G. A. Zabriskie intended to honor her grandmother, but furnished evidence for LaFollette's foes. Thus, Belle LaFollette was long concerned for her husband's health, which he sacrificed for his work. *Belle* leaves a false impression of sickness, rather than heroism, an impression Thelen endorsed. A broad-gauged modern life is wanted.

Rheta Childe Dorr
(1866-1948)

Dissident and Patriot

RHETA CHILDE DORR WAS A
feminist in the Progressive Era; her cause lay somewhere between that of
the earlier suffragists and that of the overlapping women of the first youth
movement (1910-1929). Her best seller, *What Eight Million Women Want*
(1910) helped give depth to the suffragist cause of the time, and made her
one symbol of feminism.

Born in Nebraska of gracious and traditional family, she early
joined the suffragists but sought equal social opportunity as well as the
vote. Hendrik Ibsen's *The Doll House,* which described the confining social
circumstances of women, inspired her to leave the University of Nebraska
and look for work. She found it in the post office, then became an insurance
agent. In 1890 she continued her quest for freedom in New York, where
she studied art and attempted to write fiction. Unconsciously, later con-
sciously, she followed a path then being hewn by Charlotte Perkins Gilman,
among others.

Two years later she married a Seattle businessman, John
Pixley Dorr. In attempting to continue writing and by seeking material
among rough Alaskan adventurers passing through Seattle she offended
local genteel mores. Disapproval only upset her further. In 1898 she
left her husband and with a two-year old son returned to New York
in search of a career. In choosing to retain her married name she
helped to define her ambitions, and their limits in her mind. Her

Dorr amoung suffragettes, at the Capitol. Front Line, second from left.

personal experiences in part replicated those of Florence Kelley (*q.v.*) and others of her generation of feminists.

In 1903 Dorr became a woman's page writer for the *New York Post*. She met with other woman's-rights advocates, and with them explored the lot of women in industry. As an active member of the General Federation of Women's Clubs, and other women's groups, she joined their agitation for an official federal investigation of women's work. The results of this survey opened wider fields for activists like herself.

Dorr began a series of explorations at home and abroad. She met radicals and leaders in Russia and England and reported their goals and ideas. Back home in New York she herself worked as laundress and factory hand, following the milder leads in such a work as the Van Vorsts's *The Woman Who Toils* (1903). Dorr now went through the two major traumas of her public life, in writing up her experiences as a laborer for the muck-raking *Everybody's Magazine*. It first attempted to deprive her of credit for her revelations by turning the "materials" over to one of their editors, William Hard. In the courts they only conceded her co-authorship for her articles. But then Hard reported painful factory memoirs not as requiring justice and restitution, but "positively," as women's triumphant entrance into industry.

Fortunately for Dorr she came into the hands of Ben Hampton, of *Hampton's Magazine*, then in its reform stage. (Hampton later left reform for motion pictures, in which he interested himself as author and producer.) He whipped Dorr's prose into shape, as she later gratefully acknowledged, and turned her to writing the articles which became a major Progressive writing: *What Eight Million Women Want* (1910). It summarized the march of women from women's clubs and the suffrage to her own bitter tale of the double standard which barely protected women in law.

A sample of her prose illustrates her debt to the Progressivism of the time, with its commitment to democracy, its ability to join ranks with the needy, but without false sentimentally or "literary" gestures. She is writing of a great strike in 1909-1910 which set oppressed women workers against factory employers destined for an infamous place in history:

> The strike was more than two months old when the Cooper Union meeting was held, and the employers showed no signs of giving in. It was agreed that a general strike of shirt-waist makers ought to be declared. But the union was weak, there were no funds, and most of the shirt-waist makers were women and unused to the idea of solidarity in action. Could they stand together in an industrial struggle which promised to be long and bitter. President [Samuel] Gompers was plainly fearful that they could not.
>
> Suddenly a very small, very young, very intense Jewish girl, known to her associates as Clara Lemlich, sprang to her feet, and, with the assistance of two young men, climbed to the high platform. Flinging up her arms with a dramatic gesture she poured out a flood of speech, entirely unintelligible to the presiding Gompers, and to the members of the Women's Trade Union League. The Yiddish-speaking majority in the audience understood,

however, and the others quickly caught the spirit of her impassioned plea.

The vast audience rose as one man, and a great roar arose. "Yes, we will all strike!"

"And will you keep the faith?" cried the girl on the platform. "Will you swear by the old Jewish oath of our fathers?"

Two thousand Jewish hands were thrust in the air, and two thousand Jewish throats uttered the oath: "If I turn traitor to the cause I now pledge, may this hand wither and drop off from this arm I now raise."

Clara Lemlich's part in the work was accomplished. Within a few days forty thousand shirt-waist workers were on strike.

The unadorned language, with its sense of commitment to justice, circulated everywhere. In book form, with half-million copies in circulation, it placed Dorr among the leading journalists of the time.

Dorr now had entree to the larger field of writing. Following what seemed to many the logic of the time she joined those Progressives who had also accepted the Socialist Party as the answer to society's needs. Dorr was not too comfortable among the New York elements she was required to call comrade. She held lightly to the Party program, avoiding, moreover, the more avant garde types affected by what was then known as "the youth idea": an experimental attitude toward life, sex, and the individual. The European War drew her further back to her roots, with distaste for "aliens" and then for radicals generally who saw no differences between Allied and German goals and who propagandized for peace. As she was later to write, in her autobiographical memoirs:

Down in the streets, in Union and Madison Squares and all over the East Side, scores and hundreds of loud-mouthed alien Socialists were pouring out in execrable English, denunciation of the President, of our flag, of the army and navy, and of the "capitalists" who were forcing the country into war. What did they know about America, except that we had been so senseless as to let their slave-minded lot in?... It was time they were beginning to let Americans fight.

When Woodrow Wilson (*q.v.*) drew America into the war, Dorr joined wholeheartedly in his crusade for democracy. She sent her son into the armed forces, and herself became an agitator for victory. Her book of the time *A Soldier's Mother in France* (1918) rode the tide of patriotic writing, but was finally deposited on a scrapheap along with other such writings which helped darken the fame of Progressivism, as a servant of warmongers, its great social services for a time forgotten.

Nevertheless she had one more cause which better met changing public preferences. Progressives were dissatisfied with the anti-liquor Volstead Act, which they felt harmed individual rights. Dorr contributed *Drink—Coercion or Control?* (1929), one of the writings by Progressives which merited recollection as having kept their flag flying in an era of dubious social standards; see her autobiography, *A Woman of Fifty* (1924), more accurately fifty-seven.

Lincoln Steffens
(1866-1936)

At the height of his first fame.

"I have seen the future; and it works."

LINCOLN STEFFENS WAS A muckraker and autobiographer. He won early Progressive fame which, following World War I, seemed destined to diminish due to a new popular "disillusionment" of the time. His growing radicalism, however, made him respected among dissidents, and his *Autobiography* (1931) succeeded among Franklin D. Roosevelt followers and sympathizers. A second World War and social upheaval moved his generation into history and exposed the need for a Progressive revaluation.

Steffens was the son of a wealthy California businessman; their Sacramento home later housed state governors. Young Steffens enjoyed an ideal youth. Later, the first part of his autobiography, "A Boy on Horseback," enjoyed a life of its own as published for young readers. His pleasant adventures, however, did not prepare him for studies, and he required a course in a military academy before entering the University of California at Berkeley.

He graduated in 1889 with an interest in philosophy and went on to Germany to study the subject further. Steffens broadened his concerns to take in ethics and experimental psychology. He also fell in love and married secretly Josephine Bontecou, a fellow American student. They studied together in England and France. Late in 1892 they returned to New York where Steffens was met with a parental letter informing him that he had the education he preferred, and was now on his own. A hundred dollar check was enclosed with which to begin a new life.

Steffens, well-mannered and arrayed in genteel clothing, was rebuffed by a number of editors to whom he applied, but finally received a reportorial chance on E. L. Godkin's (*q.v.*) *Evening Post.* By resourceful explorations he made himself a place as a commentator on business, where his gentility did him no harm. Steffens was not impressed by the businessmen he met, or by the politicians they patronized. The Panic of 1893, which he reported, exposed to him their weaknesses as much as those of the victims. He made friends with young Theodore Roosevelt and, among journalists, Jacob Riis (*q.v.*). In an era of personal journalism he enriched his insights with close reporting of city corruption exposed by the city's Lexow Committee. Now well-established in New York circles, he was further secured by an inheritance left him by a native student he had known in Germany. With the aid of business advisors he was able to invest his money in ways which gave him an independent income.

In 1897 Steffens became city editor of the *Commercial Advertiser.* It attracted writers bent on literary careers such as Harry Thurston Peck (*q.v.*), the Jewish intellectual Abraham Cahan, and the talented Hapgood brothers, Norman and Hutchins. They stirred Steffens's own interest in becoming a novelist, an ambition to which he clung unsuccessfully for years. Meanwhile these writers and others issued a paper evocative of the city's life and personalities. It helped Steffens determine that he could turn his experiences into a study of society.

The end of the century stirred numerous journalists and would-be writers to attempt fiction. Among journalists, Theodore Dreiser and David Graham Phillips (*qq.v.*) began novelistic careers. Ray Stannard Baker (*q.v.*), already a practicing reporter, long contemplated writing a novel, and Steffens took off a year from journalism to attempt one. Steffens's wife published a novel of woman's freedom, *Letitia Berkeley, A.M.* (1899).

In 1901, his novel undone, Steffens accepted an invitation to join S.S. McClure's staff on *McClure's.* It sought the standards of the elite magazines of the time, *Century, Scribner's* and the *Atlantic Monthly,* among others, but aimed for a broader readership and lower price. McClure sought writers who, without deadlines, would come up with important stories which would lead and direct the field. He had found Josiah Flynt who, from distinguished family, had lived deeply among criminals, and whose *The World of Graft* (1901) was a current sensation. He had Ida M. Tarbell studying for several years the history of the Standard Oil Company. With no definite plan in mind, McClure sent Steffens out to find a story in the workings of municipal government. Cities had grown at such a rate that it was difficult to perceive a pattern in their operations.

Steffens's adventures among politicians became legendary. While they unfolded in *McClure's* they created a sensation, apparently revealing a systematic pattern in cities, the bosses of which corrupted businesses, journalists, and people in government. Famous became such titles as Steffens's "Tweed Days in St. Louis" and "Philadelphia: Corrupt and Content." Steffens not only painted the faces of the real masters of great cities; he sought out those who were fighting to diminish their power. In St. Louis he gave an impetus to Joseph W. Folk, the then-obscure circuit attorney who exposed a system of bribes and sent people of community stature to prison.

Steffens's unique quality was not his exposures, which could be found in many articles of the time, but his tone. It avoided easy moralism and seemed to analyze society itself: to discover *why* it had fallen into ignoble hands. Steffens's bosses were often men of quality and compassion. They knew and shared affection for their poor constituents. They gave jobs and charity to the needy, and helped delinquents in trouble. The bosses were often loyal church members and family men.

Steffens's *The Shame of the Cities* (1904) impressed as no mere diatribe, but as a thoughtful inquiry into a condition which needed mending. Steffens was now famous, his trimmed beard and high forehead readily recognized in streets and on trains. As the Progressive era went on with new writings making impact during every year's harvest of events, his fame increased. *The Struggle for Self-Government* (1906) and *Upbuilders* (1909) featured such leaders as Tom Johnson in Cleveland and Robert M. LaFollette (*q.v.*) in Wisconsin.

Steffens gained, evidently, from the nation's need to find solutions to community problems which no boss, however talented and well-meaning could hope to control efficiently with a handful of lieutenants. Solutions appeared. Social workers and settlements, politicians and outstanding personalities multiplied. Human nature, however, powered by greed and shortsightedness, continued to protrude in human affairs. They faced Steffens's realism with practical problems, of which the least at the time were troubles at *McClure's* which caused him with such others as Tarbell, Baker, and others to secede, taking over the *American Magazine*, in which to uphold the muckraking crusade.

In 1909 Steffens was called by E. A. Filene (*q.v.*), the Boston multimillionaire merchant, to prepare a plan for raising his city out of the dust of boss-control. Steffens worked at what became his "Boston 1915" idea: one which would modernize the city and create equity among its classes. His original idea was to enlist the bosses themselves and even local criminals in building a new community. He interviewed and got to know the local leaders in business and civic pursuits. The plan was to give them stakes in each other's duties and privileges. In sum, nothing but a name came of all his efforts but they became part of Steffens's legend and his own search for a better world.

More catastrophic was Steffens's intervention in a case which literally shook Los Angeles, and the labor movement elsewhere. In Los Angeles, the anti-union *Times* building was blown up with a loss of twenty-one lives, and the unionist McNamara brothers seized and tried for conspiracy and murder. They employed the famous attorney Clarence Darrow for the defense. In the meantime Steffens had hit upon nothing less that the Golden Rule, as displayed in the Bible itself, as the only valid means for bringing peace between contending forces. Unknown to him, the McNamaras were in fact guilty as charged, and he, brought in by Darrow as a "mediator" between the *Times*'s owners and the unions, was little more than a front man for a desperate Darrow whose sole goal was to save his clients from legal execution.

Steffens was persuaded that the top men—he believed only top men could get things done—wanted a solution which took into account the internecine wars between labor and capital, and that they favored compassion and understanding. In fact, the prosecution recognized that condemning the McNamaras would only result in more public atrocities. The McNamaras were given life-sentences, but Steffens returned to a New York where he received contempt from both business people and labor sympathizers.

Recognizing that something had gone wrong with muckraking—it was breaking down into continuations of reform, on one side, and shoddy sensationalism on the other—Steffens turned to politics and international concerns. Getting to know new-President Woodrow Wilson (*q.v.*), he sought to influence his views on the Mexican Revolution, which unfolded while the great European War was changing power elements abroad. Steffens later exaggerated his influence on Wilson in the Mexican crisis. He turned to Europe when the Russian Revolution unfolded in 1917.

The next year he put himself defiantly on the line by penning an introduction to Leon Trotsky's translated book: *The Bolsheviki and World*

Peace. Persuaded that the "people" wanted peace in Russia as elsewhere, Steffens found evidence from a personal visit among the beleaguered Bolsheviks that peace was the slogan of the time. Given place on a commission to report on Russian events, he returned in 1919 with his most memorable words: "I have seen the future; and it works."

Nevertheless he had less place in the new American society than such other old muckraking comrades as Baker (*q.v.*), who found a place with Wilson himself, or Charles Edward Russell who would for the next years sustain his distinctions with books and memoirs. Steffens was little consulted respecting Wilson's Peace of Paris, and he was all but unknown during the Coolidge and Hoover Administrations. His attempt at a novel, *Moses in Red* (1926), funded by E. A. Filene, which sought Biblical sanction for modern revolution, was a flat publishing failure, entirely ignored.

Steffens's wife had died as muckraking wound down. He found a young, politically active woman, Ella Winter, whom he married and who helped draw him leftward in his thinking. She also presented him with a son, whom they named Pete. With Steffens's sense of aging, this was to him one of his imperial achievements. Disillusioned with America, and with expenses down abroad, Steffens and his family lived largely in Europe during the 1920s. He annoyed fellow-travelers of communism with his expressed admiration for Benito Mussolini as a man who got things done. Steffens himself became scornful of Progressivism, advising young Whittaker Chambers, then in his communist phase, to pay no attention to it.

He did cherish his old role in it, and through the 1920s pondered his experiences while looking for a focus suitable to a new time. His autobiography, published in 1931, gained instant success. Steffens presented a vivid picture of Progressive figures and showed a time in which progress seemed at hand. Although self-serving, Steffens's memories appeared persuasive and were set down in a narrative style which gained from his old dreams of novel writing. His tale was more complex than appeared on the surface. It ambivalencies would show up when his *Letters* were published in 1938, edited by his wife and the Communist Granville Hicks. Steffens's last years were made pleasant by the success of his *Autobiography.* Living in California, he wrote columns for the local papers in the San Francisco area. He was called upon to lecture before appreciative audiences. In 1936, some of his papers were reprinted in *Lincoln Steffens Speaking.* For some years he had been over-impressed by the disparity between his age and that of his wife; as he told her, his concerns were now that of an old man. His last years, too, had been slowed down by a heart attack in 1933. In his last year of publication he died, and was buried in the family vault in San Francisco.

Steffens's own autobiography, when accompanied with his letters, is fundamental to a study of his life. He appears in most biographies of his contemporaries, especially those of the Progressive movement. Louis Filler, *The Muckrakers* (1976 ed.) shows him in context. See also J. Kaplan, *Lincoln Steffens* (1974) and P. Lyon, *Success Story: the Life and Times of S. S. McClure* (1963).

John Marshall Slaton
(1866-1955)

Forgotten Governor

JOHN MARSHALL SLATON WAS the unsung hero of the South. His upright life as lawyer and governor of Georgia was highlighted by his unwillingness to accede to the will of fellow Georgians who demanded the blood of Leo Frank. Frank had been falsely accused of the murder of a young girl who worked in an Atlanta pencil factory of which he was superintendent. Slaton's decision cost him his political life.

Slaton's father was an educator, and he himself became a graduate of the University of Georgia. Slaton undertook a career in law which by 1899 found him the sole head of his firm. A life-long Democrat, he served in the State House of Representatives from 1896 to 1909, and was its speaker for four years. From 1911 to January 1912 he was president of the State Senate. Following the resignation of then Governor Hoke Smith, Slaton became acting Governor in Smith's place. In October of that year Slaton ran for the governorship against two opponents. His popularity was shown in his sweeping victory; he took all but ten of the state's 146 counties. Re-elected, he continued as governor until 1915.

While still in the Senate, he had cast the deciding vote in favor of a federal income tax, though states-rights partisans highly influential in Georgia had fought vigorously to defeat the amendment. Slaton had earlier supported a bill widely advocated by such populist-minded politicians as Robert M. LaFollette (*q.v.*) which curbed the power of railroads to win favors by issuing free travel passes to journalist, legislators, and others who could write or act in their behalf. Slaton had also fought to regulate insanity pleas in criminal cases, and fought also the notorious convict-lease system which gave jailed inmates over to the mercies of private contractors. He worked for other equitable bills involving Georgia's financial affairs.

In the midst of such concerns the Leo Frank case came before the court in Atlanta, and the nation. Frank was a twenty-nine year old well-regarded Cornell University graduate engineer, and a businessman, who in 1910 married an Atlantan, settled in her city, and became active in its Jewish community. The ugly murder of an employee in the factory—thirteen-year old Mary Phagan, left dead in disarray in the plant's basement—shocked him as it did all others. He immediately sought detective help in locating the murderer.

The child had visited Frank's office to get her week's pay, and then left it. It did not occur to Frank to connect these events. The city, however, was roused as it had rarely been before, even during its own anti-Negro riots in 1906. The murderer, as it happened, was close at hand, a Jim Conley who cleaned the plant. He evaded arrest until Frank himself was arrested, then became the instrument of the ambitious Hugh M. Dorsey, Atlanta's solicitor-general who at the time badly needed a court victory.

Frank had all the attributes Dorsey needed for his case. Frank was a Jew, he was a Northerner (though born in Texas), and he was a businessman, a category demagogically scorned by harassed Georgia farmers and pseudo-populists. Although businessmen had not infrequently been great reformers and innovators for the nation, the Progressive era was winding down, and its instrument of enlightenment, muckraking, was being muddled with journalistic sensationalism. The poor, the frustrated, the prejudiced of Atlanta and much of Georgia needed a victim on whom they could vent their feelings. In Frank they found the perfect target.

The case concocted by Dorsey was a travesty that, in the words put in Conley's mouth, made of Frank a molester, an exploiter of young womanhood, and, finally, a murderer who "ordered" Conley to take the child he had ruined and killed and lay her grotesquely down in the basement. Frank brought brilliant lawyers down from New York to expose this false version of affairs, only to heap further coals of fury on the torment already suffered in court by the local attendants because the lawyers were "New Yorkers"—sly, smooth, and alien. National protest from such public figures as Charles R. Crane and Jane Addams only added to Georgian hatred of those who interfered with Georgian justice. The local judge treated Conley's illogical and revealing ramblings with respect. He did not challenge Dorsey's incitements to outraged feelings nor did he suppress the groans, hisses, and outcries in the court. Frank was sentenced to be executed.

The United States Supreme Court refused to interfere. National dismay at the legal assassination only hardened Georgian determination to see it consummated. The 100,000 letters Frank received from out of state harmed as much as they helped. There were many sane people among the Georgians who recognized the disgrace their state was incurring, but only the governor could affect the decision. On June 21, 1915, Slaton sealed his own fate by commuting Frank's sentence to life imprisonment. During this period Slaton and his home had to be protected from vengeful citizens by state police, while letters poured upon them containing every manner of threat.

Frank was taken to the state prison, where he was murderously assaulted by an inmate, and was barely saved from death. Later, some of the "best people", including two former state supreme court justices, took him by force from the prison and lynched him. He died a hero, asking only that his ring be delivered to his wife, a request which was carefully carried out by men who considered themselves honorable and just.

Slaton's subsequent career touched other aspects of the state, though he himself was never given individual appreciation by scholars or public servants. He was granted an honorary L L. D. by the University of Georgia in 1922. He belonged to numerous societies, including the Georgia State Bar Association, which he served as president in 1928-29. He held membership in the Sons of the American Revolution. In the meantime, Dorsey had succeeded Slaton as Governor of Georgia. The established Jewish community of Atlanta of the time had been noticeably thinned.

It was not until 1982 that a witness, Alonzo Mann, a black who had been a teenager at the time of the killing, feeling himself close to the grave, felt compelled to make a public declaration that he had seen Jim Conley taking the dead girl down to the basement. Conley had threatened him, and his mother had warned him to keep out of the proceedings. Despite this nationally broadcast testimony, state officials initially refused to grant Leo Frank posthumous vindication. Following a long pause, he was officially pardoned.

A somewhat similar case in New York at about the same time of a miscarriage of justice gives indication that more than a "Southern" miscarriage is involved; the victims suffered in part from a deterioration of the reform impulse in American life; see Filler, *Appointment at Armageddon* (1976). Charles and Louise Samuels, *Night Fell on Georgia* (1936) was a dramatic version of the tragedy. Harry Golden's *A Little Girl Is Dead* (1963) caught more attention because of the author's contemporary celebrity.

David Graham Phillips
(1867-1911)

Voice of the Democracy

NOVELIST AND SOCIAL CRITIC, David Graham Phillips was the original target of Theodore Roosevelt's speech denouncing the "muckrakers." Phillips authored *Susan Lenox: Her Fall and Rise* (1917), the pioneer feminist novel of the time. His shocking assassination resulted in passage of the Sullivan Act, which in New York broke ground for legislative control of the purchase of firearms by civilians.

He was born in an ideal midwestern setting, the city of Madison, Indiana, on the banks of the Ohio River, south of Cincinnati and across the water from Kentucky. Behind Madison rose high hills sheltering the town. Phillips enjoyed his early years in an ample home high above the Ohio River. His father, born of a long line of farmers, was a banker and early Republican. The boy Phillips, though good natured, proved reserved among his fellows and an intensive reader. At age fourteen he was entered at Asbury College near Indianapolis, later DePauw University, the first of his family to go to college. There he drew in the free, coeducational life of the time. He was highly impressed by fellow-student Albert J. Beveridge, of poor parentage, who, like LaFollette (*q.v.*) in Wisconsin, set him an example of hard, earnest work and ambition which affected his democratic viewpoint and literary directions. A turbulent love affair caused young Phillips to leave Asbury and complete his education at the College of

New Jersey, later Princeton University. He emerged from it at nineteen determined to learn what he could about the new industrial nation America had become.

He had difficulties breaking into journalism, the Cincinnati editors to whom he applied looking with distaste at the six foot eight inch eastern-educated young man dressed in extreme fashionable clothes. He found opportunities alone, without help or recommendations and soon proved to critics among the best of journalists in the midwestern metropolis. Three years later he repeated his performance in New York, offering himself to Charles A. Dana's *Sun* without credentials as a newspaperman, and once again writing stories for the paper which placed him among such favorites as Richard Harding Davis and Stephen Crane. So far he had shown only his acceptance of Darwinian doctrine mixed with civilized aspirations. One had to survive, he believed, and so to do meant finding independence on one's own, but to human ends. As he was later to write: Man was not a fallen angel, but a rising animal.

He changed over to Joseph Pulitzer's *World* for better opportunities and a more democratic outlook than Dana's *Sun*. He initiated his service with Pulitzer by one of the most famous "scoops" of the decade: the accidental sinking of a major British ship, *Victoria,* in the Mediterranean, reported in the *World* before the news had come to the British Admiralty. Phillips disappointed Pulitzer, who hoped to make him one of his major editors. Phillips's goals were elsewhere. He wrote pieces, notably for *Harper's Weekly*, which he hoped would lead the way out of journalism, but failed to do so; and he wrote a series of *World* reports on trusts and the Sherman Anti-Trust Act which broke ground for his later articles, "The Treason of the Senate" which, after half a century, would prove of memorable importance. Otherwise, he suffered a tragic liaison with a young girl, whose death underscored for him one of his major convictions: that women must have freer opportunities and gain independence, as homemakers and in the market place.

In 1901 Phillips made his decision to leave daily journalism and find his place as a writer and novelist. His first novel, *The Great God Success* (1901) is notable chiefly as including details about his personal tragedy, but, having a newspaper theme, was seized upon as underscoring his field, and, though an apprentice work, became a fixed reference of negative commentary regarding him.

During his first independent years his articles, notably for the *Saturday Evening Post*, were more important than his early experimental fiction. They introduced his themes of midwestern values, political and social betrayal, and social revival. His first resounding success was *The Plum Tree* (1905), which sketched the rise and corruption of a political boss, contrasted with a protagonist whose ideas blended with those perceived in the career of an Abraham Lincoln and his own friend, since become a United States senator, Albert J. Beveridge.

Phillips's writing methods were by this time a New York legend. He had settled in an ample apartment overlooking New York's Gramercy Park, and there installed a draftsman's desk at which he turned out large masses of manuscript written in a difficult hand avoiding, as he said, temperament and inspiration. No matter what else he might be doing—socializing, attending theaters and concerts, or public meetings, or entertaining guests—the tall, conspicuously-dressed man with the firm mouth and handsome features who always walked could be found at his draftsman's "pulpit" beginning new chapters or books, revising articles, studying proofs with awesome industry.

The industry was grossly exaggerated. Phillips suffered illness which hospitalized him. He visited friends away from home, and took trips to his parents in Indiana. He followed the social and cultural scene in New York and elsewhere. Nevertheless his belief in work and steadiness of purpose were phenomenal, especially in a time which sentimentalized the "inspiration" of "artists" and their allegedly God-given talents.

Most harmful in time was the impression created of him as being a hasty writer, even though Phillips pointed out that nothing left his workplace before it had been reviewed and considered up to nine times, thanks to his system of having his work typed and retyped till he was satisfied. His best-known novel, *Susan Lenox*, was twenty years in the writing. His brief, fulfilled years of production, from 1906 to the beginning of 1911, completed fiction which had been in work during all the years of his aborted career and before.

Most important was the culturally naive sense of his writing being in one style. *Light-Fingered Gentry* (1907) was his New York novel. It interrelated men's and women's lives as lawyers, stockmarket manipulators, social aspirants, and public officials, maintaining an urban tone. *Old Wives for New*, published the same year, was written in Phillips's coldest prose, relentlessly pursuing the compulsions of sex, marriage and career. *The Fashionable Adventures of Joshua Craig* (1908) contrasted a rough-edged Progressive—Beveridge irrationally thought it portrayed him—with the sophisticated time-servers in

Washington politics. Its greatest novelty was to interpose the woman theme among politicians.

Phillips's most notable failure among these novels was the one from which he hoped most: *The Second Generation* (1907), his effort to express his love and admiration for his father. Although the novel included thoughtful scenes, seen individually, it fell apart as a sound record of the time. It sold well among those giving lip-service to old ways and expectations. It rated improperly with those seeking arguments demeaning of Phillips's work.

Nineteen hundred and six was also Phillips's stormy year. In "The Treason of the Senate" articles sensationally serialized in *Cosmopolitan* he attacked Senate leaders who resisted Progressive effort to bring the railroads under regulation, to enact food and drug laws, and otherwise bring the nation into modern times. Phillips's forthright attacks troubled even major reform leaders who were accustomed to having senators operating frankly as stipendiaries of major corporations. They tolerated the system of the times of having senators elected by state assemblies rather than by popular vote. Nevertheless, Phillips's articles, highlighting the senators as individuals reverberated throughout the country and were recognized as a powerful force in carrying through the Seventeenth Amendment to the Constitution (1913), stipulating popular elections. At the time the articles were all but notorious and denied book publication.

Phillips's last years fulfilled his dreams for free attention to his favorite themes. They resulted in novels largely divested of "muckraking." *The Hungry Heart* (1909) took place in a small midwestern town he had invented, "St. X," all but removed from the large city and its problems, and wholly concerned for those of an intelligent married woman bound down by a scientist-husband with outmoded marriage expectations. *White Magic* (1910) and *The Husband's Story* (1910) similarly concentrated on love, and its varied effects on men and women, the latter tale being the obvious inspiration for Sinclair Lewis's *Dodsworth* (1929).

This was the last novel Phillips was himself to see. Late in January of 1911 he was gunned down while on his way to the other side of Gramercy Park by the troubled scion of the distinguished Goldsborough family. He imagined Phillips had lampooned a member of his clan in *The Fashionable Adventures of Joshua Craig*. Phillips lingered in hospital two days, but the bullet wounds were too extensive for his life to be saved. His sister buried him in Valhalla Cemetery north of the city, where she herself later was buried.

Soon after appeared the first of Phillips's posthumous fiction, *The Grain of Dust* (1911), another of his explorations into the vagaries of love and its effect on worldly ambitions, and, the year after, his uncompromising *The Price She Paid*, which treated the problem of female independence in the arts harshly and with bare words. His evident masterpiece, *Susan Lenox: Her Fall and Rise*, meanwhile languished in drawers, the publishers being reluctant to chance its publication. When it appeared serialized in *Hearst's Magazine* in 1917, its title was accompanied with the words "America's Greatest Novel." It met with a storm of protest for treating prostitution without conventional scorn. Published in book form in two volumes it was challenged in court by the American Society for the Prevention of Vice. The publishers Appleton conceded to its stipulations, and reissued the book with a hundred pages removed: an act which drained it of its vitality and challenge.

Meanwhile in 1915 Theodore Dreiser (*q.v.*), though living a secret life, had issued *The Genius* which no more than recounted his extended sexual adventures masked as fiction. A strong anti-censorship drive headed by H. L. Mencken fought for the work on grounds of freedom of expression, and won its case, in the process winning Dreiser status as a premier American novelist. The contrast between Dreiser's culture-directed success and Phillips's appeal for suffrage to the people gave evidence that his democracy-based audience was too amorphous to maintain his good repute. Ludwig Lewisohn as influential critic observed that Phillips's books lived a sort of underground life during the 1920s, which favored other themes and treatment.

In 1931 appeared an article by the communist Granville Hicks in *Bookman,* "David Graham Phillips: Journalist." Though based on false innuendo and evidence, it was received in academe as valid and sufficient, and was used consistently as the last word on the subject, until, during the tumult of the 1960s newer commentators emerged to discover *The Treason of the Senate* and recognize it as classic. *Susan Lenox* was now seen as early feminism. Phillips's overall life and work in the context of Progressivism remained yet to be reconsidered.

There are striking contrasts in Phillips's and Theodore Dreiser's careers to be explored. Filler, "Two Gentlemen from Indiana," in R.B. Browne *et al.*, eds., *New Voices in American Studies* (1966) opens the subject, but requires further work in the light of new evidence, especially regarding Dreiser. See also Filler, *Voice of the Democracy* (1978), a study of Phillips's life and work.

George Kibbe Turner
(1869-1952)

Period Piece

ONE OF THE GREAT JOURNALISTS OF THE PROGRESSIVE ERA,
George Kibbe Turner failed to attain post-Progressive status beside that of
Tarbell, and Steffens and Baker (*qq.v.*). What robbed Turner of comparable
fame in succeeding decades gives clues to the processes which at that time
dominated change in public-author relations. Significant, too, were the issues on which the journalists built their careers, and which changed character, sometimes overnight.

Turner, an Illinoisan, attended Williams College in Massachusetts
and, following graduation, in 1891 became a reporter on the then-famous
Springfield (Mass.) *Republican*. Like many journalists of the time, he

dreamed of writing novels. He did write stories, several of which appeared in *McClure's*. S. S. McClure also published Turner's first novel, *The Taskmaster* (1902) which, like such other fictions as Mary Wilkins Freeman's *The Portion of Labor* (1901) showed the time's concern for labor-capital relations.

In 1906 Steffens, Baker, (*qq.v.*), and others left *McClure's* to edit what they thought would be a more socially-conscious magazine, the *American*. McClure had boasted that *McClure's* was only interested in publishing the facts. He now brought in Turner to fill the gap. Much troubled by the boss-ridden city government which reigned everywhere, and for which he sought a solution, he set Turner to reporting on a new form of urban operation Galveston, Texas had begun. A tidal wave in 1900 had all but reduced the city to chaos. Its leaders had in desperation thrown out political hacks and called in trained personnel as a commission to run the city's affairs.

Turner's article in *McClure's*, "Galveston: a Business Corporation," had an unprecedented effect: one that was noticed from coast to coast. Cities called for reprints; it was later estimated that some 12 million copies were circulated. Laws were passed in state legislatures making room for the new idea. For a while, *McClure's* office was an unofficial forum for exchanges and debates. By 1914, it was estimated, some 350 cities, involving a substantial percentage of the urban population, had changed their councils to conform with the idea of commission government.

Although corruption and favoritism were far from obliterated, the new idea did put municipal government on a more modern footing, and was more responsive to people's needs. McClure sought follow-ups to the Galveston achievement, and in his intuitive way, sent Turner to Chicago, notorious for crime and corrupt practices. His and Turner's original idea was to describe conditions there, using Chicago's own newspaper columns for evidence. Turner, probing the information he collected, came up with a program which provoked a fresh excitement and demand for change.

Turner actually built on an earlier campaign, fired by the British journalist W. T. Stead, whose *If Christ Came to Chicago* (1893) was a brief sensation, but which lacked program to further it. Stead emphasized the vice of prostitution. Turner built on this as central to political corruption, adding the vices of gambling and liquor. Since these pursuits were followed by ordinary people, and dependent on their patronage, they touched deep feelings in men and women. Turner's April 1907 *McClure's* article, "The City of Chicago: a Study in the Great Immoralities," was another sensation, and set off committees and crusaders everywhere to find answers to the evils revealed.

Turner's November article that same year, "The Daughters of the Poor," did more than titillate and horrify. It traced the course, this time of New York's prostitution rings, beyond its pimps, then known as "cadets," into international recruiting of girls, very often torn from immigrant families, for prostitution. All this, repulsive in its harvest of ruined lives, inspired actions which led, finally, to passage of the 1910 Mann Act. It made the transportation of women across state lines for immoral purposes subject to criminal law.

Turner was now among the very top names in reform writing and, like his peers, apparently in position to help direct America's affairs of conscience. His days of distinction, however, were numbered, his one further sensation being no more than a journalistic triumph, which featured others in magisterial roles.

McClure sent him to Boise, Idaho, where a trial of the century was forming. There in 1905 a former governor of the state, Frank R. Steunenberger, had been assassinated and a suspect found: Harry Orchard, associated with the Western Federation of Miners, long engaged in a bitter war with the mine owners. Over the years there had been deaths heaped on both sides. The miners, led by the famous "Big Bill" Haywood, gave blow for blow, but the murder by bomb of its former governor, accused of having broken promises to labor, threatened government at its source.

Harry Orchard emerged out of anonymity as a seasoned assassin. Having turned religious in prison, he responded to the queries of James McParland, a Pinkerton Police operative. McParland was notorious himself to labor sympathizers as the man who had years before broken the "Molly Maguires" in the Pennsylvania coal mines and sent its alleged leaders to the gallows. To McParland, Orchard candidly confessed numerous murders, but under the direction of Haywood. Thus, labor was on trial, rather than Orchard. The trial pitted William E. Borah, then state prosecutor, against labor attorney Clarence Darrow. The general public divided between those who felt that society's peace was threatened, and others who felt for labor in its life and death struggle.

Turner elicited from Orchard his life story and avowals, and gave *McClure's* and its book publishing house one of the memorable tales of the decade. *The Confessions and Autobiography of Harry Orchard* horrified because of the colorless and unformed nature of a drifter in and out of respectable society who ended as a murderer for hire. Darrow, in his passionate defense, compared Orchard with the upright figure of Haywood, leading oppressed workers and their families. Darrow underscored that nothing had been proved by Orchard's testimony. But he was too aware of its persuasive quality, and of the circumstantial evidence with which it connected. With powerful indirection he laid before the country the idea that tactics in war were not comparable to those among civilians. The jury's acquittal verdict appeared to accept that view; see David H. Grover, *Debaters and Dynamiters: the Story of the Haywood Trial* (1964).

Such a judgment was one of Turner as well as of his services. He could not see beneath his materials. Although he continued to write on national issues and to be read, his articles lost interest or changed shape as war in Mexico and abroad took attention from them. Turner did not reconsider them for a new time.

He turned back to fiction as a vehicle. Little of it proved memorable. His *Red Friday* (1918) sought to frighten readers with visions of a cold, machiavellian Lenin come to America and threatening democracy. It failed to persuade readers. *Hagar's Hoard* (1920) tried to reach readers with the horrors of a yellow fever epidemic of 1878, with its attendant public panic, fear, and coffins. It too made no impression. Reprinted as a "document" in 1970, its new introduction discussed epidemics rather than the story, and allotted Turner himself no more than several paragraphs.

Turner's life work can profitably be compared with that of Steffens, for light on what endures and what ends as a period piece, as society moves on.

Ray Stannard Baker
(1870-1946)

Spiritual Unrest

CELEBRATED "MUCKRAKER" and follower of Woodrow Wilson (*q.v.*), of distinguished background and journalistic achievement, Baker developed a reputation as uncompromising in his search for the facts. He went on to serve Wilson as President and to be his official biographer. Also, his "David Grayson" series, semi-fiction, semi-personal essays, circulated at best-seller level, apparently affirming Baker's roots in ordinary people. Yet his reputation did not so much fall as become dissipated, leaving uncertain traces.

He came of old New England family on both sides. Remember Baker, an ancestor, was one of Ethan Allen's "Green Mountain Boys," of Revolutionary fame. Baker's father, Joseph Stannard Baker, gained fame himself during the Civil War as a Secret Service agent and major of cavalry. He moved his family from western New York to Lansing, Michigan, then to northern Wisconsin where Ray was the eldest of six sons, all secure in their rural society and well-ordered home. Young Baker read in the family's library, with his brothers enjoyed the outdoors as they would all their lives, and was well prepared for higher learning when he returned to East Lansing to enter Michigan Agricultural College, as Michigan State University then was.

There he was impressed by Dr. William James Beal, already one of the great botanists of his time. Baker graduated without a vocation.

Following several years of work with his father, he entered the University of Michigan as a law student. Like many youths of his time he was puzzled by post-Civil War America: its expansion to the Pacific Ocean, new immigrants, cities, and cycles of affluence and economic despair. He soon left to enter Chicago journalism hoping for insight into the new world.

As a *Chicago News-Record* reporter Baker laid himself open to experiences that conflicted with the assumptions of his family and youth. He accompanied Coxey's Army of unemployed to Washington in 1893-94 where the poverty band, pleading for work relief, was dispersed by the police. He visited Pullman, Illinois, the next year, where harassed strikers of Eugene V. Debs's American Railway Union were in conflict with employer agents and federal troops. Baker's reports sympathized with the workers's needs, but held to faith in American life and opportunity.

Baker was more at ease with subjects that did not contain the imponderables of justice and need, and he advanced in reputation with articles which were precise in their handling of data and details. He was more ambivalent in reaching conclusions about key crises in human affairs. The problem was that they acutely concerned him, and that his basic evasions were not so much with his readers as with himself.

In 1896 he married Jessie Beal, the daughter of Professor Beal, and they began to build a family. Like Lincoln Steffens (*q.v.*) and others in journalism, Baker dreamed of writing novels that would embody his vision of America. He had still, however, a career to make. In 1898, he left the *News-Record* to become managing editor of S. S. McClure's Syndicate, which distributed stories and articles by such of McClure's writers as Robert Louis Stevenson and Theodore Roosevelt. But soon Baker's own talents seemed wasted in such work and he joined the active staff of *McClure's Magazine*.

The scattered nature of Baker's writing at this point can be seen in his *Boy's Book of Inventions* (1899) and *Seen in Germany* (1901). Closer to Baker's own problem was his *Our New Prosperity* (1900) that at first glance helped illuminate social processes, but in retrospect gave no sense of American issues or problems. The nation's goals and ventures, Baker averred, were soundly based. "Hard Times" that had gone on from 1893 to 1897 - came from human greed and recklessness. But they passed and the nation moved on. Baker later dropped the title from his *Who's Who* summary, but it exemplified his need for human assurances he could not consolidate.

Lincoln Steffens also out of journalism and with *McClure's,* went out into the field to find the new America. McClure assigned Baker to cope journalistically with mounting labor crises. Baker was drawn to study labor racketeering and to meet issues that established their magazine as leader in the newly discovered literature of exposure. He drew the face of corrupt labor as it appeared in Chicago, in San Francisco, and elsewhere. Especially notable was his article "The Right to Work," about a sore in the unions's sometimes desperate drive for organization that violence in employer-employee relations would not let heal.

Though Baker's work was satisfying to McClure and others who sought a middle way between individual and cooperative social goals, Baker himself continued uncertain of his path. Politically he clung to Theodore Roosevelt and then to Robert M. LaFollette (*q.v.*) as resisting industrial pirates but also the temptations of socialism. Baker hoped for a national consensus which could use his vivid accounts of personalities to win comity among warring social factions.

When McClure seemed ready to turn his magazine toward educational schemes that avoided central crises, Baker joined Steffens, Ida M. Tarbell, and others in taking over the *American Magazine* and continuing the older campaign. Baker's struggle for peace of mind, however, was not appeased. "Negro citizenship" had troubled him before, and he took hold of it again, following the 1906 Atlanta, Georgia riots against the city's blacks. His on-the-scene research resulted in his most memorable book, *Following the Color Line* (1908). Here his observations were as vivid as ever, his even-handedness the same, as he set down the explanations of white apologists. But commentators of the time could not fail to notice the impact of his accounts of inhumanity and murder which no rationale of southern feeling could dim.

Baker's innermost feelings were best displayed, though by indirection, in *The Spiritual Unrest,* in which Baker consulted religious leaders among Protestants, Jews, and Catholics who told him of the dissatisfaction with religious concerns among their communicants. Many of his informants grew in fame as the century progressed, but in their youthful vocations they spoke with a deep concern and clarity which made their statements timeless.

While he struggled with these problems, including socialism, which tempted such others as Upton Sinclair (*q.v.*) and Charles Edward Russell, a second part of Baker's disturbed mind reached another conclusion of sorts. Baker had never in his changing life forgot his deeply satisfying youth. He had all but reluctantly immersed himself in the world that paid and honored him. Also, he had settled his own family in East Lansing, where Professor Beal could enjoy the company of his daughter and grandchildren. They would all in 1910, along with Baker, make a permanent move to Amherst, Massachusetts, similarly then set among semi-rural byways.

Finally, Baker's curious impulse toward fiction, frustrated by urban clashes and corruption, found release in what became a long series of essays and vignettes describing a half-fanciful world of kindly people, love-ly rural scenes, and philosophical conversations always concluding with serene thoughts, even when they involved hard labor, unjust happenings, premature deaths. As "David Grayson" Baker published these essays as *Adventures in Contentment* (1907). They were an immediate success. As volume succeeded volume with such titles as *Adventures in Friendship* and *The Friendly Road,* popular acclaim persuaded Baker that he had struck a genuine chord in American life. He never explained why his pseudonym had been necessary.

These "adventures" embodied questions Baker's journalistic co-workers were too delicate to address to his face, though Steffens indirectly hinted at them in his 1906 letter to Baker in which he praised the pieces as "real creative art, Baker, far above and beyond reporting." In Steffens's own autobiography, as in all muckrakers's autobiographies, "David Grayson" did not exist. Steffens found occasion only to notice that Baker had taken one of Steffens's staff ideas and used it without acknowledging the source.

The real world went on, and Baker, having toyed with socialistic ideas, fixed on LaFollette as the best man to lead the nation in 1912. In that turning-point year for Progressives, Baker was outraged by the movement Theodore Roosevelt led that ruined LaFollette's candidacy and split the Republican Party. With some other disillusioned Progressives Baker turned to Woodrow Wilson, and thereafter followed him in all his endeavors.

Baker liked to think he had been an influence on Wilson's thought, but the record does not bear him out. Baker served as U.S. press director at the Versailles Peace Conference, and his books, *What Wilson Did at Paris* (1919) and *Woodrow Wilson and World Settlement* (1922) pleased Wilson followers. More interesting in many ways was the report Baker prepared at the request of the State Department on the state of public feeling and opinion in the British Island during the war: comparable in form and detail to his old "muckraking" reports, and revealing his sharp seeing traits at high moment. Once again he was the clear eyed reporter, noting every manner of detail in wartime Britain and steering clear of conclusions. Yet his report, reproduced in part in his autobiography, included nothing which would stand against the war leaders whom he interviewed and with whom he dined, and it reported faithfully all comments appreciative of the President.

In 1920, aged fifty, Baker made a major effort to renew his old career as an independent writer, using facts, history, and even statistics. His old readers, however, had disappeared into new social alignments and Baker's *The New Industrial Unrest* (1920) interested no one. Baker turned to collecting Wilson's public papers, with Professor William E. Dodd, a Southerner now based at the University of Chicago. They were published in six volumes in 1925-27. Baker himself, with access to some of Wilson's more personal papers, undertook to prepare the "authorized" biography of the late President in eight volumes. It gained him the Pulitzer Prize for Biography in 1940. In 1941 appeared *Native American: the Book of My Youth*. It captured as no earlier work by Baker the tone and integrity of his upbringing and education. Baker's follow-up *American Chronicle* (1945) was more defensive and ambivalent.

Baker's letters have not been collected, and his own versions of affairs, public and personal, are best checked against relevant accounts by his contemporaries. His six-volume *Papers of Woodrow Wilson* is wholly superseded by A. S. Link *et al.*, *The Papers of Woodrow Wilson*, which began publication in 1967, and by 1991 was in its 64th volume, with more to follow. Baker's life of Wilson was also superseded by that of Link. Of his own writings under either name of Baker or "David Grayson" only *Following the Color Line* was in significant print.

Theodore Dreiser
(1871-1945)

Suspended Judgement

Dreiser as a successful editor.

NOVELIST AND AUTOBIOGRAPHER, DREISER PIONEERED literary expression concerned for sex, and apparently for the weak and the driven. As of German-American origin, Dreiser also contributed to early ethnic assertion, though only in moderation; he himself largely assumed the social features of the American majority. Dreiser's writings had roots in late nineteenth century journalism, but became a major influence on twentieth century American naturalism.

Dreiser grew in a family in Indiana headed by religiously rigid parents and surrounded by numerous siblings. The Dreisers had once been well to do, but, were ruined by economic depression. The father, John Paul Dreiser, lost control of family affairs. His wife showed no more capacity for directing the children's impulses or ways. The girls drifted off, and of the boys only Paul found direction, becoming Paul Dresser, a successful song writer in New York. All this was to find place in literary lore as their younger brother Theodore found success there.

The most notable fact in the tall, homely man's life was the continuous friendship and cooperation he received in all stages of his development, not among traditionalists, but among dissidents and or-dinary people sympathetic to his feelings and principles, which were few but effective. Dreiser all his life strove to formulate a philosophy, collecting notes and pages in great number. How much they reflected the views of his following is matter for conjecture.

An unpromising student, he won the sympathy of a high school teacher, probably stirred by his helplessness and smoldering passion. She took steps to have him enter Indiana University. Uninspired there, he drifted to Chicago where a sister was kept by a man. Here Dreiser began newspaper work with the Chicago *Globe* and observed the vagaries of big city life. These included sudden death, fires, train wrecks, and other catastrophes. Here, too, he made his first firm commitments: life was indifferent to human hopes, and was basically futile. The only goals worth following were money, sex, and fame. A photograph of young Dreiser taken once he was established in newspapers shows him in naively flashy clothes, materializing such hopes as he had.

Dreiser continued in journalism in St. Louis and Pittsburgh, toyed with ideas of settling with a small town paper, and finally in the middle 1890s came to New York. There his brother Paul helped him become editor of a semi-advertising music magazine, *Ev'ry Month*. Dreiser found friends and work in journalism and for the popular magazines, then in their first bloom. His writing for them was strictly commercial, except that he sincerely admired the men of wealth and authority he met and whom he dreamed of emulating. At the same time he aspired to independent writing and had his friends's respect as a man of promise.

In 1898 he quelled his restless yearnings enough to marry Sarah Osborne White of St. Louis, and for a time seemed relatively settled. His plan for a novel having become clear in his mind, he undertook what became *Sister Carrie*, roughly based on a sister's life as a kept woman. Dreiser wove a thread of fate through his pages and avoided moral judgments. His Carrie drifts into life with a salesman; Hurstwood, a family man and bar-restaurant manager, becomes infatuated with her. He hesitantly steals business funds and runs away with her, is caught and ruined but permitted to go free, and takes her to New York. His own fall in life is vivid: he is a failure in attempted business, suffers worklessness and deterioration among the city's human driftwood, and is a suicide in a run-down lodging house. His final removal with other corpses for anonymous burial in Potter's Field is memorable.

Carrie's rise to musical prominence is far less convincing: she is discovered by an impresario, receives a rousing reception by audiences, and is a success. Dreiser knew nothing of the dynamics of such a career and triumph, but his narrative echoed the vague dreams of the numerous women who sat empty-handed in drab homes or lonely rooms. Carrie's sad overtones and aimlessness at the novel's end comported with their awakenings from daydreams and return to dreary rounds. The manuscript was convincing to Frank Norris, the publisher Doubleday's editor, and one who himself had learned from Emile Zola and written distinguished naturalistic fiction. Norris earnestly recommended publication and Dreiser had his contract.

He later convinced admirers that he had been mistreated by the publisher, establishing an approach he would follow for the rest of his life: he was an abused artist who had been driven to all but despair by insensitive businessmen. In this instance a Doubleday relative had seen the manuscript, Dreiser said, been horrified by its contents, and demanded that it be rejected. At Dreiser's insistence it had been published, but copies relegated to the basement. The book had not been advertised and its reception had been ruined.

So much was true, that Dreiser rejected the suggestion that the contract be dropped, and had insisted on publication. But once published the firm had taken its usual steps in sending out review copies and advertising its publication. There were some complimentary notices, but reviewers were generally not enthusiastic, and booksellers complained that the book did not move from their shelves. Dreiser's hopes for *Sister Carrie* had been too high.

Like his characters, Dreiser lost heart and abandoned himself to despair. His marriage floundered. Attempts at change of scene and rest did not help. Although he later acknowledged that his brother Paul had sought him out in a room, hopelessly inert, he did not particularize the help he received: brief physical work, then a professional regime for renewed health, for which Paul paid the cost. All this finally appeared in a manuscript Dreiser kept to the end of life, and attempted to use in parts, finally titled *An Amateur Laborer* (1983).

Aided by friends, Dreiser got hold of himself and from 1905 to 1910 was a successful commercial editor of such magazines as *Delineator* and *Designer*; as he told a fellow-editor Charles Hanson Towne, one must never deviate from the readers's slightest expectations. All this indirectly impugned the optimism and good hopes of the Progressive era and its major scribes. But in addition Dreiser never gave up his sincere respect and admiration for leaders who handled unscrupulous power. His one major tribute to higher aspirations was his purchase of his contract from Doubleday, and republication of *Sister Carrie* in 1907, when it was better received, though not significantly successful. Dreiser also worked on several other manuscripts, though temporarily bemused by practical matters.

In the curious version of candor which he later developed Dreiser put it that he had felt himself unsuited to marriage and begged his wife to release him. It appears that he could in fact have had his divorce on reasonable terms; and that, in his numerous experiences with other women he found it an actual convenience to be able to say that he was refused a divorce. His conventional career was nevertheless interrupted by his effort to win over a very young girl with relatives in his office. The scandal cost him his editorship and released him for the work which was closest to his goals.

His novel *Jennie Gerhardt* (1911) told another tale of a kept woman, whose simple dedication to a man of family and public career was cut down by his death. Half the length of *Sister Carrie*, it gave a good impression of unassuming reality. Its quality is best judged by comparing it with Fannie Hurst's more successful, but infinitely shallow *Back Street* (1931), also dealing with a kept woman, but suffused with self-pity and garish emotions. Curiously, Dreiser thought of giving Jennie a happy ending, but was persuaded by friends, including women—for whom in a sense he was a spokesman—that only a tragic conclusion was appropriate.

More ambitious was Dreiser's *The Financier* (1912) which revealed Dreiser's obsession with the rich in the career of Charles Y. Yerkes, a Philadelphian whose gambles with law cost him a prison term. Dreiser was helped by a friend who researched the court case, which Dreiser flatly reproduced; he was later to find much better artistic purpose in similar court materials in his *An American Tragedy*.[1]

The Titan (1914) continued Cowperwood's ruthless exploits in Chicago as streetcar magnate and restless sexual seeker, and helped to consolidate Dreiser's career as novelist.

In 1915 came *The "Genius"*—Dreiser in his *Who's Who* entry dropped the quotation marks around the original, possibly because he saw no reason for his early diffidence, since the novel no more than reproduced his numerous efforts to win such women as passed his way. His "character" was depicted as being an "artist," but the lengthy script made relatively little of his artistic knowledge or capacities. Nor was his concern for "chemism" as a rationale for sexual enterprises enlightening.

The novel was ultimately judged the least interesting of Dreiser's fictions, but it was the making of Dreiser himself. For it roused the rage of censors, and brought to his defense, headed by H. L. Mencken, the most visible and effective of contemporary dissident writers, as well as not a few who did not approve of Dreiser's writing, but opposed censorship.

Dreiser had already made his entrance as an autobiographer. His *A Traveler of Forty* (1913), fruit of a European tour, began his semi-candid memoirs, and, thanks to the 1910s "youth movement," made him a senior author who had broken ground for them in sexual criticism of American hypocrisy. Dreiser joined this work to a *Hoosier Holiday* (1916) and *A Book about Myself* (1922) which also included passages of autobiography purists could resent.

Dreiser issued books of undigested or patently slight character which had a place in the context of "experimental" writing then being fancied by the younger generation. With experiments continuing in the post-War years of the 1920s he was kept busy making contacts for publication and reprints. He wrote articles which claimed forthrightness, like "I Was Tempted, So I Stole," a youthful reminiscence. He looked for money in Hollywood.

It was typical of one of Dreiser's strongest traits, his retentiveness and accumulation of old manuscripts, letters, and other materials, that he held on to an actual 1906 court case: the accident or murder by a vaguely ambitious, immature young man, religiously brought up, sexually restless, of a simple factory girl he had made pregnant. Her presence had threatened his dream of winning another, more promising young woman.

But had "Clyde Griffith" really intended to kill her? In *An American Tragedy* (1926) this became the hub of the case as seen by prosecutor and defending attorney. In the light of his fumbling youth, his drab prospects, his dreams, and his humble sexual attachment, all eyes turn on the trial as it runs its formal course. An electrifying moment sees the opposing lawyers quarreling over the young people's positions in the row-boat—actually brought into the courtroom—with a man in the audience rising and shouting: "Why don't they kill the God-damned bastard and be done with him?"

Clyde is puzzled as he waits in the deathhouse for execution, where the lights dim as successively condemned men go to the electric chair—puzzled as to what he had intended, what he had or had not done. The doubt—the mitigating factor, the problem of fate—had first appeared in *Sister Carrie*, when Hurstwood had half-intended to give up his plan to steal company money, but, with the money in his hand, had seen the door to the safe accidentally shut.

An American Tragedy was a ringing success and established Dreiser as premier American novelist of his time. In many ways it represented his highest point, not only as a pioneer, or as an author confronting censorship, but as a finished master. When he visited the Soviets he was so received, and his subsequent book was entitled *Dreiser Looks at Russia* (1928). When the Depression hit America, literary groups vied for his endorsement, though his *Tragic America* (1931) embarrassed admirers as parodying his more distinguished title: it was filled with thousands of errors passing as information which had been gathered for his use by others. His blundering anti-semitism and odd social views were patiently received as by a great man who did not know better. With communists then in good odor he leaned toward them as the voice of the future.

His work in his last years was anticlimactic in the main, though *Dawn* (1931) added to his memoirs, and *The Stoic* (1947), following his death, in some fashion completed his long laid-aside trilogy. More formidable in many respects was the long series of books, by notables and their students, in and out of the literary and academic worlds, which interpreted Dreiser, almost entirely favorably.

How durable was his achievement? The papers he had tenaciously kept went to the University of Pennsylvania, where a range of academics culled materials for books, including an uncut version of *Sister Carrie*, his diaries, and his letters. His *Notes on Life* (1974), edited by several hands, finally gave some of Dreiser's thoughts to interested people; as an example:

> For, if when you die the atoms or electrons of which you are composed should disintegrate, which would mean that they would change to pure energy, and if— and this is a purely speculative idea of my own—this energy should, for some reason, coagulate as a force, you would, thereby become an immense power or unit of energy capable (assuming that thought is a phase of energy, which ma[n]y now believe), although bodiless, of continuing to think—imagine the possibilities of observation, conclusion, interest—assuming that there were endless other such disembodied and yet *thinking* units of energy to be observed by you!—perhaps even confer with! Imagine!

In addition, Dreiser was clearly the source of attitudes and ideas which influenced such figures as John Dos Passos, James T. Farrell, and, by descent, James Jones and Norman Mailer. Precisely what of inheritance he left in himself could only be guessed.

Much of the writing about Dreiser did not reach to the core of his character or achievement. Robert H. Elias, *Theodore Dreiser: Apostle of Nature* (1970 ed.) was a sympathetic, carefully-wrought study; see also Elias, ed., *Letters of Theodore Dreiser* (1959), 3 volumes. Of wide range and insight is W. A. Swanberg, *Dreiser* (1965) which makes a distinction between the liar, cheat, and egotist who was the human Dreiser, and the purveyor of truth who at his best was an artist.

NOTES:

1. A later printing of *The Financier* concluded that the give and take of court processes would deter readers from following Frank Cowperwood's financial and sexual career after prison, and printed it in small type for those who wished to get on with the tale.

Gustavus Myers
(1872-1942)

Semi-Classic

AN HISTORIAN AND REFORMER
who seemed to have attained distinc-
tion against odds, Gustavus Myers left a debatable legacy. His life was a
comment upon American expectations and ways of furthering social interests.
Myers's career contrasts interestingly with that of his brother Jerome, who
became a famous painter, at home with others of his artistic generation.

Gustavus Myers's background had traces of novelty in a
grandfather who had served under Napoleon, and a father who was a '49er
seeking gold in California. The elder Myers was, however, unreliable, a
man who could not support his family. Gustavus lived in institutions in
New York and Philadelphia. At age 14 he was at work in a factory, his
only outlet being escape into books. He began newspaper work on the
Philadelphia Record when 19, then moved on to New York to find jobs
on newspapers and to attempt articles for magazines. He had a clear, unadorned newspaper style of writing which reflected his colorless life and
experiences. Myers had, however, gained a vision of socialism, and in 1907
he joined the Socialist Party.

Myers had also developed a sense of research which, as a result
of his membership in the New York Reform Club, he now turned on Tammany Hall. He pored over old files and newspapers for information regarding its administration of public franchises. His *History of Public Franchises
in New York City* (1900) was a careful display of the documents and

associated material he had gathered. They undoubtedly revealed chicanery and fraud among the political dignitaries of New York, some of whom were still active in city affairs.

Issued under Reform Club auspices, it should have begun what became the muckraking era, and made Myers famous. Instead, it did nothing for him, even after national reform had broken open the secret operations of the time. Even more remote writings, like Charles A. Beard's *An Economic Interpretation of the Constitution* (1913), made its author known to people not involved in historical debates. Myers had no following, no institutional connections, and no insight into the many nuances of favoritism and self-interest which the public shared with the politicians. His purposes were patently good, to advance a world of fairness and equality, but they did not reach people. He was his own publisher, helped by subscriptions. According to himself, most of the copies of his book were mysteriously bought up on publication.

Myers married and raised a family. A slight, somewhat humorless man with the passive look of one whose gaze was steadily focused, as it usually was, on books opened in libraries, became fixed in a viewpoint which judged all his reading from a socialist perspective. His articles for several of the magazines, and socialist aims, as expressed in contributions for W. D. P. Bliss's *The New Encyclopedia of Social Reform* (1908 ed.), made only a pale impression. Throughout the 1900s he worked without encouragement on the study with which he ultimately became identified. Living meagerly, he was quietly scornful of his muckraking contemporaries who, with all the fanfare which accompanied their investigations seemed to him essentially shallow. His own "History of the Great American Fortunes" circulated without welcome among a variety of potential publishers.

It was finally issued (1909-1910) in three volumes by a Chicago socialist firm, Charles H. Kerr and Company. It gave Myers his first visibility in newspaper and magazine reviews. None of them, however, did anything for his personal status or well being. Socialists approved his views of American capitalists, but they did not buy his book in significant numbers. Scholars found his researches one-sided and inept. As one of them, E. D. Fite, put it in an *American Historical Review*, Myers was unable to find one fortune honestly earned. His book was a compendium of socialist rant, unsupported statements, and simple lack of scholarship.

The book did help to keep Myers employed, and he issued, through Kerr publishers, a *History of the Supreme Court* (1912) and also a *History of Canadian Wealth* (1914), neither of which made so much as a comparable impression. His private circumstances did not improve, according to a correspondence he carried on with a Boston publisher which reprinted articles he had written on psychic happenings, entitled *Beyond the Borderline of Life* (1910). This little book was supposed to have gained Myers a fee of twenty-five dollars, but though he pursued it persistently, it was two years before the publishers finally responded with payment.

More notable in Myers's life was his decision to separate from the Socialist Party. Aside from the Kerr connection, it had done little for him psychically and otherwise. The rising nationalism, thanks to the Mexican and European war situations, doubtless affected his outlook, as did the split in socialist party ranks into right-wing and left-wing sectors. But it was the eloquence of Woodrow Wilson (*q.v.*) and his evident achievements which swayed such socialists and progressives as Upton Sinclair (*q.v.*) and George Creel, and which reached Myers and many others who had had positions out of the mainstream. He announced his break with the past in "Why Idealists Quit the Socialist Party" (*Nation*, February 15, 1917), and shortly after took a job on Creel's Committee on Public Information, the main function of which was to "educate" the public on aims of the war effort. In that same year a new edition of his Tammany Hall book appeared. It was more respectfully received, but made no more impression than before.

Myers's book on *The German Myth: the Falsity of Germany's "Social Progress" Claims* (1919) maintained his established research methods, but reversed results, finding nothing which could be said for the German record. He was now in better material circumstances than he had been, and had entree to such respectable publications as the *New York Times* and *Century*. He does not appear to have suffered any qualms with respect to his methods. He had been right in his scorn of infamous fortunes, and right in justifying the war. Nor did he think of himself, as did Upton Sinclair, as having been deceived by Wilson's "golden, glowing words." His *History of American Idealism* (1925) urged his thesis as earlier books had urged theirs. Franklin D. Roosevelt's New Deal provided him with further evidence of his faith. *America Strikes Back* (1935), his one best-seller, took his usual tack of tracing and refuting foreign criticism.

A Modern Library edition of his *History of the Great American Fortunes* (1936) established it as a "semi-classic," and he followed it up with *The Ending of Hereditary American Fortunes* from which, *Time's* reviewer drily remarked, "leftists [were] not likely to crib." In 1941 he was granted a Guggenheim Fellowship in order to pursue his studies of bigotry, begun in 1921, when he published his most felicitous title, *Ye*

Olden Blue Laws. While completing his history of bigotry he became ill, died, and was buried in New York's Woodlawn Cemetery. His book was published the next year 1943. Almost half a century later, a Gustavus Myers Center was created in Fayetteville, Arkansas with a board of representatives from such organizations as the NAACP and the National Conference of Christians and Jews to publicize Myers's work and reward new writings which studied and exposed bigotry.

Harold L. Ickes
(1874-1952)

Divided Century,
Divided Man

U.S. SECRETARY OF THE Interior under President Franklin D. Roosevelt and Progressive. Harold L. Ickes was famous for his forthright likes and dislikes. He determined honesty in overseeing government contracts, and actions in behalf of the National Park Service and minorities and was an admired "curmudgeon." His legend extended beyond his death. Revelations about his private life bewildered established opinion and counseled silence rather than study and understanding.

Ickes was practically unknown, except in Chicago, until his unexpected appointment as U.S. Secretary of the Interior in 1933, though he had had an eventful life till then. Born the son of a shopkeeper in Altoona, Pennsylvania, he was raised in poverty and under rigid moral principles, before he was able to attend the University of Chicago, work his way up in local journalism, and enter Progressive politics. Always anxious and strenuously employed, he won his D.J. (Doctor of Jurisprudence) degree *cum laude* in 1907 and went on to practice law with a partner, Donald R. Richberg, also a Progressive. They often took civil liberties cases without payment. Richberg later wrote the law for Franklin Roosevelt's National Recovery Administration Act (NRA).

A Theodore Roosevelt Progressive, Ickes chaired the Cook County Progressive party during the critical 1912 election year. With Richberg he continued with the Progressive Party as it declined, bitter against those he saw conspiring to subvert its goals. The life he lived on the surface showed increasing local status which gave his name recognition with such celebrities as Hiram Johnson in California and Theodore Roosevelt nationally. Ickes had a turn in France with the YMCA, serving the 35th Division, A.E.F., during World War I. Ickes and Richberg continued their reformist agitation in the 1920s, Ickes attaining a larger visibility as the aggressive campaign manager to liberal Republicans in Illinois: a fact which Franklin Roosevelt as a liberal Democrat noticed and remembered.

Ickes also gained distinction in 1911 by marrying Anna Wilmarth Thompson of a prominent Chicago family, a woman of wealth and political status previously married to and divorced from a noted historian, James Westfall Thompson. She was known nationally as an advocate of women's rights, as an Illinois legislator, and as trustee of the University of Chicago. Ickes himself joined clubs and made his presence felt with speeches and articles. With his wife, he was visible as an advocate for Indians and conservation.

In 1932 he joined independent Republicans to fight for Franklin D. Roosevelt in his Presidential campaign against Herbert Hoover. Ickes's appointment as U.S. Secretary of the Interior after one of his heroes, Hiram Johnson, had refused the office came as a surprise. It proved to be the only major political breakthrough for old Progressives, Richberg's NRA services substantially expiring with the law itself. Charles Edward Russell, one of the notables of Progressivism, was given an honorary position in the Administration as "consultant," Roosevelt seeking to identify his New Deal with the earlier American reform tradition, but neither Russell nor anyone else other than Ickes of Theodore Roosevelt's era gained new political power.

Critics of the Ickes appointment failed to make a connection between the disastrous Teapot Dome oil scandals of the 1920s and the lag in concern for environment it exposed. Ickes brought to his long-frustrated civic feeling a testiness the edge of which patronage-seekers would learn to feel. Ickes had picked up from his idol Theodore Roosevelt a passion for conservation of natural resources. He began a lengthy reorganization of the National Park Service, and, with his own appointment as administrator of the New Deal fostered Public Works Administration (PWA) pushed conservation further. PWA was intended to help stalled business by creating new public facilities. Although it employed fewer unemployed than the Works Progress Administration (WPA), it did give a stimulus to the use of manufactured materials, the purchase of which Ickes rigidly supervised.

Ickes's labors for government became legendary. He handled all major contracts himself. He kept control of his numerous departments— Office of Indian Affairs, Fish and Wildlife Service, General Land Office, oil—worked for community ownership and minority affairs, and relentlessly fought monopoly pressure. He was criticized for not rigging jobs which would quickly put unemployed on public payrolls, but argued that august projects like the Grand Coulee Dam and the Lincoln Tunnel in New York, military and naval facilities, and the great highway from Mainland Florida to Key West not only encouraged industry, but built for the future. He emerged from quarrels as crotchety, stubborn, close-minded, unfriendly, yet so clearly an ideal public servant as to be indispensable. His offered resignations when not given his way were tabled by Roosevelt.

His publications, too, were picturesque and outspoken. His journalistic experience and decades of speech-making and civic involvement made for detailed and effective writing. *The New Democracy* (1934), *Back to Work: the Story of PWA* (1935), *America's House of Lords: an Inquiry into Freedom of the Press* (1939), and articles and interviews added fire to his program and augmented his reputation as "Honest Harold." Roosevelt, who had liked "the cut of his jib," tolerated Ickes's sharp opinions of people with whom the Administration felt it had to work, and solicited Ickes's presence and viewpoint.

Ickes was an early hater of Nazism and, as Petroleum Coordinator for National Defense (later War) built his reputation further for honesty and authority in a crucial time. Ickes emerged from World War II as one of the best-known among Cabinet members of the Truman Administration. In 1943 Ickes had published his *Autobiography of a Curmudgeon*, which drew wide appreciation. It was dedicated to his second wife, Jane Dahlman Ickes, forty years his junior, his first wife Anna having died in an auto accident in 1935. In his Introduction Ickes had written: "If, in these pages, I have hurled an insult at anyone, be it known that such was my deliberate intent, and I may as well state flatly now that it will be useless and a waste of time to ask me to say that I am sorry."

Ickes was necessarily so bemused by urgent contemporary concerns that one of his campaigns was all but puzzling. It was understandable and in character that he would be outraged by the battle the veteran conservationist Gifford Pinchot waged to resist Ickes's effort to remove Forestry from the Department of Agriculture to his own proposed Department of Conservation. But those informed in Progressivism were taken aback by his attempt to rehabilitate Richard A. Ballinger from the proved charges of attempting to give away valuable Alaska properties to the so-called "Morganheims" (Morgan, Guggenheim) interests. In the process Ickes used extreme invective charging Pinchot with cunning and fraud.

Ickes's featured article on Ballinger, seeing him as "the American Dreyfus," though printed in the *Saturday Evening Post*, made no public impression. Nor did Ickes's further indictment stir interest when published as *Not Guilty: An Official [sic] Inquiry into the Charges Made by Glavis and Pinchot against Richard Ballinger, Secretary of the Interior, 1909-1911* (1940). It did indicate that Ickes was only partially understood by journalists who focussed on passing events, and had less or no interest in Ickes's past.

Ickes resigned his Interior position in 1946, having challenged Truman's nomination of an oil magnate to the post of Under-Secretary of the Navy. Ickes's quarrel did influence the nominee's rejection. Ickes's went on to a distinguished career in journalistic commentary on issues and politics, in newspapers and magazines. He was vigorous in hatred and contempt for the demagogue Joe McCarthy. Ickes's partisanship extended not only into the present, but continued into the past. He chose the *American Historical Review*, a specialized publication, to review his bitterness regarding the Bull Moose Republican Party of 1912-1916, asking "Who Killed the Progressive Party?" and pointing his finger at one known almost entirely to historians, George W. Perkins, a Morgan Partner. Perkins had interested himself in the Progressive fortunes of Theodore Roosevelt, according to Ickes, for machiavellian purposes.

But Ickes's strongest coda to his career lay in having kept highly extensive notes throughout his New Deal years on persons seen, interviewed, and known throughout that time, on events, plans, and programs in which he had participated—all written at length with fluency, details, and clarity, obviously intended for publication. These writings were published in 1953 and 1954 as *The Secret Diary of Harold L. Ickes*, edited by his second wife, and seemed to crown his career with honor and fulfillment. They appeared classical in their fullness and dimensions, and would need only, as several commentators observed, notes and added explication as the decades unfolded further knowledge of the principals and events involved.

This might indeed be an accurate judgment, except that such explication would also apply to Ickes himself. In 1980, a researcher Graham White, having interested himself in Ickes's career, came across a memoir, written by Ickes himself, in the archives of the Library of Congress which so perplexed him that he called upon a psychologist, John Maze, to help him interpret his find. As published in *Harold Ickes of the New Deal: His Private Life and Public Career* (1985), the two set down facts which were appalling. According to Ickes, his life with Anna Wilmarth Thompson Ickes had been loveless and oppressive, at least after her discovery of his affair with another woman whom he had given a job in the Interior, and whose fiancee then husband, also job-endowed, he had sent far away on a long journey to leave the way to his paramour open to himself. Ickes's few references to Anna's last years and death, as published in *The Secret Diary*, had all been "correct" and in known character.

Anna's original will had left everything to Ickes and named him her executor. According to Ickes's own memoir, however, Anna's learning of his affair had caused her to add a codicil to her will, making her son by first marriage, Wilmarth Thompson, her executor and heir. What happened to the codicil is known only from Ickes's account. Anna was indeed turbulent in feelings, but whether she asked that it be destroyed is presently unknown. Ickes received the inheritance. His actions toward Wilmarth are known only in their results. Wilmarth committed suicide a year later, leaving a message that he could no longer live with the treatment he had suffered from his step-father.

This note, intended for Wilmarth's own wife, was turned over by the policeman on the scene to the Chief of Police, then to Ickes himself. As Ickes memorably noted in his own hand: "They [the police] perjured themselves magnificently [*sic*] and I have always felt tremendously grateful to them."

There is a strange similarity between the case of Ickes, and that of another, almost contemporary, which suggests that the subject is larger than might appear on the surface, involving attitudes not only to secret lives, but to public expectations and judgments of life within different eras. In the case of LaFollette (*q.v.*), it can be noted that, for unsettled reasons, there has been a modern historical effort to demean LaFollette, a public icon of the past. This indicates a schism between the general public, which has been untouched by the "revelations" regarding LaFollette, and a specialized academic sector which has found satisfaction in derogating Progressives. Significant figures of the New Deal, some vulnerable to "revisionist" interpretations, have been subjected to no or little neo-muckraking. Aside from strictly political lines of argument, as in the case of Ickes, no major protagonists of a critical school have come forward to raise questions of character among Progressives, which could have reached as far as President Roosevelt himself. For reasons yet to be publicly spelled out, reference sources are silent on matters reflecting on individuals of the era.

A case in point, then, somewhat similar to that involving Ickes, and almost contemporary, would be that of James M. Landis, born a generation later than Ickes in 1899, educated at Princeton and Harvard, a law clerk to Justice Louis D. Brandeis, but by only 1935 chairman of the Securities and Exchange Commission, than Dean of the Harvard Law School, then, among numerous other honors, Director of the Office of Civil Defense, and Special Assistant to the President. In 1963 Landis confounded the law courts by coming before them for failure to file income taxes for a five-year period. He spent most of his thirty-day "sentence" in hospital for a "neurological problem," but the next year a one-year suspension from law practice in New York went into effect. He was found dead shortly after in the swimming pool of his Westchester County home, with no details provided in the press. Although his career was too extensive and significant to evade, conventional references made no attempt to probe its significance.

Landis, however, was no former Progressive with principles founded in national traditions. He had been a product of Twenties self-indulgent prosperity which he was able publicly to control by comporting with liberal principles. Ickes could only overcome his native Progressive principles by separating them from the complex relations and temptations in which affluence had placed him. Those who found his memoir, White and Maze, sought to interpret it in terms of psychology. Unfortunately, psychology deprived of history could only feebly follow the apparently catastrophic pocket in Ickes's character. Those who wanted to forget the memoir deprived Ickes of his right to understanding. They wanted, in short, to forget Progressivism as infringing upon their "new history." But to do so was to distort actual history. This involved not only Ickes, as well as the Landis phenomenon, but the generation of Progressives, many of whose lives also involved bizarre details which helped to round out the human aspects of their major achievements and concerns.

The White, Maze revelations were not beyond controversy. One professional historian thought that Ickes "wanted" readers to know he was a cad and a crook. But the question of just what Ickes "wanted" continues open. His memoirs also included an account of the distorted life he had lived as a "guest" in the Anna Thompson household, and her imperious manipulations of both men's feelings. Ickes's emotional humiliations, both as "guest" and, following her divorce, her husband, had been extreme: so much so that, he wrote in his private memoir, he had hoped not to return from his service with the A.E.F.: death was preferable to once again being whipped up by her taunts so that she could enjoy her ecstasies of triumph. Ickes's extra-marital affair in Washington was not with an innocent woman, but with one who had negotiated a place in his needy, emotional life. The precise details governing the codicil's place in Anna's and her lawyer's keeping was uncertain, and did not allow for quick judgment. Anna may have shifted her position one way or another, dealing as she was not with a manipulable husband, but with the U.S. Secretary of the Interior. Aspects of the matter required further research. As for the distraught Wilmarth, who patently, to his death, expressed malice toward his stepfather: judgment wanted further to be deferred. The Ickes memoir was only at the beginning of its career.

Meanwhile, accounts of Ickes in conventional sources continued inadequate. Although his positive achievements would undoubtedly be recalled, as Americans sought to sum up their century, they would never again be able to maintain the fatuous admiration of Ickes which had previously passed for comprehension.

Ickes's *Secret Diary* also needs to be reconsidered in the light of his revealed memoir, as does his *Autobiography of a Curmudgeon*. His partner Donald R. Richberg's own Progressive memoir, *Tents of the Mighty* (1930) helps throw light on their hopes and disappointments, as, indeed, do many other memoirs. See also H. M. Hooker, ed., *History of the Progressive Party*, by Amos Pinchot (1950), brother of Gifford Pinchot. E. T. James et al., eds. *Notable American Women 1607-1950* Vol. II, (1971), has a careful, though obviously incomplete, sketch of Anna Ickes's life and work. Nothing substantial has yet been added to the White, Maze revelations, either pro or con.

T.H. Watkins, editor of *Wilderness*, and a long time conservationist, in 1990 published a biography of Ickes, *Righteous Pilgrim: The Life and Times of... Ickes*, which set down once and for all the Ickes of conservation, public service, and man of integrity. It made all but nothing of the White, Maze revelations. They await an era concerned once more for the New Deal and its protagonists.

Arthur Ernest Morgan
(1878-1975)

Social Engineer

ENVIRONMENTALIST, PRO-
gressive educator, and theoretician of
community, Arthur Ernest Morgan
achieved in all these fields, which included the creation of the Miami
(Ohio) Conservancy District, a landmark flood control system, precursor
of the Tennessee Valley Authority (TVA), of which he became first chairman. In addition, his revival of the then failing Antioch College as an
experimental institution, a spearhead of the Progressive Education
Association, and his canon of writings and work on community
structure raised questions of how or why he could have been, as he
was, substantially forgotten.

Morgan was the child of St. Cloud, Minnesota parents, his father
being a surveyor and water control artisan whom his wife, of Puritan New
England character, considered a ne'er-do-well because of his easy manners
and drinking. Young Arthur adored his mother and early showed introspective tendencies and a desire to attain her ideal of manhood. This included
high moral standards and public service.

Graduating from the local high school, Morgan went west to
see the world. He saw the World's Fair in Chicago, stopped at Denver
where he viewed its gambling and drinking with distaste, and enrolled
in the University of Colorado. He quickly discovered in himself a

lack of interest in formal study, and returned home where he learned from his father to survey and drain and direct water according to farmers's and community needs.

These pursuits were then in a low state of development, the ample and apparently endless expanses of American terrain scarcely seeming to require them. Nevertheless Morgan was in an era which needed better control of nature. Morgan in Minnesota helped legislators revise state wetlands codes. In 1905 his father retired and he took over his business. Two years later he joined the United States Department of Agriculture as a drainage investigator, and in 1910 formed his own engineering company in Memphis to handle drainage problems for land developers and build canals and levees. This work took his teams from Tennessee to Louisiana, the southwest then being notorious for its untended wetlands. In the course of his work Morgan won legislators in several states to sharpen their land codes so as to curb unscrupulous speculators and incompetent surveyors.

He also observed the inept farming techniques which eroded large stretches of southern land, and evidently learned from Hugh Bennett's (*q.v.*) experiments to protect the top soil against wind and rain by contour tillage and other means. Although Morgan in this era did very well financially he was uninterested in money and lived with great simplicity. He had married and lost a wife by death ten years earlier. In 1912 he married Lucy Griscom, a Quaker and graduate of Wellesley College, who shared many of Morgan's ideals. They worked together for the rest of their lives, Morgan himself associated with Quakers, though not officially of any sect.

In 1913 occurred the great flood of Dayton, Ohio, one of the worst in American history, which did vast damage in the metropolitan area.[1]

The flood drew the energies of the city's leading citizens, notably John H. Patterson and Col. Edward A. Deeds of National Cash Register, who marshalled forces to repel vandals and protect Daytonians. Deeds also raised two million dollars for flood control and recruited Morgan to study the means for obtaining it. Morgan's thorough study of flood experiences at home and abroad resulted in a massive organization of men and equipment. It also gave him his first large opportunity to link related activities for health and civility. He built comfortable places for the workers, and encouraged them to good conduct and even reading. He also maintained an open shop while holding good relations with unions. Dayton was a very conservative town.—during the coming intervention in World War I it would make widely known and notorious to radicals the idea of the "100% American," the title of which Upton Sinclair (*q.v.*) bitterly novelized.

Morgan credited Col. Deeds (left) with the will and determination which resulted in the building of the Miami Conservancy District.

The actual dams and reservoirs were arranged in ways calculated to receive water in orderly and controlled fashion. Morgan created the concept of a dry dam ready for all emergencies, as distinguished from one in use, but capable of taking an estimated overflow. Although this necessarily increased costs, it prepared for the worst, helping the chances for saving lives.

Morgan's vision of the "social engineer" was to crystallize later, but his evolution from engineer to social engineer proceeded from his pragmatic tasks to community service. The Miami Conservancy District was recognized as a milestone in engineering, and made Morgan famous in high circles.

As he had turned from wetlands to flood control on a social level, Morgan now turned to one of his earliest dreams, which was to build a life worth living not for one person but for many. He had as a youth read Edward Bellamy's *Looking Backward*, with its description of a cooperative civilization, and also the much less profound *In His Steps*, by Charles M. Sheldon, a Kansas minister, which was a sensation in the 1890s: a tract in novel form intending to lead people to follow Jesus Christ's example. The novel had the distinction of selling more copies than any book of the time other than the Bible. Morgan was not the most sensitive of readers, and, being self-taught, was capable of serious esthetic errors. But the meaning of a well-lived life seemed clear to him. He and his wife discussed plans for a home and school in which they could carry out their ideas for reasonable education and community.

Morgan began with a school in the Dayton area, to which he and his wife called progressive educators, and in which they carried out experiments of the kind John Dewey had made famous in his Chicago experimental school. Morgan also sought and thought he had found a site in Massachusetts (later Ted Shawn's center for study of the dance) for his projected community. Instead, his attention was called to Antioch College, twenty miles from Dayton. It had been famous under Horace Mann in the 1850s as sponsored by the Christian Church and with an open policy toward women and blacks. It had faded to a degree in the post-Civil War decades, though attracting several notable teachers and supporters. By the end of the century it was at the end of its resources and in 1920 threatened with closing. Morgan now undertook to revive it as a college which insisted on live teaching and learning, with relevance to the present.

Morgan set aside his engineering in favor of social engineering. He helped found the Progressive Education Association, of which he became president. He called for teachers with a realistic sense of their disciplines, and who repudiated rote learning. Morgan instituted a work-study system, which was not quite so new as it then seemed. Horace Mann had also used students as workers, sometimes quite relevant to the teaching and missionary goals of some of them.

Under Morgan work was to be as meaningful as reading. His own experience inclined him toward practical matters, and he found jobs and support from such important people as Charles F. Kettering, inventor of the auto-generator and the self-starter and president and general manager of the General Motors Research Corporation. But he also sought out leading educators, including John Dewey, for furthering his and his students's aspirations. Horace Mann's towers—once the highest in Ohio—vibrated with students's lighter moments, but they also heard endless debates and discussions over goals in life and means for attaining them.

Much that Morgan himself projected for his school disappointed him, especially as related to moral commitment, but Antioch enjoyed a fame such as it had not had since Mann's time. It was an inspiration to other progressives who moved in areas which little concerned Morgan, like the arts and world affairs. However, when the challenge came to tame the Tennessee River and make its rapids and dangerous turns less threatening to those who used it or lived in flood range he responded to it.

Morgan did not so much flee a failed educational experiment, as his critics alleged. Morgan was critical of others, but he was also critical of himself and was aware that he was not a charismatic personality. To some degree he was envious of those who were and as a result made mistakes in judging the worth of some individuals. But such ruminations were not central in his thought, and certainly not in his results. Strategic was the fact that he had set certain educational factors working which could affect his own site, or others. Experimental study programs (notably "independent study") grew in many colleges, as did "work-study" programs. He was not bound by any one experiment.

The Tennessee Valley Authority was a product of Senator George W. Norris's solicitude for the natural resources he saw tied into the Tennessee River's great flow. The government during World War I had begun a dam at Muscle Shoals to generate power for much-needed nitrogen. Found unnecessary, the project was left unfinished. Its potential was seen by Henry Ford's people, who offered to make it a site for private industry. Norris saw the Tennessee River as a national heritage which should not be given away, and he saved it for the nation.

A decade later the new President Franklin D. Roosevelt, fighting the Depression and seeking to open job opportunities and tie them with hope-breeding messages to a desperately needy public hit upon the Tennessee Valley as involving more than only a dam or even several dams which could cut ravages on farms and people when "flood seasons" came. Electricity and much else could be generated to build the dignity and wealth of the region. Government service, flood control, ideals of community—all came together to suggest Arthur Ernest Morgan for the task.

The years 1933 to 1936 were the fruitful years of Morgan's TVA chairmanship. He laid elaborate plans for the dams, but also for the towns which were to benefit from the waterpower. As he had shown concern for his workers at Dayton, he took account of the needs—as he saw them—of the people who lived along the Tennessee River. He helped choose his colleagues on the supervising board, Harcourt A. Morgan (no relative), university president and agricultural expert, and young David E. Lilienthal, protege of Supreme Court Justice Felix Frankfurter, the LaFollettes in Wisconsin, and of Senator Norris.

There were political problems, with which Morgan was impatient. Paradoxically, a crucial disagreement between Morgan and his associates involved Wendell Willkie of the Commonwealth and Southern, which supplied power to some of the people in the region, though with little ambition to expand services. Morgan himself had long been suspicious of the public service concerns of vast corporations. He should then have been at one with Harcourt Morgan and Lilienthal, who believed that public power should be expanded, with Commonwealth and Southern adjusting its capacities to those created by government pricing and improvements.

But now Arthur Morgan was persuaded that Willkie was sincerely progressive in his willingness to cut his company's profits in favor of help to the tens of thousands in the state who had never known electricity in their homes, and who needed help to obtain it. Private industry, Morgan thought, should take precedence over government.

Moreover, Morgan would have expanded education to farmers, cultural as well as practical, in effect obtruding upon their very life-styles, which involved traditional preferences in home living and entertainment, as well as farming methods and products. One congressman read condescension and patronage into Morgan's program which he denounced as offensive.

A curiosity of Morgan's "chairmanship" which he had encouraged in his democratic faith—was that as chairman he had no more rights or perquisites than either of his colleagues. He could thus be outvoted on every issue, and he was. There can be no question but that he became paranoid, particularly as others among the top executives of TVA massed in support or sympathy with Morgan's opponents. This crisis continued into 1937, when President Roosevelt, in a series of distressing incidents, felt constrained to drop Morgan from all connection with TVA.

From a ready point of high visibility, Morgan's "major" career was over at the age of sixty; but from the standpoint of service and ideas, a valuable era lay before him. For practical purposes, his career at Antioch College was over. New administrations took over, undertaking "experiments" which did not touch on his goals. He continued to focus on rational approaches—he had no concept of the irrational in human behavior—which would bring harmony and results to the wider sections of society. As Progressives had seen the family as the basic unit of happiness and self-fulfillment, Morgan saw the small town as the independent integer which kept society free and creative.

In 1944 he published a major work on Edward Bellamy, whose *Looking Backward* was often seen as a "utopia," but which had actually—a novel—spurred the movement which created the famous Populist Platform of 1892, much of which was later written into law. Many in the 1930s noted that the New Deal seemed to follow Bellamy's logic and demands in some detail.

To some, Morgan's book seemed a mere expression of admiration for Bellamy's work; but they missed the point, though clearly expressed.

To Morgan *Looking Backward*, and Its follow-up novel *Equality*, was an experimental plan for better times, or what he termed a *pilot plant*. Morgan had experience with pilot plants; before the Miami Conservancy dams had been erected, he had built them in miniature, with actual water piped through the tiny sluices to show how they would react to material conditions. Morgan had conceived of his college as a "pilot plant" for others to observe. So the Bellamy plan loomed in his mind: as a first draft for future action, a projection meriting study.

Similarly original was Morgan's *Nowhere Was Somewhere* (1946), which conjectured that Thomas More's *Utopia* was in fact not a "utopia" at all, but an actual account of an early exploration which had taken ad venturers, perhaps driven from course by winds and tides, across the sea to Peru. It had already puzzled scholars that More's book contained descriptions which fitted Peru, but that it had been written *before* Peru was officially discovered. All this gave Morgan a chance to analyze the Peruvian civilization as he had Bellamy's, in a book which is yet to be seriously examined.

In his first decade following his TVA service Morgan involved himself deeply in the details of small-town organization, and received numerous calls to address civic bodies about their problems and the nation's. This did not create a new career for him, but he did not seek one and was content to live, as he always had, the life of simplicity. He initiated a community school at Celo, North Carolina. In 1948-1949 he served on a University Education Committee in India, his recommendations resulting in the establishment of rural universities directed at improving Indian rural living and agriculture.

At home he initiated projects for "green belts," care for the elderly, and the use of local properties which made his Ohio town of Yellow Springs in some ways better known to civic groups than the college itself. He worked vigorously from 1957 through 1960 to stop a Corps of Engineers plan to flood Seneca Indian land in Pennsylvania in behalf of a dam they wished to construct, Morgan urging that an alternative plan could be found. Although he was defeated in this crusade, it furnished him with the inspiration for a book which combined engineering history and social purpose, *Dams and Other Disasters: a Century of the Army Corps of Engineers in Civil Works* (1971), written when Morgan was ninety-three. His last book, published three years later, *The Making of the T.V.A.* showed him with his head high and vision unshaken. Although it failed to interest the general public and journalists of the day, it was also true that TVA

The building of the Miami Conservancy District, precursor to the Tennessee Valley Authority.

itself was no longer in the news. Both could await the larger judgments of history.

Morgan left a large canon of writings, biographical and regarding his enterprises. Several merit mention: *My World* (1928); *The Small Community, Foundation of Democratic Life (1942); The Miami Conservancy District* (1951); and, for his educational work in India, *The Rural University* (1950). Three studies present interpretations of Morgan, two by Antioch-associated writers: Clarence J. Leuba, *A Road to Creativity* (1971) and Walter Kahoe, *Arthur Morgan: a Biography and Memoir* (1977). Roy Talbert, Jr, *FDR's Utopian: Arthur Morgan of the TVA* (1987) is highly documented, but fixed on a dubious "utopian" concept which equates Morgan's life with failure. See also Carl M. Becker and Patrick B. Nolan, *Keeping the Promise* (1988), which vividly recaptures the flood of 1913, and the building of the Miami Conservancy District.

NOTES:

1. So severe was it that associated floods in the Great Miami River complex were relatively little noticed. A modern masterpiece, Helen Hooven Santmyer's... *And Ladies of the Club* (1982) devotes some pages to the effect of flood waters in nearby Xenia, Ohio.

Upton Sinclair
(1878-1968)

Crusade
for Socialism

HE WAS A SOUTHERN AUTH-
or and socialist, whose active years
touched American life at many
points, and whose influence was felt around the world. Although much
of his impact diminished or declined when age encouraged him to retire,
he left a residue likely to engage scholars who did not separate culture
and society.

The basic fact of his life—wholly ignored in his lifetime—was that he
was of a southern tradition which gave him an objective view of the disorder
in northern states. His people had been naval officers. Sinclair's father failed
in the Navy and became a salesman in New York: a weak, gentle man, according to Sinclair, who could not resist drink. Sinclair's mother had been a Baltimore belle, raised for ladylike activities which withered in dreary New York
tenements. From time to time she took her boy to visit her and her husband's
spacious homes in Baltimore and Virginia, where the contrast was permanently written on his mind.

He proved to be a bright and firmly moral child who graduated gram-
mar school at twelve and had to be accommodated in classes before he undertook a combined high school and college curriculum. At age fifteen he sold a
story to the popular magazine *Argosy*, and found his vocation as a writer.

Thereafter he was the support of his mother with pulp paper novels for Street and Smith, novels of derring-do. There were often to be noted by critics as allegedly giving him his "simplistic" style of writing. It was not realized that Sinclair, as a dedicated romantic, sincerely believed in the high code of principles his pulp-paper heroes maintained. In time he was to learn the world's ways and to gear his idealism with reality.

He took his high ambitions into the twentieth century, having run through City College of New York and learned independently the gamut of disciplines pursued at Columbia University. He did this by beginning courses, acquiring the syllabi, then transferring to other

Serving on the Monitor: Sinclair's grandfather in background and a comrade

courses free of charge, meanwhile studying the contents of language, history, philosophy, and other subjects while writing his Street and Smith yarns and also dispensing and collecting tickets on a city street car.

Finally finding his mundane labors intolerable Sinclair took his new Shelleyan idealism into serious fiction. His first efforts were rebuffed, and having kept a journal of his frustrations, he had it published as real, printing an item in the newspapers that its author had committed suicide. *The Journal of Arthur Stirling* (1903) won him the notoriety he needed, but still did not establish him as a novelist. *Manassas*, his historic effort on the Civil War, did not sell. Living in the country on borrowed money with a young wife, Meta Fuller Sinclair, and child, and having "discovered" socialism, he practiced austere living and the violin, while his wife was kept busy at idealistic labors worthy of himself.

Laborers working under the harsh and nauseating conditions in the Chicago stockyards had fought and lost a strike against their packing house employers. It occurred to the editor of the Socialist *Appeal to Reason* that there was a proper theme for a novel, which he commissioned Sinclair to write. *The Jungle* was torn off at white heat after seven weeks spent in the stockyards in 1904 observing and working under its oppressive conditions. It was published in part in the *Appeal to Reason*. David Graham Phillips (*q.v.*), himself just then building his career in fiction, and reading installments in the *Appeal*, wrote Sinclair an unsolicited letter of earnest appreciation Sinclair never forgot. Faced with the constricted publishing practices of the time, and tailoring the book to them, Sinclair created an air of notoriety which could not be quelled. As published by Doubleday, Page and Company in 1906 (the same company which had unsuccessfully published Theodore Dreiser's (*q.v.*) *Sister Carrie*—the edited version of *The Jungle* opened wide a scandal in impure food production which resulted in passage of the historic Pure Food and Drug Act of the same year.

The continuing fame of Sinclair's first masterpiece has obscured the fact that three generations of readers passed over remarkable pages which were never challenged in any language in which it was read. A feature of the great strike at Packingtown had been the black strike-breakers the Beef Trust owners had called in to keep their plants operating. Sinclair, with his southern background, had no problem in seeing them as they were: brutal laborers who carried knives and drew Chicago prostitutes to join them in their rough sports. They were an embarrassment to both the white "comrades" who dominated the socialist movement and who ignored the social problems the blacks represented, and to respectable blacks seeking equity in society.

Sinclair himself was sincere in his socialist professions, but the banners he held up for thirty and more years represented a crusade led by whites which was intended to serve all others as well.

Sinclair's next several years were filled with events which kept his life and career turbulent. He put the money which poured in from *The Jungle* into an idealistic commune in New Jersey he called Helicon Hall. There, inhabitants were to work and refine ideals. It attracted noted visitors and such tenants as Sinclair Lewis, then a Yale graduate seeking a path. Helicon Hall earned a name in annals of the time, though it burned down the next year. Harry Kemp as a college boy had written Sinclair and been welcomed into his home. He ran away with Sinclair's wife. Kemp went on to write verses which chanted freedom, but put him closer to the Richard Hovey of *Songs from Vagabondia* than to Walt Whitman. He later became a Cape Cod character. Sinclair's former wife called Sinclair publicly "an essential monogamist," as though, Sinclair commented, there was something wrong with that.

Sinclair began a long career of informal comment to readers about his life and views, but in addition he sought seriously for durable prose. *Samuel the Seeker* (1910) had a Voltairesque brightness, but failed to capture attention. *Love's Pilgrimage* (1911) sought to pin down his mystic faith in enduring love, without his eye-catching novelistic techniques. *Sylvia* (1913) and *Sylvia's Marriage* (1941) again sought a contemplative prose, and in addition broke ground with the startling introduction of gonorrhea. Here Sinclair followed Ibsen, who had brought on stage the diseased spectre of *Ghosts*. Sinclair's canon of writings still remained enigmatic.

King Coal (1917) was less promising. It no more than reminded the reader—who needed no reminder—of the ugly war in the coal regions of Colorado several years back which had cost not only miners's and company deaths, but those of laborers's women and children. Sinclair's unveiling of these events was shallow in comparison with the reality. Closer to reality was Sinclair's story of *Jimmie Higgins* (1919), the socialist name for their rank and file workers, humble in talents but steadfast in principles. For Sinclair by 1919 had passed with numerous friends through the fires of American intervention in World War I. He had seen the Socialist Party split into pacifists and revolutionaries on one hand, and President Wilson (*q.v.*) supporters on the other. He himself had joined Wilson in his "crusade for democracy." Disillusioned with war's results, Sinclair's *100%: the Story of a Patriot* (1920) sought to make amends to those who had suffered from the brutality of unbridled "patriots."

These events, and the Bolshevik victory in Russia, did not lose Sinclair his following in the 1920s. This was because of the unfolding of a literature of skepticism which not only took in socialists, but such anti-patriots as H. L. Mencken. Sinclair had already instituted what many called his "great pamphlet" series: a survey of American establishments, aiming to show them as dominated by the great American corporations: *The Profits of Religion* (1918); *The Brass Check* (1919), analyzing native journalism; *The Goose Step* (1923), examining American education; *The Gostlings* (1924), American schools; *Mammonart* (1925) and *Money Writes!* (1927). With satire and anecdotes Sinclair strove to show these basic disciplines of life curbed and strangled by mercenary forces.

Were his charges true? Had he pilloried American misleaders for the future to condemn? Till World War II his thick, many-paged pamphlets circulated in great numbers from Sinclair's very own press as his defiance of a capitalist civilization. He found pious leaders in the church who showed no mercy to tenants in church-owned tenements. He caught the *New York Times* in patent falsehoods regarding American union leaders and the Soviet Union. Using irony and indignation, he scorned leaders in education for hounding such manifest men of learning and courage as Scott Nearing, and mercenary writers who were pampered by affluent editors, while educators and writers of talent suffered suppression and outcast status.

The problem lay in Sinclair's equation of money with falsehood: the "economic interpretation." There was falsehood and suppression also in socialist news and education. He himself, for all his hatred of liquor which had blighted his childhood, for many years helped hide the fact that Eugene V. Debs, a socialist "saint," had a liquor problem, among other party scandals. Sinclair was partly gullible, partly not candid in not noticing the excesses of cruelty practiced by Soviet masters.

Separating truth from falsehood even before unions gained over-bearing power and socialist regimes made an art of falsifying the news was a discipline requiring independence and intensive search for right and wrong. The limitations of Sinclair as pamphleteer were the limitations of his sympathetic readers.

Those limitations were revealed when he sought to raise funds for a press which would truly correct the errors or distortions of the "kept" press, the "indoctrination" of schools and churches, the false art of fiction writers. Sinclair waged his campaign for several years, then gave it up. Obviously it was the public itself, his cordial readers and acolytes, who failed to deliver the money and talent wanted for his dream of unadulterated truth to take on reality.

Meanwhile his personal art and life continued. He had married a Mississippi belle, Mary Craig Kimbrough, whose spirit matched his own, and set up a permanent home in Pasadena, California. There he poured out a constant stream of world-wide correspondence and debating matter, as well as the fiction which was to be his bid for posterity's attention. During the 1920s his major efforts were recognized as being, first, *Oil!* (1927), a novel inspired by the Teapot Dome scandal. It temperately probed the character of an oil producer in the field and the various personalities who peopled western life. Sinclair's control of events made for a picture of Twenties living to which later readers could turn and feel enlightened.

The next year Sinclair issued a two-volume *Boston* in similar temper, but dealing with the case of the anarchists Sacco and Vanzetti who had died in the electric chair the year before having, as H. G. Wells put it, walked to their doom for seven long years. The problem, which Sinclair then assumed did not exist, was to determine whether they were or were not innocent of the payroll murder of which they were accused. Did Sinclair's interlarded fiction affirming their blamelessness merit suspension of reality? Later evidence created a veil of doubt.

Worth noting in a study of Sinclair's art was Sinclair's four-act drama, *Singing Jailbirds* (1924) as effectively using expressionistic techniques, but also in its excellence calling attention to Sinclair's numerous other writings in drama, short fiction, and other fields which might stimulate readers to broaden their sense of what Sinclair had accomplished in his long life.

The 1930s saw him working to turn his fame into political credit, running for Congress and the governorship of California. In the trying years of the Thirties he was able to reach voters more seriously. Creating the concept of EPIC ("End Poverty in California") he became one of many messiahs who promised to lead the desperate and despairing into the promised land. His remedies were only what, as a socialist, he had offered all his active life: production for use, work for the needy; but in 1934 he posed a threat to the established order by winning the Democratic nomination for governor. Although he was defeated, it is likely that the threat he and other challengers represented pushed President Franklin D. Roosevelt into further New Deal commitments.

Sinclair had always been an exponent for rational living and inquiry into unestablished territory, and all his explorations resulted in books, such as *A Home Colony* (1906), *Good Health and How We Won It* (1909), *The Fasting Cure* (1911), and *What God Means to Me* (1936). His *Mental Radio* (1930) involved explorations which reached beyond the corporeal frame, and, with age, more and more took his attention. He was persuaded that his wife was able to make contact with other minds, and his examples of projected vision were impressive to professionals in mental fields. He himself came to believe that the mind had an independent existence, and would survive, at least for a time. Albert Mordell (*q.v.*) who contemplated writing a book about Sinclair, and who was a weathered skeptic, was unconvinced. To Mordell, Sinclair put the question: "What would you say, if Einstein found our experiments impressive?" (As he had.) Mordell's response was: "I would then look into Einstein."

By the 1940s Sinclair had lost much interest in lesser controversies, and was retrospective in his outlook. He still had his ability to view recent events as substance for novelistic treatment, and conceived the idea of a special agent who would have secret dealings with matters of major importance. This was actually his oldest idea, his 1904 *Manassas* having brought into one canvas not only Abraham Lincoln and the soldiery of the Civil War, but all other major protagonists. He had also a number of times used a specially-endowed upper class agent, to whom the problems of the world would come as a revelation, as they often had to Sinclair himself.

So began the "Lanny Budd" series of novels, into which Sinclair poured the reading and information of a lifetime, to carry his hero into world-ranging scenes and situations. Upton Sinclair had his last bestsellers, this time in six stately volumes of fiction: *World's End*, *Between Two Worlds*, *Dragon's Teeth*, *Wide Is the Gate*, *Presidential Agent*, and *Dragon Harvest*. Intellectuals's responses ranged from irony to ill-concealed contempt, but Sinclair himself believed he had been born to write the series, and hardly followed their comments. An interesting comparison could be made between his series and the later conservative William F. Buckley, Jr.'s "Blackford Oakes" series of novels.

Following his wife's death, Sinclair married again and quietly moved into retirement, into his eighties still straight and good-humored, photographed smiling next to his books, piled to the ceiling. He lived in a nursing home, to be nearer to his married son, Daniel. In his last year, left alone by the death of his third wife, he could be seen still smiling, in a wheel chair.

Sinclair wrote several autobiographies, and his second wife, Mary Craig Kimbrough Sinclair one, *Southern Belle* (1957); he issued a memorial volume of the work in 1962. His papers went to the Lilly Library, Indiana University, where two bibliographical volumes were soon produced; he had published one of his own as early as the 1930s. Numerous books included chapters devoted to him. An interesting comparison can be made between Floyd Dell's *Upton Sinclair: a Study in Social Protest* (1927), Dell having been a companion of Randolph Bourne (*q.v.*), and Leon Harris, *Upton Sinclair: American Rebel* (1975). In 1988 was published a new edition of *The Jungle*, after accident revealed a mass of papers which restored the one-third additional material of the original manuscript.

Vachel Lindsay
(1879-1931)

"I Am the Gutter Dream"

Vachel Lindsay was poet of the Progressive Era, much more so than Edwin Markham (*q.v.*) though not perceived as such because of a time factor. Born and raised in Abraham Lincoln's Springfield, Illinois, Lindsay acquired a populist dream of a singing, sensitive people receptive to poetry, and, from his family, a belief that evangelical religion was a well-spring of beauty.

He attended Hiram College in Ohio and art school in Chicago, and taught in YMCA programs, but felt drawn to meeting people face to face with his message, especially in the rural settings of his upbringing. Later in the 1900s he undertook tramps in the countryside, from Illinois to New Mexico and through most of the southern states seeking to persuade housewives and farmers of what became his Gospel of Beauty. These journeys are memorialized in his *The Tree of Laughing Bells* (1905), which he distributed, and *Rhymes to Be Traded for Bread* (1912). He also developed what became his platform manner, of dramatic reading, accompanied with gestures and postures of various kinds intended to reflect those of the people from whom he learned.

Moving into the 1910s, Lindsay made contact with poetry journals of the newer generation of youth, which was moving rapidly away from Progressive attitudes toward bohemian goals and a new individualism and elitism.

Lindsay, open to more democratic intonations and rhythms, was actually more advanced in them than most of the younger poets, embracing as he did Negro, popular preacher, dancing, and rural rhythms. His poem "General Booth Enters into Heaven" caught the just-deceased evangelist's ecstatic vision, and lifted to popular visibility the idea of poetry as it had not been since Markham's "The Man with the Hoe" had literally gone around the world. Lindsay's book, headed with "General Booth" as the title poem in 1913 established Lindsay's vocation. It was augmented by *The Congo and Other Poems* (1914), with the title poem's astonishing invocation of Negro rhythms and other verses reflecting American ballads and folk heroes. His poems also included such more austere masterpieces as "The Eagle That Is Forgotten," remembering John P. Altgeld, Progressive governor of Illinois, and, in the second volume, "Abraham Lincoln Walks at Midnight."

The success of his books promised good things for poetry and himself. It brought him before a new youth which proclaimed itself ready for explorations of the human psyche, and even before some of their elders who were preaching for a more open society.

All but stunning was Lindsay's total engagement with General Booth as

> He saw King Jesus. They were face to face,
> And he knelt a-weeping in that holy place.
> Are you washed in the blood of the Lamb?

Others who the poem amazed could, if only for the poetic moment, catch from Lindsay his awed and hallowed feeling. They could vibrate to his tremendous energy as in his invocation of "Bryan, Bryan, Bryan," though the stirring elections of 1896 were now far away, and Bryan less of the leader and inspiration that he had been in that year.

With Lindsay, they could wake in the night to "The Ghost of the Buffaloes," as they had once thundered across the Plains, and join the Plains Indians as

> They rode long-horn cattle, they cried "A-la-la"
> They lifted the knife, the bow, and the spear,
> They lifted ghost-torches from dead fires below,
> The midnight made grand with the cry "A-la-la"...

Johnny Appleseed... John L. Sullivan... the Bronco That would not be Broken... And the college yell, which Lindsay turned into—transformed—into "The Kallyope Yell:"

> Proud men
> Eternally
> Go about,
> Slander me
> Call me the "Calliope"
> Sizz...
> Fizz...
>
> I am the Gutter Dream
> Tune-maker, born of steam,
> Tooting joy, tooting hope.
> I am the Kallyope.
> Willy willy willy way HOO!—

and on and on till;

> Prophet-singers will arise,
> Prophets coming after me,
> Sing my song in softer guise
> With more delicate surprize;
> I am but the pioneer
> Voice of the Democracy...
>
> Whoop whoop, whoop, whoop
> Willy willy willy wah HOO!
> Sizz...
> Fizz...

Although Lindsay now had entree to poetry and intellectual circles he was in fact a product of older schools. His attempt to find a soul in the new motion picture world resulted in no more than an oddity along his tragic path. *The Art of the Motion Picture* (1951), like his immature emotional fancies regarding the actresses he met, no more than revealed his light grasp of reality. This was also true of his later *The Golden Book of Springfield* (1920) which imagined a utopia where there was in fact a political machine, in a community subject to trends which were rapidly transforming what he recalled from his childhood. But before then Lindsay published his *The Chinese Nightingale and Other Poems* (1917), with its immortal title poem and such other memorable ones as "The Ghost of the Buffaloes," which recalled the prairies before they had been trampled by determined adventurers.

Ludwig Lewisohn, in his once-admired but academically rejected *Expression in America* (1931) thought that Lindsay was evidence that a poet must believe something, even if it be nonsense, but this no more than patronized a well-based talent. Lindsay's best poems caught the spirit of a people he knew, who had been sustained in hardship and struggle for advancement—later called "upward mobility"—by a faith in the benign purposes of life and in the destiny of their country as a leader of nations. This faith was tested by Lindsay's career as a spokesman for his people.

He had a living to earn, and moved into giving poetry recitals mainly under college English Department auspices and before women's clubs and gatherings. His excited deliveries of his most famous poems, notably "The Congo," which everyone then wanted to hear, with its vivid sketches of African blacks "pounding on the table, /beat[ing] an empty barrel with the handle of a broom," his vaudeville motions and inflections provided thrills to otherwise bored students and matrons. It soon became evident that Lindsay's Gospel of Beauty was a lost cause among them. Lindsay endured a decade of such labors before economic depression made audiences even less receptive to aesthetic messages which did not speak to material gain and political solutions new to poetry.

Meanwhile Lindsay had himself been impressed by times which swiftly changed from war to prosperity then to a new realism and newer naturalism. The easy camaraderie of pre-war Greenwich Village in New York and the Midway of Chicago had become more formalized as publishers, theater groups, and even lecture circuits rose in social status and financial consequence. Friends and acquaintances outstripped Lindsay in audience response and influence. The Twenties were a time which linked Edwin Arlington Robinson and Robert Frost as stars in poetry. Edna St.Vincent Millay was wider read than any of them and more visible, as were Carl Sandburg and—striking a new and adverse note—T. S. Eliot.

Lindsay could no longer conjure up the enthusiasm which had enabled him to bring to life the Anti-Saloon League as well as the Democratic National Convention which nominated William Jennings

The poet before life deserted him.

Bryan, the call to Armageddon with which Theodore Roosevelt had thrilled the nation, The Calliope, "tooting hope, tooting hope, tooting hope," and the shade of Johnny Appleseed moving across Ohio and Indiana scattering seeds to make apple trees which had inspired his own wanderings. Lindsay had always been something of a child, and now, though himself a family man with children of his own, he wrote children's poems which critics, staying abreast of current sophistication, saw not as having their own realm of reality, but as a falling off from earlier poems which were now less read than before. Some seemed remote. Others, like "The Congo," had the potential for offending ideologists, who smelled "racism" everywhere.

Lindsay became paranoid. With no talents for social adjustment, with politics and metaphysical verse turning attention from him, Lindsay suffered insecurities which extended to his own wife. He had nowhere to go or look. He swallowed Lysol; a searing death which did not come soon enough. His last words were: "They tried to get me. I got them first." He was buried in Oak Ridge Cemetery, December 7, 1931. Mark Harris's *City of Discontent* (1952), about Lindsay and his world, was insightful and empathetic. Edgar Lee Masters's *Vachel Lindsay: a Poet in America* (1935), though by a friend who had also written unforgettable poems, suffered from Masters's own frustrations and bitterness.

Ahead lay more catastrophes. Robinson and Frost died in the good regard of scholars and neighbors. The Youth uprising of the 1960s shook the scholars and emptied the neighbors of poetry, leaving it in the hands of a new elite which practiced "self-expression" as poetry. For a summary of their principles, Elizabeth Hardwick, "Wind from the Prairies," *New York Review"*, *September 26, 1991*, which demeans not only Lindsay, but for good measure Carl Sandburg and Edgar Lee Masters as jinglers and non-poets.

Hugh Hammond Bennett
(1881-1960)

"Father of Soil Conservation"

HUGH HAMMOND BENNETT was a public servant of the kind which rarely struck the general imagination. Yet, as in the famous phrase commemorating Sir Christopher Wren, entombed in St. Paul's Cathedral, if one wished to see Bennett's monument, he had merely to stand in any well-kept farming expanse in America to feel his presence.

Bennett was born in North Carolina on his father's large but badly eroded farm which supported his many children and others. Young Bennett never forgot the rude farming implements the family and workers laboriously employed to draw a living from the exhausted land. Raised tall, spare, and strong, like one of many poor families of the time, "Big Hugh" labored over-time to acquire the money to advance his education. He entered the University of North Carolina in 1897, had his stay there was interrupted for two years while he worked to gain further funds. In 1903 he won his degree in chemistry.

Beginning with work as a surveyor of soils in the U.S. Department of Agriculture, Bennett never looked back. A friendly, endlessly energetic man, Bennett not only found soils fascinating—he ultimately knew all soils, in the country and abroad—but was an evangelist in imparting the messages for farmers and experts they contained. His goal was to save the land, badly worn wherever it had been mishandled by lumbermen and one-crop farmers who had girdled trees to kill them, planted tobacco, and otherwise removed natural protections from the soil.

By 1906 Bennett was soil scientist in his Bureau of Soils, administering surveys which ultimately took him across the country, talking to everyone he encountered and storing up their complaints and experiences. In 1909 he became supervisor of soil surveys, and made the first of his numerous visits abroad, working with others to determine soil needs in the Panama Canal Zone. Bennett returned often to Central America with a committee concerned for a boundary dispute between Honduras and Guatemala, and, in 1923-24 for rubber-producing soils in Ecuador, Venezuela, and Brazil. Earlier he had explored Alaskan soils as a preliminary step to the building of the government-owned Alaska Railroad. He later helped with setting up of the Territory's Chugach National Forest.

Bennett's main concern was building a program of soil conservation which would be a continuing process of soil maintenance, there being none in the United States when he began his work. He saw precious topsoil with its natural minerals being continuously washed away through rains and on inclined planes, and pondered means for maintaining it under natural conditions. Needing laws to establish scientific measures, Bennett employed dramatic devices to reach the imagination of those who could help him to establish policy in soil conservation. Thus, addressing an assembly, he would lay a towel upon a table, pour water over it, then tilting it by two corners let the spectators see the water run off to the floor. Bennett promoted for America contour tillage, which became a staple of farming, its irregular lines preventing water from accumulating in a run-off. He also explored mulches which held in the earth and kept water from dislodging it.

His greatest coup took place in 1935 when he sought Congressional approval for a bill for the first time establishing a soil conservation service. Bennett seems to have taken inordinate steps to determine when a dust storm might reach Washington, where he was to testify before a Senate committee on the urgency of the proposal, it having been a year which had created havoc on farms. His dust storm reaching the Capitol on time and darkening the chamber created a sensation. His Public Law 46 was passed into law in record time. Bennett was made chief of the Department of Agriculture's new Soil Conservation Service.

Bennett was now able to accomplish what he had worked for: to establish soil conservation as a matter of national policy, to be administered under government direction by trained personnel. It was a far cry from 1928 when, by earnest argument, he had managed to persuade Congress to grant him $100,000 for work on erosion problems. He now drew up 1700 Soil Conservation Districts, with a program to differentiate their needs and expand means for ministering to them. Although his work had touched numerous individuals and areas over the years, it had taken a major drought and a critical economic depression to enable him to further his cause.

Bennett himself never let up in his study of soil conditions at home and abroad. His own home, "Eight Oaks," outside Falls Church, Virginia, was a model of farm care. Bennett's fame was strictly limited. Although he was sometimes seen as dour and over-concerned for soil, he was in fact a cheerful, friendly person, interested in people as well as land. Active to the end, he died of cancer, July 7, 1960.

Bennett himself wrote much, his articles, speeches, and official reports helping to trace his career. Thus, his collaborative *The Soils of Cuba* (1928) spoke of its people, as well as of the sugar they grew; one of its problems was transient workers who, permitted to grow their own food would be less likely to wander away from steady employment. Bennett's own book, *Soil Conservation* (1939), reflects his style as well as substance. Wellington Brink, his colleague and biographer, in *Big Hugh: The Father of Soil Conservation* (1951) brings out the picturesque in his crusade. See also D. Harper Simms, *The Soil Conservation Service* (1970). Bennett's career in some ways complements the first part of that of Arthur E. Morgan (*q.v.*) and others of a social service, Progressive generation.

Grenville Clark
(1882-1967)

Prophet of World Order

Gᴿᴱᴺⱽᴵᴸᴸᴱ CLARK
was both a patriot and
peace advocate, whose long civic services were all but unique in his time. Born of and reared by a wealthy liberal New York family, he attended Harvard University and its law school, where his friends included the later Supreme Court justice Felix Frankfurter.

Clark completed his graduate studies in law in 1906, then entered the New York law firm of Carter, Ledyard & Milburn, in which Franklin D. Roosevelt also performed as clerk. In law Clark was a "generalist," in time taking fraud, real estate, bankruptcy, and insurance cases. He was soon known for his persistence and energy in his work. It more than made up for his relatively moderate legal distinction. Tall, charismatic, and determined, with a formidable jaw, he rose quickly in his profession. In 1909 he and old college friends set up their own firm. It included Elihu Root, Jr., son of the U. S. Secretary of State. A second partner, Francis W. Bird, interested Clark in Republican and Bull Moose politics.

The country in 1914 faced the challenge of what was then the European War, with a military establishment which lagged in many departments. Under-financed by Congress, it still used cannon for its training and maneuvers which had seen service in the Civil War. Clark saw the need for private initiative if the nation was to heed former-President Theodore Roosevelt's call for military preparedness. A friend of Major-General and Chief of Staff Leonard Wood, Clark planned to warn the public of what he saw as a national emergency. Together and with others, he and Wood set up the Military Training Camps Association, of which Clark became president. In a time of President Woodrow Wilson (*q.v.*) neutrality, the Association earned some popular distaste as provocative, designed by men of wealth for class purposes.

The Plattsburg (New York) Training Camp entered into history as representative of the "Preparedness" movement, even though the Association spread its camps around the country and trained an estimated 80 percent of later combat officers. Still later the Association became the Reserve Officers Training Corps (ROTC).

A lieutenant colonel in the Adjutant General's Office, Clark undertook to direct the recruiting and training of 130,000 technicians for army service. When President Wilson himself joined the preparedness effort, Clark was among those justified by events. But his mind was already on the anticipated peace which, like Wilson, he planned to make secure. He emerged from the war to become for almost half a century the most vigorous figure in America to seek guarantees for world peace, outside radical perspectives.

During the 1920s and 1930s Clark explored legal means for pledging nations to seek peaceful solutions to international problems. He also, however, sought political alliances which would curb the actions of international adventurers. With the League of Nations an evident failure, his major hope lay in Clarence Streit's "Union Now" proposal, which would have drawn together free nations into a compulsory union, limiting sovereignty when necessary and enforcing peace.

Among major figures Clark interested in this view were John Foster Dulles, Henry L. Stimson, Christian Herter, and Franklin D. Roosevelt himself, for whose election in 1932 and 1936 Clark had labored through a national lawyer's committee. In addition, Clark and Felix Frankfurter gained Stimson's appointment as Secretary of State. A Clark associate, John L. McCloy, was added to Stimson's staff as advisor on disarmament. Clark's own contribution to the disarmament controversy of the time was a book, pressing the "Union Now" solution, *A Federation of Free Peoples* (1939).

Clark made a principle of keeping himself in the background, preferring to direct individuals into aspects of his work. He became famous among initiates for his lengthy and expensive telephone calls at home and around the world, his calls to individuals ranging from President Franklin D. Roosevelt in Washington to Josef Stalin in Moscow. Clark was persuaded that the peace he sought must involve the U.S.S.R., and later Communist China. This stigmatized him to some conservatives as left-wing—or, to some radicals, in Lenin's phrase, a "useful idiot." Clark gave such views of his work little attention, and maintained contacts and friendships as he pleased. One such was Edgar Snow, an international correspondent, known for his sympathy with communist goals.

Clark patently followed a path of principle. Thus, he was long involved in Harvard affairs as alumnus and trustee, and a personal friend of its president James B. Conant. Certain differences, however, became so serious, notably concerning the transfer of collections in Harvard's Arnold Arboretum to Cambridge, that their relations cooled. Roosevelt, too, incurred Clark's displeasure with his "court-packing" plan of 1937, though Roosevelt was sufficiently the public man to be patient with so liberal and useful an associate as Clark.

Clark's personal life had its private aspects during which he enjoyed such activities as bird watching and duck hunting; his Harvard quarrel had partially involved the fate of a duck population. He kept his home and law offices in New York and an estate in Dublin, N.H., where he mixed private and public business. For almost fifty years he was married to Fanny Dwight of Boston, with whom he had three daughters and a son. Following her death he married Mary Brush James, widow of the painter William James, son of the philosopher.

Clark's particular cause outside of peace was civil rights, for which he worked with such associates as Roger W. Baldwin of civil liberties fame. Clark fought in court and out for such rights as those of Jehovah's Witnesses, who protested their children being forced to salute the American flag. He supported the idealist Willard Uphaus, whose "World Fellowship Camp" attracted numerous visitors whose names Uphaus refused to give Federal investigators, for which he suffered prison. Clark himself was refused permission to visit China with his friend Snow.

Black civil rights intensely concerned Clark. He put up $20,000 of his own money as bail for blacks arrested in the Freedom Rider cases. In 1962 he supported the radical William Worthy's right to a passport to Cuba, the Castro revolution which Worthy reported sympathetically. Clark worked closely with the National Emergency Civil Liberties Committee which handled issues in the field, and in his will left half a million dollars to the NAACP Legal Defense Fund.

His major goal, however, continued to be world order. An hiatus in this campaign occurred when World War II created another national crisis. Clark in 1940 chaired the National Emergency Committee for Selective Service and himself wrote the Selective Service Act of that year. During the war he served as an aide to Secretary Stimson. In 1944-45 he chaired the Citizen's Committee for National War Service.

Once the war ended he returned to the problem of peace. The detonation of the A-bomb in 1945 rang an alarm bell for him as for others. It inspired him to redouble efforts to ensure world order. In his search he found help in the Harvard Law School authority Louis B. Sohn. Clark also convened an emergency gathering of authorities at his Dublin home. Just how much hope he had of reaching cooperation with the great communist leaders is not known, but there was influential opinion which did nurture such hopes. Secretary Stimson and Roosevelt himself had entertained the idea of sharing the secrets of the A-bomb with Stalin, on grounds that not doing so would sow suspicion and alienation in war-time allies. This, too, was the opinion of the physicist Niels Bohr, and of Frankfurter.

Clark and Sohn's *A Plan for Peace* (1950) aimed to employ the United Nations when feasible, but to move beyond it if necessary. With numerous revisions, comprehending courts, finances, membership, and a Bill of Rights, the privately-printed *Peace Through Disarmament and Charter Review* further matured the Clark-Sohn findings. Of 3,000 copies printed, Clark distributed 2,000 to leading figures around the world. A digest of this work was also widely disseminated and consulted.

In 1958 came *World Peace through World Law: Two Alternative Plans*, to crown Clark's labors in the field. One plan revised the UN Charter, the other supplemented the UN with a world security organization. During the 1960s there appeared further variations of these basic works.

In perspective, Clark was the Twentieth Century equivalent of William Jay, son of the first Chief Justice, whose legal training and turn of mind also resulted in basic strategies for bringing great powers to bargaining tables and in impeding or preventing wars.

In the 1940s Clark suffered ailments which forced him to resign active law practice. A later heart condition confined him further to his Dublin home. The increase in his disabilities made friends of Clark anxious to have him granted the Nobel Peace Prize. They overcame his objections by pointing to the attention it would draw to his proposals. His death, January 12, 1967 put an end to their project. The liberal Unitarian minister Donald S. Harrington conducted memorial services in Dublin and New York.

Mary Clark Dimond, one of Clark's daughters, collected essays by friends and colleagues in *Memoirs of a Man* (1975), edited by Norman Cousins and J. Garry Clifford. Also helpful are Clifford and Samuel R. Spencer, Jr.'s account of Clark's work on the Selective Training Service Act of 1940, *The First Peacetime Draft* (1986), and Gerald T. Dunne, *Grenville Clark, Public Citizen* (1986).

Norman M. Thomas
(1884-1968)

Old-Style American

Norman M. Thomas was a pacifist and Socialist Party leader, whose manifest integrity, warmth, and clarity of purpose gave his party credibility. His causes contributed to changes in the social structure of his time. He was reared in Marion, Ohio, where Warren G. Harding ran his newspaper, the *Daily Star*. As a boy Thomas helped deliver it to subscribers. Thomas always thought well of Harding; he had seen the future President as kindly and equitable toward his employees and as one who had paid them better than union wages.

Thomas's father was a clergyman, and on both sides of his family the boy could view upright and notable predecessors. His guiding principle became morals. It won him respect and also derogation before gaining him wide approval in the last years of his life.

When his father moved their large family to Lewisburg, Pa., Thomas attended Bucknell University for a year. He went on to Princeton Theological Seminary, his grandfather and father's school, graduating from it in 1905. In a time which drew earnest clergy to "Christian socialism," he sought East Side settlement work in New York. Thomas was ordained a Presbyterian minister in 1911. Wealthy congregations were open to him, but he chose a pastorate in the East Harlem Church and chairmanship over Presbyterian social service agencies.

Thomas married a social worker, Frances Violet Stewart, whose inheritance freed him for civic causes. He soon found one in which affluence helped little: resistance to the war and propaganda machines which rolled about him once the country intervened in World War I. Thomas became a conscientious objector. Tall, decisive, and an eloquent speaker with a rich baritone voice, he was fearless in resisting bullying and aggression by police and others supporting war measures at home as well as abroad. He was already a member of the Fellowship of Reconciliation, which attracted many ministers. He now joined with Roger Baldwin to set up the National Civil Rights Bureau, later the American Civil Liberties Union.

Disillusioned with what he saw about him as products of capitalist rule, and at one with socialists and others who were suffering abuse and prison for anti-war protests, he became a member of the Socialist Party in 1918. Afraid that his notoriety might harm his settlements and other projects, Thomas resigned his pastorate. His experiences contributed to his pacifist masterpiece published in 1923, *The Conscientious Objector in America.*

Thomas's rise in the Socialist Party was swift, and, considering its past, it promised effective political service. Populists in the 1890s had offered a semi-socialist program of expanded government services which was all but preempted by Theodore Roosevelt and Woodrow Wilson (*q.v.*) in the 1912 elections. They also included the socialist standard-bearer for President, Eugene V. Debs, whose over 900,000 votes seemed to promise an even greater future. Debs in 1920 all but repeated the 1912 performance. It soon became evident, however, that Debs's new endorsement had been a protest vote against the late war, during which Debs had been jailed for denouncing the Espionage Act of 1917 which had been used without mercy against aliens and radicals.

Now there was a changing of the guard. Debs died in 1926. Dan Hoan, socialist mayor of Milwaukee, was unwilling to give up so strong a post for a presidential nomination. Although Thomas as the new socialist leader polled only 267,420 votes in 1928 in the twenty states in which he was on the ballot, he was far from a symbolic candidate, despite the economic prosperity. There were deep pockets of poverty in the land. Textile companies in the South, where wages were low, roused strong-arm men against would-be union organizers, sent by A. J. Muste, like Thomas a pacifist minister, and for many years one of his closest friends.

Thomas himself had been active in the Passaic, N. J. textile strike of 1919, and supported other such movements in the Twenties. Thomas had no intention of being a mere socialist symbol. His book *Prosperity?* (1927) one of many books to come, developed a program and approach which he took into his 1928 campaign, and which were subsequently to influence that of Franklin D. Roosevelt's team, when they took over after the 1932 elections. Thomas projected a public works program, old age pensions, unemployment insurance, and shorter work hours. He was then suspicious of the League of Nations, suspecting it was more prone to war than peace. As to the Soviet Union, he shared with many workers and others the hope that despite shortcomings, it was laying foundations for socialism, and urged official recognition.

Despite Thomas' best efforts, his warm personality and wit, constant traveling and writing, his party suffered a decline in the 1930s. It fell between New Deal measures on one hand, and the propaganda and trade union aggressions of the communists, helped by Soviet Union prestige and direct aid, and maligning all partisans outside the fold as "social fascists." Thomas' own work was both educational and practical. He and Harry W. Laidler organized the League for Industrial Democracy. A member of the militant faction of the Socialist Party, Thomas cooperated with Muste in seeking labor and political alliances which would resist the rule-or-ruin actions of the Communist Party. In 1937 Thomas visited the Soviet Union and saw enough to discourage his old tolerance of its dictatorial control.

"Splinter groups," including Trotskyites, Lovestoneites, and others attempted a new socialist beginning with an American Workers Party and gained some influence in such worker-based organizations as the United Auto Workers and the International Ladies Garment Workers Union. Although the group made some impress on labor developments it failed to build a political base and drifted into the Socialist Party. Thomas's main role continued to be one of favoring peace and civil rights. He helped fight the Ku Klux Klan in Florida. In 1938 he made national headlines by being jailed in Jersey City for defying an edict against socialist meetings by Mayor Frank Hague, a Democratic Party stalwart.

In 1940 Thomas, desperate to keep America out of war, horrified liberals by cooperating with the America First Committee in protesting threats to neutrality. Actual war following Pearl Harbor found Thomas unable to resist helping. He proposed "critical support" of the war effort, meaning that he and his friends would not hesitate to criticize the government when it permitted harassment of vulnerable people like Japanese-Americans. He made his last campaign for the presidency in 1948, by then having been widely recognized as having been a firm voice for civil rights and peace, the last patently necessary in a nuclear-bomb infested world. W. A. Swanberg's *Norman Thomas, the Last Idealist* (1976) seemed to suggest that idealism was no longer practical in the world of its time.

Albert Mordell
(1885-1979)

Sedate Radical

CRITIC AND LITERARY adventurer, Albert Mordell broke ground in freethought and materialism in traditional literary interpretation, and pioneered Freudian thought in readings of standard literature. Mordell's discovery of lost writings, notably by Lafcadio Hearn, but including such others as James Russell Lowell and Henry James suggested the unused potential in over-formalized study.

He was born and raised in Philadelphia in a family which took seriously study and its Jewish heritage. Mordell's father, a Hebrew teacher, had brought an old World learning to their new home. Albert Mordell's younger brother, Louis J. Mordell, became a noted Cambridge University professor in pure and applied mathematics and an F.R.S. (Fellow of the Royal Society). Mordell chose a more complex path for influencing his times.

He received the superior education offered by local famed Central High School, and spent a number of years in probing liberal and socialistic possibilities for a career, in odd jobs and fugitive writings in Philadelphia and New York papers. He then served an apprenticeship with a Philadelphia lawyer, after which he and another brother opened a law office which provided for them during the next half-century.

Mordell's interests were, however, in literature. A quiet, sober man somewhat under average height, and, following his stormy years, with formal manners and address, he appeared on the surface the least likely of men to entertain unconventional ideas. His first, self-published pamphlet of some eighty pages, *The Shifting of Literary Values* (1912), however, contained the seeds of what would become his first memorable book. Mordell ventured far, from Jack London to the internationally famous litterateur Georg Brandes, to find reviews and approval. The idea that literary values were not either "immortal" or ephemeral was novel at the time and brought out protests and approval from a surprising number of journalists, reviewers, and writers of public stature. The *London Academy* found the pamphlet of interest, as did young Floyd Dell in the *Chicago Evening Post*. William Lyon Phelps of Yale University liked it, as did the *Book News Monthly*. Mordell thought it had stimulated a Britisher Ernest Killett as late as 1929 to write his *Whirligigs of Taste*. Mordell followed up these and other leads to develop his career as litterateur.

Mordell's theme became in 1915, also privately printed, *Dante and Other Waning Classics*. Its thesis was striking, that writings continued viable so long as their basic materials comported with palpable phenomena. To the extent that they contradicted reality, their impact weakened. Dante, then, continued to draw "our" attention because of the human feelings to which he appealed. His fantasies of Hell and Heaven had comported with the superstitions of his time, but increasingly they could not satisfy generations which had learned the material facts of the known world. Dante's lengthy descriptions of a non-existent Heaven and Hell lost followers as science advanced. So Dante's readership waned, and waned further while Mordell wrote.

Mordell applied his method similarly to John Milton, whose Lucifer came to him as a bore, to John Bunyan whose pilgrimage Mordell saw as abstract and unpersuasive—he thought Bunyan lost an opportunity by not describing "Vanity Fair," which could have been interesting—to St. Augustine, Pascal, and others. Mordell provided an interesting Appendix of such notables as Poe, Emerson, and Goethe who had expressed in print or privately their dissatisfactions with touted "classics."

In his methodical way, Mordell sent copies to living influential authors and was later able to print their approving comments in another printing of his book. It did not make Mordell famous, but it gave him prestige to pursue his work especially among liberals and socialists of the time. Meanwhile he had been impressed by newly published Freudian hypotheses and Freud's own interpretation of Johannes Wilhelm Jensen's novel *Gradiva* in 1907. Mordell was a steady and formidable reader in home and foreign literature all his life, and, having grasped the psychoanalytical principle early and grown with it, was able in 1919 to emerge with a pioneer work of strong originality.

He himself was the least erotic of men, a bachelor linked to his scholarly pursuits; yet his *Erotic Motive in Literature* broke ground which subjective reading and empathy had not fathomed. Dreams, the Oedipus Complex, unconscious author motivations, projections, all these and more were unfolded through writings which had been read and approved for generations without any sense of revelation regarding their authors, their disturbed psyches and unconscious confessions. Mordell having opened the way, he was liable to patent errors, esthetic and factual. But Swinburne, for example, was being innocently admired for writings which plainly reflected his own school experiences as a flogged junior—wounded, as Swinburne later set down in private papers, in ways which unfitted him for a normal sex life.

Mordell's book was widely reviewed, even headlined, in a spectrum of anger and admiration and in the most influential journals. H. L. Mencken, who had fought for Dreiser's (*q.v.*) right to free expression, was sufficiently annoyed to ask who cared how authors wrote their books. The *Nation*, the *Atlantic Monthly*, the *New York Times* saw Mordell as foul-minded, a voyeur, without cultural sensibility, and the like. Simeon Strunsky, just then gaining influence on the *New York Times*, wrote a satire elsewhere pretending to find sex in the works of Euclid. Support came from Havelock Ellis and Freud himself.

The poet Conrad Aiken challenged Mordell to find sexual innuendo in Henry James: a challenge which would soon turn upon itself as psychological studies multiplied concerning James. Mordell carried on this strain of his interests in *The Literature of Ecstasy* (1921). By then, Freud and Freud in literature were rising mountain high, and the theme became generally familiar.

In 1919 Mordell opened a new vein of writing, even while following older themes. He became an early admirer of Dreiser at the same time that he continued to turn endless pages of old magazines and newspapers for light on developments among American and Foreign authors. His Dreiser and related contacts—Mencken, Frank Harris (*q.v.*), the publisher Horace Liveright—availed him little at this time, for he was primarily a critic rather than a figure in literary circles. Working between academic and general themes in local Philadelphia papers and fugitive essays he was largely kept out of going cultural affairs. His books spoke for themselves, rather than for him.

But in reading old files Mordell became aware of materials which had not been gathered by earlier critics and literary historians, and these drew him to still other files of periodicals. His first coup in what he called literary "detecting" was publication of a group of articles which Henry James had earlier written but never reprinted; Mordell edited them and Liveright reprinted them in 1919 as *Traveling Companions.* In 1920 Houghton Mifflin published Mordell's collected and edited *The Function of the Poet*, by James Russell Lowell. Neither of these finds, nor others, opened academic vistas of popularity to Mordell, but they contributed to his visibility and encouraged his further researches.

Mordell's greatest find, one that would bear his imprint thereafter, was Lafcadio Hearn, whose strange career marked him as a genius, though to a cult rather than a general readership. Hearn had come to America aged nineteen from a mixed English-European background and lived twenty harried years as a journalist and writer mainly in Cincinnati and New York. Half-blind, he wrote with a unique sense of color. Believing himself ill-favored, he sought female companionship among blacks. He leaned toward the exotic, was less discontented in French and French writing, and wrote and translated tales which showed sensibility more than personality. He left a trail of fugitive writing which no one troubled to study or collect after he left for Japan in 1890. There he became Japanese in name and at Tokyo University, where he taught English and American literature. He married a Japanese, became a father, and in *Japan* (1904) and other books impressed on American readers the fan and cherry-blossoms legend which, despite the Russo-Japanese War would inadvertently deceive absent-minded Americans until 1941.

In 1923 appeared Hearn's *Essays in European and Oriental Literature*, arranged and edited by Mordell. The next year came his *Karma and Other Stories and Essays*, and *St. Anthony and Other Stories*, the latter volume being Hearn's English translations from Maupassant, and the following year Hearn's *Occidental Gleanings*, culled from the *Cincinnati Enquirer*, on which he had served eccentrically. The title enjoyed some recognition in America, but because of Japanese pride in possessing Hearn, his family and work, began to build a reputation in Japan for Mordell himself which was higher than at home.

Mordell continued to break ground. His *Notorious Literary Attacks* (1926) was the best such collection of invidious criticisms of famous books as seen by contemporary critics. Mordell's lengthy introduction was enlightening about critical principles and changing standards.

In 1933 Mordell published his least controversial volume, *Quaker Militant, John Greenleaf Whittier*: a surprising volume, since Whittier was conventionally situated in academic lore as a rural poet. A century had passed since the abolitionists had been firebrands in America, and fifty since Whittier had died. His role among them had been quietly put on the shelf among academics and forgotten. With research which brought out scores and hundreds of verses by Whittier which had been uncollected, and activities as journalist, editor, and political figure which had affected events, Mordell quietly integrated the whole into the poet's life. Mordell revealed Whittier as a disappointed lover and male coquet, one who suffered nervous ailments obviously related to his repressed inner life.

The book was well-received despite the all but cosmic changes which had grown up between the antebellum world of the old crusaders and the new world of Darwinism and Marxism as well as a profound Depression which was changing it further. *Quaker Militant* was Mordell's last general publication, aside from his literary discoveries.

Yet he was to have one more turn of visibility which, at the time, seemed to promise to open wide expanses larger than those he had at home already penetrated. E. Haldeman-Julius, born Emmanuel Julius and a contemporary of Mordell, raised in Philadelphia, had made a start in socialism and journalism, and in 1919 undertook what became his famous or notorious "Little Blue Books": small volumes printed on pulp paper and held together with staples. They ran in the hundreds, then thousands of volumes, priced from ten cents to tall "books" for a dollar and less in volume purchases.

Haldeman-Julius (he had married Marcet Haldeman, who accompanied him in his enterprises) offered classics, often with lurid, eye-catching titles, from the ancient Greeks to contemporary debates, emphasizing radical ideas, erotica, free thought, and tales and poems which could be readily consumed by anyone, at lunch break or as a tool for self-education.

The millions of copies of Little Blue Books which Haldeman-Julius disseminated seemed to optimists like Upton Sinclair (*q.v.*) an adjunct to socialist mass education, a prelude to socialism itself. Long range judgment suggests that it fed Progressive aspects of the time, and faded with them, leaving little residue. But the rubble included some of Mordell's most relaxed and candid memories and ideas.

These seem to have been sparked indirectly by Haldeman-Julius himself when in 1949 he published two volumes of hastily written autobiographical notes, *My First Twenty-five Years* and *My Second Twenty-Five Years*. These taller volumes contained interesting details regarding his early socialist experiences and later publishing exploits in Girard, Kansas, which had earlier been a socialist publishing center and from which had been issued the once-famous *Appeal to Reason*. Ruined by World War I, it became the base on which Julius, as he then was, built his popular press on free thought, quasi-leftist principles similar to those the publisher Lyle Stuart later exploited.

Haldeman-Julius poured out an endless stream, not only of Little Blue books, but also of newspapers and magazines filled with scraps of information and opinion, letters, and other easy to read matter. Mordell read Haldeman-Julius's reminiscences, thrown off in his *American Freeman*, and his memories of older Philadelphia. He was stimulated to hunt out with camera and research old buildings and landmarks associated with the early Julius and himself. Mordell walked over the historic terrain of Kensington, Northern Liberties, and other Philadelphia sections, photographing scenes relevant to both of them and commenting on their past and present occupants who included such personalities as W. C. Fields, and such sites as the Labor Temple where Karl Marx's First International had been officially laid to rest. The result was a pamphlet, one of Haldeman-Julius's "Giants", *Trailing E. Haldeman-Julius in Philadelphia and Other Places*.

Patently parochial, though at its best an example of local color, the pamphlet opened the way to other Mordell publications, too hastily assembled and erratic in quality, yet containing observations and information which helped put a yeasty-changing time in perspective. *Haldeman-Julius and Upton Sinclair* ("the Amazing Record of a Long Collaboration") was not especially illuminating, and was filled out with gossip about "Haldeman-Julius' early authors." *Sham-Smashers at Work* no more than drew shallow free thought materials from the publishers' *Monthly* and his *The Debunker*. Mordell here added his own correspondence with Georg Brandes to fill out the pamphlet, contributing a genuine literary footnote. Still using materials in Haldeman-Julius's files, Mordell compiled *Frank Harris and Haldeman-Julius*. More substantial was Mordell's evidence that his patron's clamor for Eugene V. Debs's release from prison—Debs had been jailed for opposing American involvement in World War I—had helped gain Debs his freedom.

Mordell's long correspondence and association with Theodore Dreiser contributed revelations regarding Dreiser's secret life in still another Haldeman-Julius pamphlet, as usual along with disparate materials bearing on free thought. Dreiser had considered a Philadelphia divorce, with Mordell acting as his attorney. With Dreiser in 1951 occupying a curious place in American writing—assumed outstanding, yet of little actual weight in contemporary fiction—the essay had almost no visibility on the scene.

Mordell continued methodically to organize and add to old and new materials; as late as 1961 he published a book, based on new findings of William Dean Howells-Henry James items. However, he had patently slowed down. Many old associates were dead, new impulses were taking over in the academic and publishing markets.

A new economics served Mordell. Reprinting entered into the mass market with Lyndon B. Johnson's effort to create a greater New Deal by subsidizing libraries as well as even street gangs. Reprint houses were formed to seek out and make available a forest of titles which had not been able to survive on popular demand. Many of Mordell's major writings had a surprisingly modern ring, embodying as they did skepticism and even sex; and they reentered print. His Japanese reputation stayed steady, so that although his Haldeman-Julius-sponsored view of T. S. Eliot's critical "deficiencies" had no impact on Eliot lore, as reprinted in Japanese it is likely that it was Mordell's opinion, rather than Eliot's prose, which was there taken more seriously. Mordell spent retirement years in Miami, Florida. His passing was noticed only in his own city.

Mordell's major writings displayed his scholarship and the contours of his mind, but his Haldeman-Julius pamphlets best offered details about his actual life and relations. In one of Haldeman-Julius's scrapbook-and-article publications, *The Critic and Guide*, for 1950 appeared a somewhat amateur attempt to follow Mordell himself in his literary adventures: Abraham Bronson Feldman, "Albert Mordell: a Prophet Not Without Honor." Mordell's major papers are in Special Collections at the University of Pennsylvania Library.

Randolph Bourne
(1886-1918)

Youth Legend

WORLD WAR I DISSIDENT AND youth movement advocate, Randolph Bourne was a hunchback whose courageous appeals for peace made him a legend in the 1920s and after.

He was born in Bloomfield, N.J., in a conventional family of women who had been deserted by the father. Bourne proved a brilliant student who learned, however, that he could never be accepted by peers in normal circumstances. After graduating with high school honors in 1903 he felt driven by conscience to contribute to the family's needs by filling onerous jobs, but left empty-handed in 1909 and with no evident future. He entered Columbia College where he met challenging students, was impressed by John Dewey's pragmatic philosophy, and himself won distinction as editor-in-chief of the student monthly and by having an article on youth's destiny accepted by the *Atlantic Monthly*, the first of such acceptances. As a major in sociology he gained his Bachelor's degree, and his M.A. with a thesis on Bloomfield. In 1913 he published his *Youth and Life*, a manifesto hailing contemporary youth as forerunners of a better time.

Having won Columbia's premier Gilder Travelling Fellowship, he spent a memorable year abroad, meeting literary and political notables in England and on the Continent, observing strikes and student life, and being on the scene when Germany's Kaiser Wilhelm declared war against the Allies. Back home, wearing the cape and beret which became one of his life patterns, he entered into the bustling social and cultural life of New York's Greenwich Village and began work.

His entering wedge was education. Investigating a progressive educational system in Indiana then much in the news, he wrote *The Gary Schools* (1916) praising its emancipating qualities for the young. He followed this with *Education and Living*, a book of essays, the next year, which gave him further opportunity to use the loose sociological training he had acquired.

Bourne, however, was interested in a broader vision for human expansion, and the *New Republic*, begun in 1914, gave him the outlet he needed. He became its "contributing editor," which meant little more than that his varied essays and articles on novels, poetry, the cities, feminism, immigrants and settlements, individuals, and American cultural wants were welcomed and paid for. He was a friend or acquaintance of such luminaries of the time as Van Wyck Brooks, Walter Lippmann, the poet James Oppenheim, the sociologist Elsie C. Parsons, the editor Alyse Gregory, and numerous others in the arts, at universities, and in Bohemia. Indeed, there was scarcely a visible New York figure in those related fields whom Bourne did not seek out and find, and impress with his searching mind and aspirations.

As Bourne's friend John Reed came to symbolize youth's turn to radicalism, Bourne, aided in part by his infirmities, which put the patent egotisms of this first twentieth century youth movement out of his reach, came to represent its finer hopes and projects.

With war now far advanced in Europe, Bourne turned to pacifism as a vital means of preventing America from being drawn into its toils; and here his academic credentials came to his aid. The American Association for International Conciliation was rooted on Columbia University's campus, having been founded by its president Nicholas Murray Butler. For its publications Bourne contributed pamphlets. But in his edited book, *Towards an Enduring Peace* (1916), Bourne was able to bring together essays by such international figures as Romain Rolland, renowned for his novel *Jean Christophe*, roughly based on an ideal Beethoven. Rolland was just then at odds with his own country for being embroiled in war. Bourne also printed the views and resolutions of socialists and neutralists at home and abroad. He was helped to define his stand by the fact that peace was actually a la mode at the time, the President himself, Woodrow Wilson, professing a neutral position. The quality of Bourne's convictions was yet to be tested.

Bourne's ardent nature was well appreciated. He played the piano with notable verve. His conversation was earnest and with

The young college editor. Behind him, with moustache, is Alfred Knopf, later a famous publisher.

substance. His prose was clear and varied, particularly in his less journalistic essays. Although he drew his ideas from others, ranging from Cardinal Newman to John Dewey, he gave them a flare and relevance. His idea, for example, of a "trans-national America," generously mixing races and people in uplifting measure, he borrowed from the philosophy teacher Horace M. Kallen.

The *New Republic* was his bread and butter during the major portion of his public life, but he was eager to contribute beyond it. He and his friend Van Wyck Brooks dreamed of an emancipated culture and literature, and he wrote for and consorted with the editors of *The Dial, The Seven Arts,* and the radical *Masses.*

Bourne's dream of freedom and peace was abruptly curtailed by President Wilson's call to arms in April 1917, and his subsequent call for war, war to the uttermost. Bourne had, sensing the change in public feeling, printed articles appealing to reason. He urged that intervention would give priority to the least humanistic social feelings and attitudes. America was stronger, more able to influence events and a just settlement by standing outside, than by being drawn into and identified with massive military operations. With the *New Republic* committed to Wilson's policies, and with other organs subjected to censorship and closing, Bourne found himself more and more reduced from a public figure to an occasional contributor.

He considered joining the activist, pro-Bolshevik intellectuals, along with Reed and Max Eastman. He turned inward, beginning a novel in which he recalled the feelings of his early youth. He prepared a stoical paper in which he viewed the monster State as overwhelming and unassailable. His familiar circles were broken up by clashes with authority and alienation. John Dewey's pragmatism, Bourne concluded, worked in peace time, but was useless in times of crisis.

His health, always delicate, was further impaired by poverty, winter-cold, and evident discouragement. Although he continued to dream in private letters of a new writing which would attack America with irony, satire, and distaste, he saw little about to inspire hope. He succumbed to bronchial pneumonia: a loss to dissenters they found it difficult to accept. *Untimely Papers* (1919) included his last efforts at persuasion. Brooks edited *The History of a Literary Radical* (1920) which, though it reflected the editor's major literary concerns did not deviate far from those of Bourne.

Bourne was well-remembered as a principled humanist in the 1920s, and for his radicalism in the more political Thirties. Thereafter, his most effective, if partial, image persisted in John Dos Passos's novel, *1919* (1932):

> A tiny twisted unscared ghost in a black cloak hopping
> along the grimy old brick and brownstone streets still
> left in downtown New York, Crying out in a shrill
> soundless giggle *War is the health of the State.*

Louis Filler, *Randolph Bourne* (1966 ed.) sought a balanced portrait of his life and work. John Adam Moreau, *Randolph Bourne— Legend and Reality* (1966) worked at details of his life among family and friends, and found many of a personal nature. His *Letters* (1981), too, repay reading.

Allan Nevins
(1890-1971)

An American Heritage

HISTORIAN, TEACHER, AND journalist, Allan Nevins was the giant of his time among historians, overtopping the best by the sheer magnitude of his original researches. Although his prolific writing encouraged some people to slur his labors, the high quality of his major writings and even routine ones gave them no alternative to appreciation but silence when possible, and neglect. He was a measure of the status of history in public consciousness when he died.

Born on the farm in rural Illinois, Nevins was raised to hard work and also keen pleasure in basic living when it did not retard growth: nature, good companionship, and above all reading. A romantic, he could not understand people who had not had a season with Dumas, Stevenson, Scott, and James Fenimore Cooper. He drew American lore from home roots, building on it a sense of the past and larger present.

Nevins, become a sturdy, medium-sized young man, proud of his Scottish past. He received his Bachelor and Master degrees at the University of Illinois, taught English for a year there, then joined the *New York Evening Post* in 1913 as an editorial writer. The paper still bore the marks of William Cullen Bryant's long and rigid attention to clear writing and

Jacksonian thought, as well as of Edwin Godkin's (*q.v.*) later impeccable style and Old World liberalism.

Here at the *Post* Nevins developed his own power of clear statement and hard attention to facts. Although he stayed current to new versions of liberalism refined in Woodrow Wilson's (*q.v.*) era, much of his mind and heart was in the past. He retained a constant delight in Godkin's old satiric journalistic prose, reading it not as bitter and derogatory but as penetrating. He himself practiced a more temperate approach toward new democratic phenomena which had outraged the older journalist: New Immigrants from Europe, unions, ethnic politics, and the attitudes of brash new youth of the 1910s.

While continuing on the *Evening Post* until 1923, Nevins also prepared himself for work in literature and history. He took satisfaction in writing for the *Nation* (1913-1918), also Godkin's former preserve. Godkin's standards were there maintained by Paul Elmer More, a journalist and religious conservative who had served on the *Evening Post*. Nevins esteemed him, along with James Russell Lowell, the greatest among American literary critics.

He began his career in history with an effort to link it with literature in the life of Robert Rogers, a frontiersman who fought in the French and Indian War, was an explorer and embroiled with Indians, and who had been controversial in the Revolutionary years. Rogers had published memoirs and a crude but pioneer play *Ponteach* (1766)—Rogers's version of "Pontiac"—which Nevins issued with a biographical introduction. In 1922 he published *The Evening Post*, covering highlights of its and its editors's journalistic career, and the next year edited *American Social History as Recorded by British Travellers*. In 1917 he prepared a volume of general import, *Illinois*, for a series on the states.

His major career began with a masterpiece in which he took special pride, *The American States During and After the American Revolution* (1924). It was unsubsidized and unheralded. Nevins simply made his way through archives up and down the older states scouring them for fresh light on the politics and life of the states in transition. Although he picked up the literary editorship of the *New York Sun* in 1924, and followed it with editorial work on the *New York World*, he now had entree into academe, which was then rigid in deference to the Ph.D., which Nevins technically lacked. In 1927 he was received in Cornell University's history department as an assistant professor, and while there completed a volume in a history series, heavy with footnotes but still highly readable and informative, *The*

Emergence of Modern America (1927). Now a patent academic prize, Nevins was offered an associate professorship in the History Department of Columbia University, which he accepted. Several years later he attained his professorship. Although he continued to be a maverick (*q.v.*) among academics, with the articles, reviews, formidable encyclopedic entries, and essays and books of all kinds which kept him in public places as well as in hallowed halls, his publications loomed so high in accordance with professional standards that would-be challengers could scarcely raise questions without exposing themselves to notice.

Two basic questions were involved in the scope of Nevins's research and the way he met inevitable caveats. Much that he did—edited collections of essays, solicited studies, even books—were prepared as he liked, and did not stir adverse opinion. Nevins thought one should not write of a person or institution one did not himself like, but if one was not willing to defend the project in open technical forum the result was obviously in legitimate question.

Nevins recognized this when he issued in 1934 his *History of the Bank of New York and Trust Company 1784 to 1934* (1934), probably with the cooperation of bank officials. It involved interesting people beginning with Alexander Hamilton. Nevins had a good regard for Hamilton and others treated in the text, but he did not list the book among his works. He did list his *Life of Henry White, Diplomatist* (1929) among them, and though he liked his subject, White lacked notable qualities: he had been a State Department appendage with few ideas and little impact.

On the other hand, there was Nevins's extensive article in the *Dictionary of American Biography* on Oakes Ames, who had been accused of malfeasance in the 1872 Credit Mobilier scandal relating to the building of the Union Pacific Railroad under Congressional authority. Nevins in his article responded vigorously to the generally accepted charges against Ames, filling his refutations with detail and authority. He did the same with an article on Helen Hunt Jackson, famous for her novel *Ramona*, which scorned American policy toward Indians. Nevins held that in historical terms, interesting as were her books in the field, they were sentimental in not dealing with the reality of Indian-United States intercourse.

Increasingly he was able to gain entry into sources of material not available to others, and his inclinations drew him to central figures in American life around whom controversy and vital events had once swirled. His first major work in the public view received the Pulitzer Prize. *Grover*

Cleveland (1932) was definitive, and Nevins's *Letters of Grover Cleveland* the next year lent solid support to the biography.

Nevins's implicit contention in his books, was that Cleveland was a man of courage and right thinking. But many Americans in 1932, in and out of academe, were not happy with their Depression prospects. They were sympathetic to the Soviet Union and fearful of war. They took only minimal joy in the stolid Cleveland who had threatened war with England over a "Venezuelan affair," helped break if only by indirection the Pullman Strike of 1894, and been patient with a run on the United States Treasury— a run which J. P. Morgan Company had stopped on hard terms to the Government. Political History was then at high in academe, but there were skeptics among students who only moderately joined Nevins in his appreciation of the picturesque aspects of torchlight parades and big-fisted Irish toughs who dominated the city polls at election.

Less controversial on the face of it was Nevins's magisterial study of *Hamilton Fish* (1936), President Ulysses S. Grant's aristocratic Secretary of State who kept his President from blundering into war on several occasions. It, too, won the Pulitzer Prize for History. By now, Nevins was one of the distinguished sights on Columbia's campus, a good natured looking man who attracted increasing numbers of students seeking entrance into history. Nevins set other students to typing the edited diaries of Presidents and others he was preparing for publication. He set still others to attempting mastery of subjects he thought needed doing, or re-doing.

Nevins was genuinely affable but he was far from naive. He recognized envy and bad faith, especially in competitive New York. His historical concerns were intense enough to put him above most of the trifling ambitions of associates great and small. His unceasing work, in the midst of a calm and protected family life became legendary, and he made firm decisions, often resented, barring or permitting entry into his most private affairs.

Nevins was forever in and out of the great Columbia library, moving swiftly from the book stacks, carrying perhaps thirty books for use by a graduate student, or to his own car for transportation home. His *The Gateway to History* (1938) scanned the entire field from primitive and ancient history to modern historical methods and directions. In always clear, individualized terms and with countless felicitous examples: the world of a man who was wholly engaged by his subject.

He was often off campus on research elsewhere or on other engagements, to the chagrin of students whom he had congratulated on the largeness and complexities of their subjects, and whom he would help only if they seemed serious. Meanwhile he had in hand, among other numerous projects, a life of the elder John D. Rockefeller, who had apparently been pinned to the wall in muckraking studies by Henry Demarest Lloyd, Ida M. Tarbell, and others, but whom he now implemented with vast materials from the Standard Oil Company and Rockefeller family themselves. Nevins's formidable two-volume study, *John D. Rockefeller: The Heroic Age of American Enterprise* (1940) met little direct challenge. It was "establishment" history, discontented reviewers averred. But the book being for anyone, rather than only academics, their disquiet made little impact, certainly on him. A completely revised later edition of his book was entitled *A Study in Power*. Nevins often returned to his older books for revisions and additions, and gained profit as well as satisfaction from the new printings. Later still, with a collaborator, Nevins issued a formal three-volume study of Henry Ford with separate titles (1954-1963) covering the firm and family's papers in exposition of Ford's rise into modern times.

Nevins was partly impelled in his work by a hunger for readers, reading what they pleased, but reading. What is the use of history, he cried in one review, if the book he was reviewing perversely passed by railroad records and special studies to make patently false judgments which besmirched the facts. Believing as he did, Nevins not infrequently went out on limbs to defend and aid historians he saw as sound, whatever their political tendencies. On one occasion he testified in court to the integrity of an author of whom another, more skeptical historian observed privately: If he is not a member of the Communist Party, why isn't he?

To encourage reading, Nevins sponsored publication of *American Heritage*, intended to popularize history for the quasi-educated public. He was the driving force behind what became a movement, started in Columbia but spread elsewhere, of reaching public figures for often protracted interviews which would draw from them intimate details regarding other significant public figures and events. Innumerable reels of interviews by his students were gathered for careful use by responsible scholars. He himself donated a manuscript of his own autobiography for study in Columbia's Oral History Archives.

Nevins received numerous honors and degrees at home and abroad while never stinting his own research and observations wherever he might be. He took World War II honors as a government publicity chief in England and New Zealand with modesty and a goal of service, and an alert sense of propriety. He feared being misconstrued. A student commented on the shelves of new jacketed books in his Columbia office which "looked" as though they had not been read. He later observed that Nevins had torn off the jackets so that the scene might not be misread.

He was well aware that times were changing, and that many of his deep enthusiasms were considered old hat or worse by new pretenders, but he quietly persisted in doing what he could for the intellectual world which made a difference to him. He would have wanted a full-scale biography of E. L. Godkin, but could not find a proper person to do it. He was troubled that James Fenimore Cooper was thought to be fit only for young readers, and in 1954 issued a volume of selections from the Leatherstocking Tales with a lengthy introduction and continuity. It showed time and attention given to the sumptuous volume, for which Reginald Marsh provided illustrations. Nevins's plea was for romantic literature, but he rejected the view that Cooper's frontiersmen and women did not comport with the facts. Mark Twain had shown no mercy in downgrading Cooper, and Nevins gave Twain short shrift. He took elaborate pains to compare the romantic vision with the facts to be found in travelers, scientists, and historical accounts.

He had long contemplated a multi-volumed history of his favorite period, the Civil War and post-Civil War era, to be continued till his death, and was always off to see archival materials on a subject he planned to cover in short or longer space. Nevins did not revere materials for their own sake, and constantly threw letters and memoranda in wastebaskets when they had done their work. Those who were bewildered by the magnitude of his fulfilled projects were driven to imagine that Dumas-like he had hosts of investigators preparing research and drafts of chapters, perhaps books, for him foreman-like to oversee and arrange. They could not imagine him as what he was: a devotee of history and culture who remembered whatever had touched him and whatever he had done, who knew just what he needed to know and went out to find it. He had trained a generation of scholars and worked along with them to obtain the information they needed and he could himself use; his several score introductions to books gave insight into his process of learning, as in the case of the distinguished biography of Samuel F. B. Morse (*q.v.*) which he sponsored. Nevins's only problem was time, and that he had mastered as well as anyone could.

From the 1940s to his own death, from final services to Columbia through "retirement" which he took in the Huntingdon Library in California, he worked at his series. The first two volumes, *The Ordeal of the*

Union, over a thousand pages of narrative and analysis, scanned the American scene for factors since the 1840s which were building toward a climax. They were published in 1947. Three years passed during which he prepared his two-volume *The Emergence of Lincoln*, with all the currents that emergence comprehended. It took nine more years before *The War for the Union*, in two volumes again, entered into all the complexities of personalities, fortifications and assaults, and the leaders military and political of the two great opposing sections could be explicated. The final two volumes brought together all these factors and developments while hymning the theme of victory. As Lincoln had, so Nevins saw victory only in the preservation of the Union. These final two volumes were copyrighted not by Nevins but by his wife, for Nevins himself was gone.

He had looked forward with gusto to dealing with the post-Civil War decades, but never gave time to philosophizing on such matters. History had sufficed for him, in whatever era. The volumes he had completed were his masterpiece, and, going forth to the larger American public, rather than narrowly to the academic establishment, gave evidence that not only would they flourish there, but would continue to do so.

As noted, Nevins provided an "Autobiography" for those who sought to know him better. For working purposes—always a priority to him—his own writings were ample for insight into the mental world he inhabited, and his ways of viewing the world and its people.

Nevins's major writings as well as some minor ones are firmly in print, his *Ordeal of the Union* distributed by the Book of the Month Club. There must in due course be a review of the place of historical classics amoung general readers and those directing historical study. One inquiry could begin with *Reader's Catalog* (1989), compiled by scores of editors and consultants covering all of history and culture in some 40,000 selected titles, many patently ephemeral. Yet not a single category carries so much as a mention of Nevins. See also *The Oral History Collection of Columbia University* (N.Y., 1964).

Maury Maverick
(1895-1954)

Noblesse Oblige

S PECTACULAR UNITED STATES Congressman and mayor of San Antonio, Texas, Maury Maverick was identified with civil rights causes and New Deal issues. Noted for his family name, he worked intensively to give it personal meaning, and succeeded to an extent. Well read in liberal traditions as well as an activist, he forged a radical style which seemed justified by the dour prejudices he defied.

He was born in San Antonio, Texas and famous at birth because of the meaning his grandfather Sam Maverick had given his surname; as a cattleman early in the nineteenth century the older Maverick had refused to adopt a brand along with other cattle owners. He had thus won title to any strays his cowboys came across. The family had distinctions which went back into American history. A Sam Maverick was one of the Bostonians who fell before Royal rifles at the Boston Massacre. Matthew Fontaine Maury of Virginia, modern discoverer and charter of the Atlantic Gulf Stream, was another distinguished forebearer on young Maverick's mother's side. Maverick's father, a quiet gentleman, dealt in Texas real estate less venturesomely than had his own father, who had been a follower of Sam Houston during the hectic period of Texas rebellion and Independence.

Young Maverick admired his father, but it was the spirit of old Sam Maverick which spurred him as he worked his way through childhood and adolescence. He matured at Virginia Military Institute and the University of Texas, from neither of which he received a degree.

During irregular schooling he had worked at odd ranch jobs, but was never far from books about the nation and history. The Alamo, in San Antonio, scene of Texas rebellion, was never out of his memory. He admired such popular spokesmen as Tom Paine and Robert M. LaFollette (*q.v.*), and later thought George W. Norris, who had led the "revolt" against "Czar" Joe Cannon, head of the U.S. House of Representatives, the greatest living American.

In 1916, aged twenty-two, Maverick was admitted to the Texas bar and began to practice. On the country's entrance into the then-European War he joined the Army as a first lieutenant and was assigned overseas where he promptly found himself in the front lines. In the battle of St. Mihiel he brought in twenty-six prisoners by himself. At the Argonne he was severely wounded and, though recovered, suffered pain all his life. In 1920 he married and began to raise a family.

Maverick was set on a political career despite the Texas conservatism of the 1920s. He took an open stand against the Ku Klux Klan, was energetic and conspicuous in local politics, suspicious of corruption, and an organizer of committees. His Citizens League issued publications and quarrelled with local leaders. For a living, Maverick built houses and was elected County Tax Collector, but with the coming of the Great Depression he shifted his priorities. Unemployment disturbed him. With friends he personally visited hobo jungles, dressed shabbily. Out of his experiences came a "cooperative camp" to serve needy people. It functioned with some success and public approval.

Maverick soon distanced himself from conservatives in his district by adopting attitudes which inspired his foes to call him a "communist." His goals, however, were not in that direction. He was an early New Dealer who scorned the radical cliches of the time. He did indeed fight for Negro and Mexican-American rights—the latter had previously been classified as blacks, and as such been oppressed by the poll tax, which he also opposed. In his 1935 run for Congress, these and other crusades cost him conservative civic respect and popularity, but they also gave him enough votes to win against serious local antagonism.

Maverick now had a national forum on which to move, and he took up work in Washington with zest and a program. Somewhat below average height, with threatening overweight, but quick-moving and with expressive gestures, he looked somewhat like a southern version of Fiorello La Guardia,

Maverick liked to run over to Mexico and bring back animals for the zoo.

New York's picturesque reform mayor. Maverick brought bustle and excitement to Congress. He was soon known to the nation for his work especially among young ambitious congressmen, eager to help direct and publicize New Deal measures. It was a tribute to Maverick's leadership that his legislative colleagues were soon known as "the Mavericks."

His issues were those exposed by the Depression crisis, but he made them partly his own by full-hearted agitation and appeals which brought his principles and experience into focus. Maverick, on radio, in the press, and in Congress denounced slums and approved Federal action favoring the needy and unemployed. Above all, he stood flatly against suppression of opinion especially as fostered by committed anti-communists, and in the Tydings-McCormick Bill of 1935-1936 intended to punish with criminal charges attempts to disaffect soldiers from their duty. Maverick came to Congress a pacifist, and though he worked with President Franklin D. Roosevelt on much legislation, he broke with the President on the issue of peace. Later hatred of fascism turned Maverick to national preparedness, emphasizing air defense.

Maverick's Congressional service was also the high point of his writing, not only on political issues, but also social and historical. He sought the company of professional litterateurs and was friends with writer Sherwood Anderson, himself uprooted from Twenties concerns. Maverick was especially close at the time to H.L. Mencken, whose crackling prose influenced his own. He published articles and essays, and even book reviews, using his outlets as a forum for his own purposes.

In 1937 he increased his public image with forceful support of anti-lynching legislation: the one southern congressman to do so. That year, too, he published what became a best-seller, *A Maverick American*, a mixture of personal autobiography and experiences bearing on the social scene. Encouraged by its good reception, he went to work on another book. It became *In Blood and Ink* (1939), a serious effort to plot the course and meaning of the Constitution, written from his liberal perspective.

In the meantime, his own Congressional District in Texas had divided into Maverick and anti-Maverick forces. In 1937 he was hard put to win re-election, but managed to do so. Giving and getting no ground, he took his stand against President Roosevelt's own Vice-President, Texan John Nance Garner, whom he dubbed a reactionary. Standing a third time for re-election in 1939 Maverick was unable to pull it through. Running for mayor of his home town San Antonio that same year he stood on firmer ground. A century before his grandfather had assumed the title of mayor. A winner this time, Maverick brought to his city a program of civic improvement which continued to interest the nation.

As mayor, Maverick made himself a byword to conservatives not only in San Antonio but elsewhere across the nation. Slum clearance, public health, and a clean sweep of patronage and corruption were old issues to him, and on the surface hardly intended to wound. But when allied with such other issues as the poll tax and the rights of avowed communists, they took on a lurid hue. Maverick's restoration of an old Spanish village, "Villita," in the city's center housing the Alamo added charm which even conservatives could not openly criticize. His determination to permit communists to use the city's auditorium for a public meeting, however, was too much for town patriots to bear. The meeting was stormed by an estimated 5,000 enraged citizens, the attendants driven out and the auditorium vandalized.

Maverick served only one term of his memorable mayorship. The imminence of war opened his last career as a public man. In 1940 he joined with Adlai E. Stevenson and others to organize a committee to Defend America by Aiding the Allies. He became an assistant in the Office of Price Administration, but soon shifted to the War Production Board which he served throughout the conflict, especially as dominant figure in the Smaller War Plants Corporation. This he infused with his own energy by way of allocation of funds, speeches, publications, and general visibility. He added a word beside his own name to the language by denouncing "gobbledegook," bureaucratic babble, as an impediment to necessary war measures.

The war over, Maverick continued to make himself heard through correspondence and concern for public issues. He was well regarded by President Harry Truman and had good prospects for a return to government. In 1951 he prepared to run for Congress, but a heart attack called off an actual campaign. His old war wounds had never given him peace, and contributed to his final decline, which he recognized and for which he prepared. Maverick's strenuous activity had never been for mere preferment. It had been his American, or Texan, version of *noblesse oblige*, and was so recognized when he died.

Maverick's own autobiography reflects the sequence and tone of his affairs, and is studded with innumerable details of personal and public nature. See also Richard B. Henderson, *Maury Maverick: a Political Biography* (1970).

Stephen Vincent Benét
(1898-1943)

Poet of the Nation

POET AND STORY-TELLER, Stephen Vincent Benét is best known as author of *John Brown's Body* and the fantasy, *The Devil and Daniel Webster*. Of no famous literary school or tendency, he is yet to be given an identity among native traditions.

Few authors, however, came of more tradition-conscious family. Of Spanish descent, Benét's forebearers had left Minorca to settle in St. Augustine, Florida. His father, grandfather, and great-grandfather were Army officers, the last two graduates of West Point, and his family moved about according to Army orders. Born in Bethlehem, Pennsylvania, young Benét was taken to Benecia Arsenal, California, from which, in the distance, he saw San Francisco burning, following the 1906 earthquake. Other moves took the family North and South. In a highly literate household, the boy grew to be a deep reader from early childhood, all but ruining his eyesight in the process.

He was also retentive, absorbing the details of official Civil War accounts from bookcases at home, as well as romantic poetry in several languages and eras. Benét published his own first collection of verse, *Five Men and Pompey* in 1915. A second book of verse, *Young Adventure*, issued in 1918 while he was still at Yale University, showed his continuing commitment to poetry. But meanwhile, with America committed to World

War I, he attempted to gain acceptance into the Army by memorizing the sight-measurement chart. Exposed and rejected he returned to finish his course at Yale, graduating in 1919, and receiving his master's degree a year later.

In the next several years he studied at the Sorbonne on a scholarship, met Rosemary Carr and married, and set up in New York as a writer. He was doubtless helped to make beginnings by his brother William Rose Benét and sister Laura Benét, who were both secure in metropolitan literary editing and writing. The talent, however, was all his own. It took him into verse, short stories, and novels, the best of which was perhaps *Spanish Bayonet* (1926), an historical fiction of early America. Generally, his work divided into historical themes with forays into fantasy, and tales centered on contemporary life as it affected educated New Yorkers. In 1924 his brother William, along with the litterateurs Henry Seidel Canby and Christopher Morley founded the *Saturday Review of Literature*, intended for just such people, about and for whom Stephen wrote.

Benét's decade-long writing had displayed skill, his always-active reading, and imaginative construction. It showed independent judgement and generous social sympathies. A number of pieces were memorable, among the poems "American Names," "Ballad of William Sycamore," and several others; among the tales, "Jacob and the Indians," and possibly "Johnny Pye and the Fool Killer." But in sum they were too light to resist alone the winds of change. Benét's determination to undertake a long poem with no sure sale in sight, and on the Civil War he presented suddenly to his family. But, according to his brother, the decision did not surprise them. Stephen had been too long absorbed in related themes. He had lived North and South, and taken the feelings and attitudes of all American sections to heart.

In an era, the Twenties, which made much of cynicism regarding America, past and present, and found more delight in visions of Paris than in anything back home, Benét went regularly to the New York Public Library, where he took notes and sketched verses suitable to his tale of war, its major figures, and the ordinary women and men who were to fight and suffer by events. He read histories, memoirs, accounts of battles and of the numerous places in which people lived or to which they came. He pored at length over Abraham Lincoln's words and deeds, and those of such others as Jefferson Davis, and Robert E. Lee. And though he plotted the lives of slaves and their search for freedom, he was generous to the dreams of their owners and of the free white southerners who believed in their cause.

Benét had his own resentments regarding Americans who were unappreciative of Poe and, a bit later in his own time of Vachel Lindsay (*q.v.*). He thought often "of some well-dressed gentlemen/ And well-fed ladies I have met at times/ Who spend their years despairing of the Republic/ And trying ways to beat an income tax...." But he held to a larger view which saw beyond the evident failures to matters larger than any of them. Benét devoted two intense years to what became *John Brown's Body* (1928). It won him the first Pulitzer Prize for literature and changed his life.

Unique in that era of writing was the variety of poetic styles he created in order to unfold the stream of events accompanying the Civil War: of homes North and South emptied of their men, with such of those left behind as "a tall woman... cooking much in an iron pot," or, in Virginia, holding a plantation together with steel fingers under the velvet glove, though "never well since the last child died." Benét had songs for the blacks and songs for soldiers on both sides. They echoed happier days of love and frolic, or cast shadows caused by people fighting each other who were less different than their accents and slogans declared.

Most subtle were the long narrative sections telling of armies forming, fighting, regrouping—poetry made from recorded phrases and passages in old newspapers and books, by leaders, commanders, and common soldiers. They ran from almost direct prose, too sober or painful to be chanted, in the concerns of a Lincoln or a Lee—ran from them to free verse forms which carried the burden of hard conditions of war or premonitions of worse to come. They told not so much what humble people said or proud leaders declared, as what they meant.

Quite special was Benét's six-page "Invocation" to the lengthy tale, and to the American born of new land and conditions:

> They tried to fit you with an English song
> And clip your speech into the English tale.
> But, even from the first, the words went wrong,
> The catbird pecked away the nightingale.

Benét, searching for the essential American, projected words intended to comprehend all Americans, but, however the finished result was viewed, he defined a program for himself. *John Brown's Body*, through a signal public success, won no consensus place. Edgar Lee Masters, though himself a poet, said that he would not read a book about John Brown, though Brown was scarcely in it: a burnt fuse, rather than a presence. Allan Tate, an influential critic of the time and apologist for the Confederacy, referred to Benét's "hair-raising defects," but did not explicate his judgement.

Benét took a 1926 Guggenheim Fellowship and his family to France, where he wrote most of *John Brown's Body*, then, following its success, finally settled in New York again. The Thirties were not generally fruitful for his art. The era of Depression questioned the nation in ways he had not foreseen. Nevertheless, he answered the question in one work at least which more than sufficed to save the decade for him.

"The Devil and Daniel Webster" first appeared as a short story in 1936. It told of a New Hampshire farmer tempted by hard times to make a pact with the devil, exchanging his soul for better luck. Called to fulfil his part of the bargain Jabez Stone desperately pled with Webster to save him. Webster called for a jury, which came in ghostly array at the Devil's call: Simon Girty, the renegade; King Philip, bitter Indian chief in a devastating colonial war; the pirate Teach; and others: all certain to find for the Devil. And Webster, curbing his fury, faced them as men of once finer instincts, and as Americans. He pled his client's cause in the name of what they had been, and others were.

The New Deal writer, Arthur M. Schlesinger, Jr., criticized the tale as false, since the real Webster would have agreed that the Devil's contract was good law; but in so arguing, he underscored the reality of Benét's tale, which, in fact, recorded Webster's well recognized love of the Union and its finest hopes. "The Devil and Daniel Webster" was a runaway triumph as a tale, then as a memorable motion-picture, and, finally, as an opera, for which Benét wrote the libretto.

The coming of World War II stirred all Benét's patriotism and need to serve. He had in work another large-scaled plan for a poem describing the founding of America in Virginia. His "Invocation" was even more powerful than that which had introduced *John Brown's Body*, in its passion for America and faith in the message it had for an embattled world. Left incomplete by Benét's death from overstrain, it contained echoes from Elizabethan England, and a vivid capturing of such personalities as Sir

Walter Raleigh and John Smith. The fragment, *Western Star* (1943) gained Benét his second Pulitzer Prize, though posthumously.

Little noticed was his short, interpretive book, written for the Office of War Information, intended to introduce American history to uninformed new Americans and foreigners. *America* (1944) was no work of art, but in its humility, and earnest effort to communicate the idea of the nation, it reflected something of the guiding force Benét had found in life.

Charles A. Fenton, *Stephen Vincent Benét: the Life and Times of an American Man of Letters* (1958); see also Fenton, ed., *Selected Letters* (1960), and Benét's own 2-volume *Selected Works* (1942). A magisterial work on Benét, finding his true place in the saga of America is yet to be studied and divulged.

Ben A. Botkin
(1901-1975)

The Artist and Folklore

FOLKLORIST AND LITTERATEUR, Ben A. Botkin created and popularized the concept of "Folk-Say," which broadened understanding of folk resources and led it away from narrow and condescending academics. His *Lay My Burden Down: a Folk History of Slavery* (1945) broke away from sentimentality and propaganda. His *A Treasury of American Folklore* (1944) opened the field wide for national reminiscence and empathy.

Botkin was of second-generation Russian-Jewish background, like Charles Angoff (*q.v.*) raised in an ethic community of Boston, and like him of scholarly temperament. Botkin's brother Henry also revealed talent, though in painting. Botkin's acceptance for admission to Harvard University was a sensation in family circles, which included the Gershwins, then living in Brooklyn, New York. Botkin bore a strong family resemblance to his cousin George Gershwin, just then profiting from the success of his song, "Swannee," and rapidly building a career as a song-writer.

Of poetic and romantic temperament and a good student, Botkin was slow to develop goals. He graduated from Harvard in 1920 and took his Masters degree a year later at Columbia University. With ethnic capacities implemented by the lore of western civilization, he first took an instructorship at the University of Oklahoma, then spent several exploratory years back in the New York area looking into ethnic neighborhoods, taking graduate courses at Columbia, and experimenting with articles and materials.

He returned to Oklahoma convinced that folklore offered a key to his ambitions, and also undertook graduate work at the University of Nebraska under the folklorist Louise Pound. This forced a long apprenticeship on him as he also met academic demands on his time, and conformed to English Department requirements. Botkin's dream was to unite the perceptions of high art with those of folklore, but it moved slowly. He was held back to a degree by the genteel academic antisemitism of the time and place, and by his own diffidence. Although he had notable wit and good humor, he also suffered the anxieties of slow professional advancement and the resistance to change he encountered.

The 1920s were a sparkling time for George Gershwin and his lyric writing brother Ira; their popular music flourished in such successes as *George White's Scandals*, *Lady Be Good*, and *Strike Up the Band*. George Gershwin himself dazzled critics with his *Rhapsody in Blue* (1923), *Concerto in F* (1925), and *An American in Paris* (1928). Henry Botkin also grew in art circles of the Avante Garde. For Ben Botkin it was an era of study, the preparation of his thesis, and expanding his acquaintanceship with older and newer writers who responded to western influences.

Part of his ambition was reached in his edited *Folk-Say: a Regional Miscellany*. It appeared in four volumes (1929-1932) and drew together notable writers. They included among established writers Carl Sandburg, Mary Austin, and the western sage J. Frank Dobie; among younger writers Erskine Caldwell, Henry Roth, later author of the esteemed novel *Call It Sleep*, and the folklorist Vance Randolph; and among blacks—whom Botkin unconventionally studied and knew—the scholar Alain Locke. As Botkin later summed up his experiences with "Folk-Say," he drew into his net Indian legends, tall tales, old timers's reminiscences, old songs, slang, dialect, and local-color. There was local protest against some of the mildly off-color materials, enough of it to discourage further issues of the publications, but Botkin had made his point: folk lore was not different from literature, but part of it.

In 1934 he made his second attempt to attract literary people who also represented the West as lore and in his magazine *Space* published writers all of whom would make their mark. These included the poets John Gould Fletcher and Winfield Townley Scott, writers of Indians and cowhands Joseph Matthews and Stanley Vestal, storytellers Paul Horgan, August W. Derleth, and David Cornel DeJong. He also tutored George

Gershwin in Negro lore which entered into Gershwin's *Porgy and Bess*. It began its career in 1935, three years before a brain seizure unexpectedly killed the composer.

These activities, which were continuously interrupted by college duties, took Botkin through most of the Great Depression. In 1938 he obtained leave to join the Federal Writers Project of the Works Progress Administration (WPA) in Washington to edit their Folklore enterprise. Writers on the Project were sent or assigned South to cull tales and songs known to those living in backwoods and small towns, especially lore which might be lost if the living failed to pass on their reminiscences and notions to investigators. A notable feature of this program was the lore known to ancients among the blacks, some of whom had been born before Emancipation and even in slavery, and whose experiences and fancies had been unexplored. Botkin organized the work and instructed the writers. He edited the manuscripts which they turned into their supervisors.

He was faced with the choice of whether to return to Oklahoma, or resign his position there, and decided to stay on in Washington, even though the Government-funded Projects were in jeopardy from critics who opposed Federal financing of the Projects. Also, war was reaching America, and military jobs and related activities were taking precedent over other civil operations.

For a time it appeared that Botkin had miscalculated. A married man with small children, he needed a full-time salary. An interim Library of Congress project involving Federal Writers Project materials was followed by a "resident" fellowship for arranging folklore materials. He was, however, about to come into more stable and fruitful times. His slave memoirs were accepted by a university press. Archibald MacLeish, then Librarian of Congress, appointed him chief of their Archives of American Folk Song. There he met a constant flow of interesting authors, musicians, and folklorists, some, like Charles Seeger became his particular friends (Seeger was the brother of Alan Seeger, whose poem, "I Have a Rendezvous with Death" shared fame with "If I Should Die, Think Only This of Me," written by England's Rupert Brooke. Had Seeger lived, he would have been uncle to Pete Seeger, the dissident folk singer.) One friend called forth a touch of Botkin's wit, when he described him as a friend, philosopher, and guide, gently calling attention to his inversion of the adjectives.

As momentously, Botkin was assigned by a publisher to prepare an anthology of American Folklore.

For the next several years Botkin was, not without trepidation, involved in preparing his vast anthology, unsure of what might come of it. As he told a friend: I keep sending them ideas and sample materials, and all they do is send me checks. On its appearance, tastefully prepared, and with a heralded preface by Carl Sandburg, *A Treasury of American Folklore* was a ringing success, with the affluent publishers envisioning a series of such volumes to entertain and instruct. There were academic complaints. A Richard Dorson sought a minor crusade against what he termed "fake lore," arguing that Botkin made no distinction between anecdotes, quips, literary work, and "true" folklore, involving conscientious comparison of sources and variant versions of the matter involved. His critique had little practical influence. Botkin resigned his Library of Congress position and moved to Croton-on-Hudson, New York, to be nearer his publishers.

From his home he issued a variety of volumes. None was quite so successful as the first *Treasury*, but all were welcomed and approved. Botkin took particular satisfaction in his *Treasury of Western Folklore*. His *Treasury of Southern Folklore* gained from the imprimatur of the distinguished southern historian Douglas Southall Freeman. *A Treasury of American Anecdotes* (1957) ("Sly, Salty, Shaggy Stories . . . from the Grassroots and Sidewalks of America") annoyed a few academics, but was welcomed by the uninitiated, as was also *Sidewalks of America* (1954).

In 1966 a fellow-folklorist, Bruce Jackson, edited *Folklore & Society: Essays in Honor of Benj. A. Botkin*, a festschrift and 23-page bibliography which reminded readers that their folklorist had also indited poetry, and even explored verse for regional qualities. Early in the 1970s a stroke unexpectedly interrupted Botkin's ever-exploratory career, which dove-tailed oddly with those of his brother and the Gershwins. The stroke did not respond to treatment, and he died in a nursing home. He was buried in nearby Sharon Gardens, in Valhalla, New York.

Although Botkin's was largely a life of the mind, he mixed with numerous contemporaries, his colleagues on the Federal Writers Project being of a distinctively varied sort, with reminiscences of all sorts to contribute. His acknowledgements of helpful individuals in just one book, *Sidewalks of America*, took more than a closely-printed page. Bruce Jackson's introduction to *Folklore & Society* succinctly traced his career. His own writings reflect his interests and opinions. His library, at the University of Nebraska, contains a wide range of them. See also Jerrold Hirsch, "Folklore in the Making: B. A. Botkin," in *Journal of American Folklore* 100 (1987), the author promising a larger work.

Thomas E. Dewey
(1902-1971)

"The Future
of America
Has No Limit"

KNOWN AS "MAKER OF THE MODERN REPUBLICAN PARTY," Thomas E. Dewey was wider known as the man who almost became President of the United States. His failure to attain what seemed all but in his hand threw light on factors which determined public choices in America.

He appeared to come from nowhere when, in 1935, he emerged as a vibrant prosecutor of criminal gangs which held formidable sections of New York City business in thrall: a young man no more than half a dozen years out of law school. Actually, he had come by way of Ann Arbor out of the modest town of Owosso, Michigan, where his forebears included a founder of the Republican Party. His grandfather, George Dewey, a newspaper editor, participated in the historic Jackson, Michigan, meeting where dissidents came together in 1854 to set up the new party. His father George Dewey, Jr. carried on the elder Dewey's work as editor and also served as postmaster of Owosso under President Warren G. Harding. His boy Tom from early boyhood displayed family traits of rigid adherence to duty, never missing a school day, and earning money from earliest years by selling and farm labor while also working on the family newspaper.

Tom Dewey had a rich soprano voice, and first went to the University of Michigan to develop it. He then went on to New York to mature it further as well as to follow Frances Hutt, another student of voice, who had a scholarship to continue her studies and who was soon to be his wife. Dewey concluded that his voice was not good enough to make him rich and famous, and turned to law for a career. He took quickly to it, garnered friends and associates, and soon became the protege of a newly-made U.S. Attorney for the Southern District of New York, George Medalie, whose chief assistant he became. Dewey concentrated on racket cases in his office, rackets having become the major plague of a desperate, Depression-ridden city. They were being languidly looked at by the local District Attorney's office.

Dewey brought an unprecedented efficiency to the rackets indictments he put into motion. He gathered and trained investigators who explored accounting books, telephone bills, commercial paper, and other sources to set up cases for which racketeers and their enforcers had no preparation. He bypassed politicians and protectors of criminals to confound them in court, and himself protected informers who helped build up cases against rings which terrorized poultry, milk, kosher meat, and other merchants, cases which won headlines in the national press and exposed ring leaders to fascinated readers and civic anger. The young man from Owosso not only stood up to such legendary masters of crime as Waxey Gordon and Lucky Luciano and their highly-paid attorneys. He won key verdicts of guilty and long prison sentences, dispersed rings, and won freedom for oppressed thousands of businessmen large and small.

Dewey himself was threatened with death during his momentous and drawn-out campaign. He somehow avoided direct assassination, though he came regularly to work without protection from his modest uptown apartment, and though he could readily have been cut down on his way home or to his office. One plan for assassination was apparently set for execution, but for some reason not followed through. It would appear that his rapid rise and national popularity disoriented the racket leaders, who had worked mainly through local arrangements, and who were terrified by the national glare which Dewey generated.

Dewey's rise to fame was spectacular. Humphrey Bogart played Dewey in a "Gangbusters" film. He became District Attorney for New York. Streets were named for him. In 1938 he was matched as a Republican against a well-admired veteran Democratic Governor Herbert Lehman; and though defeated put up a strong fight. In 1940 he became a contender for the Republican nomination for President, and though beaten by Wendell Willkie's backers made a creditable showing.

In 1942 he became Governor of New York and quickly revealed administrative ability of a high order. With World War II on he cooperated with the Federal government and military in ways which kept his name high beyond state lines. There was nowhere else for Republicans to look for their candidate to oppose Franklin D. Roosevelt in 1944. Dewey took their nomination for President with all but incredible confidence; Roosevelt, he told them, was the easiest Democrat of all to beat. An example of his eloquence as imparted to enthusiastic followers seems in order:

> What are we offered now? Only the dreary prospect of a continued war economy after the war, with inter-ference piled on interference and petty tyrannies rival-ing the very regimentation against which we are now at war. The present administration has never solved this fundamental problem of jobs and opportunity. It never can . . . it has never even understood what makes a job. It has never been for full production. It has lived in chattering fear of abundance . .. Is America old and worn out? Look to the beaches of Normandy for the answer. Look to the reaches of the wide Pacific . . . Look to the miracles of production in the war plants in your own towns . . . The future of America has no limit.

Here was no "me-too" Republican, let alone a little man on a wedding cake, as malice suggested; and voters sensed the difference. The soldiers's vote helped Roosevelt's margin of victory look somewhat better, but Dewey was able to return to Albany with head high, to compile a notable record as Governor. The Thomas E. Dewey Freeway cut nine-hours of driving time from New York City to Buffalo. He made budget savings which set pork-barrel projects aside for the benefit of public health and handicapped New Yorkers. Dewey furthered civil rights legislation in defiance of Republican stipendiaries.

All this was made known to the nation when the Republicans took advantage of post-War dissatisfaction with Truman Administration scan-dals, its docile obeisance to labor, its ambivalence toward radicals. Dewey was given his second chance at the Presidency, and, matched against Truman, seemed now to many the man needed for valid reconstruction of national goals. His whistle-stop appearances were well received. His calls for new energy and patriotic endeavors applauded. Truman could depend on official labor and Federal deployment of funds, but Dewey, frankly representing capital, could appeal to those who recalled his phenomenal prosecutions and knew his executive ability.

What then turned the balance toward Truman in those last days of the campaign? Dewey himself thought he had matured too early, and had not learned the wisdom that came of studying public feelings and wants. This was, to an extent, true; like another self-made success, Herbert Hoover, he was remote from his auditors, appealing to their desire for a leader more suitable to a corporate head than to a President. And yet he had been better rooted among people than even Hoover, raised in poverty and with supreme technical capacities.

But Dewey had not only left Owosso, Michigan; he had abandoned it, visiting it only while his mother was alive in the house built by their grandfather. Dewey's 486-acre working farm in rural New York was fairly earned; he had gained little financially from his crusading years in New York, and he deserved his prosperity. But on his mother's death it did not occur to him to give the house which had sheltered three generations of Deweys to the city as a keepsake, a memorial to distinction, an aspiration to other Owosso youth. He sold it for $11,000 he did not need. Shallow as the public appeared at times, it noted that Truman, though loyal to disloyal friends, never abandoned his modest house in Independence, Missouri, or turned his back on its people. "I'm a Jackson County Democrat," Truman said, "and proud of it." Not the most memorable of statements, but giving a sense of place and even purpose.

Dewey went back to being governor until he tired of it in 1955, and left to enter high level law and join Nelson A. Rockefeller as the leader of an Eastern Establishment of Republicans. He helped make Eisenhower President by defeating Robert A. Taft's drive for the 1960 Republican nomination, and he was an advisor to Richard Nixon. Indeed, he was scheduled to visit the White House on a fateful day chosen by advisors as the best man available to talk straight to Nixon about his need to reorganize the nation's intelligence system which was then inadequately coping with turbulence in and off the streets.

Dewey was gracious toward people who appreciated his sharp insight into issues and circumstances, and genuinely friendly toward a variety of others. Yet, following a game of golf with friends in Miami, Florida, he returned to his motel alone, and lying down to rest before departing, his bags all neatly packed and ready, he died in his sleep.

Dewey's own *The Case against the New Deal* (1940) is historically of interest. Richard Norton Smith, *Thomas E. Dewey and His Times* (1982) surveys him and his world with sympathy and insight. It is significant that Dewey could not bring himself to complete his own autobiography. Competitive to the end, he could not face his private self in ways which demanded revisions as well as visions.

Charles Angoff
(1902-1979)

Ethnicity and Art

LONG IDENTIFIED WITH having assisted H. L. Mencken (*q.v.*) in his conduct of the *American Mercury*, but, following that period, a veteran editor, novelist, biographer, and English professor, Charles Angoff was sufficiently obscure to raise questions about the durable in American culture.

Angoff was born in Minsk, Russia, but brought by family to Boston in 1908; he was naturalized in 1923. A Harvard A.B., he began work on Boston newspapers. In 1925 he was suggested as an assistant when Mencken, with the support of his publisher A. A. Knopf, undertook to issue the *American Mercury*. This job put Angoff in immediate contact with many of the most vibrant and well-known writers in New York, and, by mail and through visits, with many of them elsewhere. Angoff quickly established himself as an associate of Mencken, as well as one who took from him the burden of maintaining contacts and negotiating articles and terms.

Angoff later noted that many people, during the years when the *American Mercury* was in vogue, imagined that it was a large, organized firm, bustling with editors, readers, sub-editors, and others. In fact, it took up an office in Knopf's publishing firm, its "editorial board" consisting mainly of Mencken, Angoff, and George Jean Nathan, when he could be persuaded to pay attention to anything beyond the theatre. They mainly read manuscripts, made recommendations, solicited suggestions, wrote brief reviews, jeered at the "booboisie," and carried on magazine business. Thus, Edwin Markham (*q.v.*), on a venture, sent in his *Ballad of the Gallows-Bird* for consideration. It struck Angoff's attention, and he passed it on the Mencken, who liked its ballad measures but off-handedly rejected it as too long for the magazine. It was only when the two of them were out walking in town, and accidentally met Markham that Angoff was reminded of the *Ballad* as unfinished business, urged it upon Mencken, and received his consent to go ahead with publication.

Mencken was skeptical of academe and, being of German descent, somewhat of the Jews—considerably, as his 1989-published diaries revealed—and took pleasure in needling Angoff with invidious remarks about Harvard, its accent, professors, and president, whose name he pretended he could not remember; and more discretely about Angoff himself, whose learning, staid ways, and ethnicity Mencken found ripe for irony as stuffy and genteel. Angoff seems to have realized that Mencken, and Nathan, with whom he was more relaxed, were the stuff of literature and biography, and to have kept lengthy notes on their private sayings and ways.

The Twenties were Angoff's happiest years. He did little writing in that time, confining himself to giving absorbed attention to the litterateurs and others whom his work and connections permitted him to know. A pamphlet he wrote for the socialist-sensationalist publisher E. Haldeman-Julius became one of his Little Blue Books which, in sum, introduced millions of readers to pieces ranging from classics, often given eye-catching titles, to controversial sketches. Angoff's pamphlet, *The Real Aims of Catholicism* (1928), aired prejudices which Angoff never acknowledged in later summaries of his own work.

The Great Depression killed the *American Mercury* vogue. Mencken lost his interest in cultural subjects, and turned to vilifying the New Deal. Angoff himself became the *Mercury's* managing editor, and editor in 1934-35, after which it became a strongly conservative publication. He himself joined the *Nation*, then was an editor on the *American Spectator*. There with George Jean Nathan and others he attempted unsuccessfully to keep up a saucy voice in a gloomy, doctrinaire period.

Angoff went on to be a "contributing" editor on the *North American Review*, a distinguished name. He was embarrassed when it was made notorious, its publisher Joseph Hilton Smyth being arrested in 1942 as a Japanese spy. Other Angoff editorial connections included another turn with the *American Mercury* (1943-1950).

Meanwhile Angoff's own career as a writer began with a catastrophic effort to survey at length and from years of reading the sweep of American writing. The academic establishment then being still in traditional hands it was able to turn thumbs down on what were to have been the first two volumes of Angoff's *A Literary History of the American People* (1931). The volumes died without defense as irresponsible and inept. There was bitter contrast for him in Ludwig Lewisohn's then-successful *Expression in America* (1931), which was backed by Lewisohn's European literature studies and Freudism.

Over the following years Angoff explored, with several publishers, his interest in classical music, which was cordially noticed, and in verse, which made no impression though Angoff found activity and publication with the Poetry Society of America. He also published several anthologies.

These developments went along with his increasing concern for his Jewish roots, including his own family members, who became the subject of a series of novels surveying the feelings and adjustments of Jews in the New Immigration of the early twentieth century. Angoff found a publisher, Thomas Yoseloff, whose faith in Angoff was whole-hearted, and who gave him full scope for his work. *When I was a Boy in Boston* (1947); *Journey to the Dawn* (1951); *In the Morning Light* (1952); *The Sun at Noon* (1955); *Something about My Father* (1956); *Between Day and Night* (1959); *The Bitter Spring* (1961); and *Summer Storm* (1963) made up a canon of autobiography and fiction which placed Angoff solidly in the forefront of ethnic writing.

Its particular quality was that it did not present itself as picturesque, but as the thinking and activities of a segment of new Americans becoming part of the whole. Angoff's work in the genre received substantial attention in its time. When larger attention turned to such people—as it had once done to "local color," patronized by such older Americans as George Washington Cable, Edward Eggleston, Sara Orne Jewett, and Mary Noailles Murfree ("Charles Egbert Craddock")—Angoff would perhaps gain presence by that interest. His and Meyer Levin's anthology, *American Jewish Literature* (1970) was made formidable by inclusions from the writings of Lewisohn, Henry Roth, Daniel Fuchs, Saul Bellow, and others, as well as Angoff and Levin.

Angoff's most striking appearance as author involved his 1956 book on Mencken. It was denounced in a *New York Times* review as a work of malice, the reviewer warning celebrities against confiding in such people as Angoff. Since the reviewer did not challenge the content of Angoff's book, it appeared to be a plea for bowdlerized portraits. Among other things, Angoff reported Mencken as having said that he celebrated Edgar Allan Poe's birthday by urinating on his grave in Baltimore. A Mencken biographer suggested that Mencken had perhaps amused himself by shocking Angoff. The publisher, possibly seizing an advertising opportunity, took out a full-page advertisement defending his author for telling the truth. He later had occasion to say that the book had sold well.

Also notable was Angoff's salute to his favorite era, *The Tone of the Twenties* (1966), consisting of essays on personalities he had met or known. Although there was a self-serving note in some of the portraits, they were low-keyed enough to give off an aura of accuracy and to contribute to knowledge of the subjects.

Angoff through these several decades made efforts to establish himself in academe. He moved from a turn in Kansas City to turns elsewhere. He finally established himself at Fairleigh Dickinson University as an editor for their press, then as a professor in their English Department. Several of his books expressed his sense of the passing of good things, and of life itself. *The Bell of Time* (1967) and *Prayers at Midnight* (1971), among other books recorded his reluctance to leave the beloved scenes of his youth and early manhood.

How much of his work would survive his demise it was difficult to say. Angoff himself was not a vibrant figure, but his roots ran deep, and their place in the nation's lore was known. His study of Mencken and of Mencken's era was secure: it was a unique record.

No significant writing sought out the essence of Angoff's career. *The Old Century and the New, Essays in Honor of Charles Angoff* (1978) contained relevant matter.

Merrill Moore
(1903-1957)

*"There was a Man
Who Borrowed
the Sea..."*

MERRILL MOORE WAS A POET
who achieved a unique notoriety because of the rumor that he wrote excessively, and only in the sonnet form. His observed excesses, too, included
a long series of writings in his chosen field of psychiatry, service to his
country in World War II and in China, and a rounded private life.

As a very young man he associated with the original Vanderbilt
University "Fugitive Group," and contributed to their poetry, but in time was
gently separated from their legend, as he was from individual poetic associations. His publications received brief comment, sometimes no more than titles,
rather than criticism.

Born in Columbia, Tennessee, he came of notable family, his
father John Trotwood Moore being a respected regional novelist and
librarian, his mother Mary Brown Daniel Moore rating also as a
writer, as well as being her husband's successor as state librarian.
Young Moore himself took his high school enthusiasm for poetry to
Vanderbilt University where, as friend and associate of Allen Tate and
John Crowe Ransom, he worked with and contributed to their publication *Fugitive*. Following graduation from Vanderbilt Medical School
in 1928, Moore served a brief local internship, then made for Boston

where his skills and professional reputation grew in its hospitals and private practice.

As a psychiatrist trained under a colleague of Sigmund Freud, he expanded his medical connections. He had already settled deeply into his pattern of self-expression in the sonnet form. He explored the changing literary field, ranging from that of Thirties "social significance" to Fifties and later "self-expression" and found himself increasingly alone, especially as his writing of sonnets increased, first by the hundreds, then the thousands.

Moore had found that his social and professional concerns took more of his mind than did the writing of verses which, indeed, scarcely placed demands on his overt consciousness at all. This gave his few critics who were goaded by his publications to comment on them too little to work with. Their meager finding, such as it was, was that Moore wrote too much. True poetry required high absorption in details and alternative readings in the forms and phrases of changing contemporary poetry. It should involve such icons as T.S. Eliot, Kenneth Fearing, Theodore Roethke, as well as Tate, Ransom, and their friends.

Moore, however, trusted his own psychology, and in the course of writing found that a phrase, a word, a line of words—the sonnet form taking shape itself—roused sufficient inner impulses to make the poem a prompt extension of his several lives.

Over the years, Moore's sonnets explored every variation of rhyme and rhythm. They made the mere form all but inconsequential to his particular sense of feeling. As he said:

> You are mistaken in your naive guessing
> That novelty is now my chief desire,
> You fail to see the thing that I am stressing
> Is not these ashes but the former fire....
>
> So I ask humbly of a race of men,
> No—nothing new, only the old again.

Of such was Moore's "normal" sonnet. But he had so much stirring in his round life that his poetic completion could scarcely be considered a "sonnet" at all:

> He stroked the cats on account of a specific cause,
> Namely, when he entered the house he felt

That the floor might split and the four walls suddenly melt
In strict accord with certain magic laws...
So in he always stepped. Before him went
Always his shadow....

One critic thought Moore did not choose his words, or "correct" them, carefully, though it is obvious that Moore's work as a psychiatrist lay behind much of what he did choose to set down, and needed to be grasped for adequate interpretation. All Moore's critics expressed their group attitudes, rather than individual insights, and never had examples to offer as evidence. One problem they had was how to shunt Moore aside without opening gates for him to enter readers' minds. Thus, Moore's poem on "Robert Witt" could have suggested Edwin Arlington Robinson's un-forgettable poem on "Richard Cory"—Moore admired Robinson—but that would have opened gates for Robinson, who was no longer in vogue. So Robinson's poem with its thrilling conclusion had to be laid aside as "evidence" against Moore:

Whenever Richard Cory came downtown,
We people on the pavement looked at him...

So on we worked, and waited for the light
        And went without the meat and cursed the bread;
And Richard Cory, one calm summer night,
        Went home and put a bullet through his head.

Moore had it that:

When Robert Witt dies, it will be decorously,
He is spending this summer at Peckett's-On-The-Hill.
There is something very polite about everything Robert does.
He can smile and I've often seen him laugh fit to kill...
He's one of the best doctors and, I think, a gentleman.
He lives alone, in comfort, on Commonwealth Avenue...
He will probably give his books to the medical library,
And Robert will lie in his coffin very still.

Over the years in his several roles as poet, psychiatrist, citizen, soldier, and family man, during which he fathered four children—

Moore explored many languages, regularly including French, German, and Spanish, which found expression in surprising rhymes, metaphors, and topics, as illustrated by his later volumes of *Clinical Sonnets*. Moore melted his flashes of poetic impulse into a vocabulary which was, or could have been, suggestive to readers who had not been put off by his lack of "reputation;" and instructive in the areas of objectivity in verse as well as emotion.

As a doctor he saw patients continuously, and there is still to be a portrait of the many-sided artist and technician they and others knew.

One vignette comes from Josh Logan, theatre and motion-picture director, who in 1940 suffered a nervous breakdown and found himself in the hands of a "tall, balding [man] with a protruding paunch. His eyes were close together and his cheeks pushed far apart by layers of fat; he was a perfect Modigliani subject." Moore looked to Logan like a fugitive from an asylum, and was amazed to learn that he was a doctor who lectured and had lectured for twenty-five years at Harvard Medical School.

Moore won Logan's confidence not by authority or restraints, but by persuading Logan to "take advantage" of the "elation" he was experiencing—he was in the "high" period of his manic depressive breakdown. Moore's cultural interests served Logan well, for he could direct Logan's high-tension language and ideas toward recovery. (Logan, *My Up and Down, In and Out Life* [1976]).

Moore as psychiatrist was a major in the United States Army during World War II, and a lieutenant-colonel in China in 1946. He then resumed a life of medical service in Boston—a life which also included long-distance swimming among other enthusiasms, a life which took him to the theatre as well as out-of-doors.

Although his life as artist had been too firmly taken away from him by a la mode practitioners for him to profess seriousness in its pursuit, Moore seems quietly to have probed the poetic scene to determine where and how he could communicate aspects of his poetic life to others. Louis Untermeyer, the poetry anthologist, a longtime friend, kept up with Moore's production of verses, and advised him regarding them. William Carlos Williams was also a friend, and at one point even a patient, as well as being also in the medical profession, though with status among the avant garde. He could not help Moore's visibility among poets, but he did not hinder. It remained for one of Williams's biographers, a Reed Whitmore, in a single passage of his book, *William Carlos Williams, Poet from Jersey* (1975) to acknowledge Moore's long friendship with Williams as involving no more than an "acquaintance."

Moore evidently lived too strenuously for the physique he carried, dying at no more than 54 years of age. Although he increasingly wrote and spoke modestly about his poetic inclinations, it is obvious that he quietly probed all possibilities to receive a hearing. He published 16 volumes of poems, the first two from *The Fugitive* being privately printed, the last, *Fugitive Sonnets*, finding The Poet's Press in Glasgow, Scotland, in 1954. In between were *The Noise that Time Makes*, printed by the prestigious Harcourt, Brace, which made him notorious, Moore's publications went on through *Clinical Sonnets* (1950) and *More Clinical Sonnets* (1953) to *Verse Diary of a Psychiatrist* (1954).

Should his verse or life trouble or interest an investigator in time, he would not be able to proceed without careful reference to Henry W. Wells's *Poet and Psychiatrist: Merrill Moore* (1955), a work which followed Moore's life with care and regard. Wells was born in Sewanee, Tennessee in 1895. He took his degree in literature at Columbia University and joined its faculty as a specialist in Elizabethan poetry. He quietly expanded his interests to take in such poets as Emily Dickinson and Wallace Stevens, and the state of American poetry, to all of which he committed books. In older age he read and wrote deeply in Chinese, Japanese, and Indian literature, and as a still older academic was curator of the Brander Matthews Museum in Columbia's literature department. He died in 1978.

His book on Moore individually examined some 200 of Moore's poems. Moore's final paradox was to issue, through Wells, two years following his own death, a manuscript of—not sonnets, this time, but quatrains. *The Phoenix and the Bees* had its historical roots, as Wells could not resist noting in his introduction, but more important, it gave evidence or further evidence, of Moore's turn of mind, in this case as concerned for life and death. Moore invoked classics and ephemera, puzzling over bees honey and Phoenix's innumerable transitions. In long lines Moore noted that:

> There was a man who borrowed the sea
> Day by day in a spoon of memory.
> When in the end he had spooned it all away

He looked behind him—there a new sea lay.

And in short lines:

> Bees are hatched
> And some are lost
> But bees never
> Count the cost....
>
> Bees swarm
> In their hive,
> The colony
> Will survive.

Wells himself observed that "such poetry as Doctor Moore's is ultimately more rewarded by silence than by either exposition or praise."

Acknowledgements

Charles Angoff, p. 263; Otis Historical Archives/Armed Forces Institute of Pathology, Washington, D.C., p. 57; Bergengren Memorial Museum, Madison, WI, p. 126; Gertrude Botkin, p. 254; John J. Burns Library, Boston College, p. 74; Francis A. Countway Library of Medicine, Boston College, p. 267; Dartmouth College Library, Clark Collection, p. 217; Nancy Gallin, p. 263; Hargrett Rare Book and Manuscript Library, University of Georgia Libraries, p. 156; Jerrold Hirsch, p. 254; Lilly Library, Indiana University, pp. 194, 201, 202, 222; Carleton Mabee, p. 18; Terrellita Maverick, San Antonio, TX, p. 244, 246; The Miami Conservancy District, Dayton, Ohio, p. 192; Vernon R. Alden Library, Ohio University Libraries, p. 90; Special Collections, University of Pennsylvania Libraries, p. 226; Philadelphia Jewish Archives, Balch Institute for Ethnic Studies, p. 226; Schlesinger Library, Radcliffe College, pp. 67, 118, 148; State Historical Society, Madison, WI, p. 138; Madison-Jefferson County Library, Madison, Indiana, p. 160.

Appreciation to **Saralee R. Howard-Filler**, whose imprint is on all aspects of the printed book.

And to **Emily Arma Howard Filler** *and* **Louis Graham Howard Filler**, *whose heritage in the American past is both a privilege and a trust.*

Index

COLOPHON:

*The text in this book
is set in Times, an
Adobe Postscript typeface
which is based on
Times New Roman,
originally designed
with Linotype in mind
by Monotype.
Type design supervised
by Stanley Morison,
1932.*

*The book was produced on
a CompuAdd 386 computer
with Xerox Ventura Publisher 2.0
with Professional Extension
(GEM version).*

*Book and cover jacket
designed and produced
by Diana L. Grinwis.
Pencil illustrations
rendered by Richard Geer.*

*Film halftones by
Litho Color Service, Lansing, MI.
Page output by
Desktop Productions, Lansing, MI.
Offset lithography and binding
by BookCrafters, Inc., Chelsea, MI.*